environmental policy
and
administration

ENVIRONMENTAL SCIENCE SERIES

Asit K. Biswas, *Editor*
Department of Environment, Ottawa, Canada

Published

Dynamics of Fluids in Porous Media
Jacob Bear

Scientific Allocation of Water Resources
Nathan Buras

Environmental Policy and Administration
Daniel H. Henning

In Preparation

Systems Approach to Water Management
Asit K. Biswas, *Editor*

Computer Simulation in Hydrology
George Fleming

Air Pollution: The Emissions,
The Regulations, and the Controls
James P. Tomany

environmental policy
and
administration

Daniel H. Henning

Department of Political Science, Eastern Montana College,
Montana University System,
Billings, Montana
and
Department of Government and Public Administration,
United College, The Chinese University
of Hong Kong

american elsevier
publishing company, inc.
NEW YORK LONDON AMSTERDAM

AMERICAN ELSEVIER PUBLISHING COMPANY, INC.
52 Vanderbilt Avenue, New York, N.Y. 10017

ELSEVIER PUBLISHING COMPANY
335 Jan Van Galenstraat, P.O. Box 211
Amsterdam, The Netherlands

International Standard Book Number 0-444-00137-9

Library of Congress Card Number 73-7685

Library of Congress Cataloging in Publication Data

Henning, Daniel H
    Environmental policy and administration.

    (Environmental science series)
    Bibliography: p.
    1. Environmental policy--United States. I. Title.
II. Series: Environmental science series (New York,
1972-   )
HC110.E5H46   301.31'0973   73-7685
ISBN 0-444-00137-9

Manufactured in the United States of America

To Dorothy, Tundra Dawn, and Forest Daniel,
and to Environmental Quality
for Future Generations

CONTENTS

Contents

Contents

FOREWORD

I am happy to have been asked to write the Foreword to Professor Henning's book on the administration of environmental policies. To undertake the writing of a coherent, synthesizing book on environmental policy and administration requires a considerable measure of fortitude. The task is difficult. When, some years ago, I proposed to write a book on the subject of the environment as a focus for public policy and a challenge to modern society, I was assured by many of my colleagues that it could not be done.

One evidence of the difficulty of producing singly authored books on environmental politics and administration is that there are relatively few of them compared to the numerous anthologies which exist on the subject. The demand for environmental studies in American universities broke in upon academia with unanticipated force and magnitude. Publishers, who in 1966 and 1967 were writing polite letters of rejection for manuscripts on environmental policy, were, by late 1968 and 1969, "beating the bushes" for suitable, textual material to meet an heretofore unanticipated need. The most expeditious way to meet this need was to fashion a textbook from previously published articles relevant to various aspects of environmental policy.

Most of these anthologies emphasized the politics of environmental pollution, but their content was determined as much by the availability of the literature as by considered judgment as to what the field of studies really required. Many of these anthologies were, and are, very useful, but they do not easily provide the coherent view of the subject matter that a book by a single author can provide.

It is for this reason that Professor Henning's study is a welcome addition to the literature. His book emphasizes the background of the environmental policy movement in the efforts that preceded it for the conservation of natural resources. As a resident of the Montana "Big Sky" country, the conservation of natural resources comes quite naturally to Professor Henning, although he has not forgotten that the environment most immediately experienced by most Americans is urban. To the growing literature of environmental policy and administration, he brings in this volume his own particular insight and background, and thus enriches a field of study in which no single work can be expected to be definitive. Various viewpoints and orientations are needed and it is good to have Professor Henning's contribution.

Lynton K. Caldwell
Chairman, International Union for Conservation
of Nature and Natural Resources,
Commission of Environmental Policy,
Law and Administration,
and Arthur F. Bentley Professor
of Political Science and Professor
of the School of Public and Environmental Affairs,
Indiana University, Bloomington, Indiana

PREFACE

In the final analysis, politics and government will determine environmental survival and quality through the policy and the administrative process. The state of the environment has recently become a dominant, and permanent, policy issue for the general public, and the executive, legislative, and judicial branches of government, with billions of dollars being spent on a variety of programs. On the federal level alone, there are some 80 agencies directly or indirectly involved in environmental affairs. Moreover, the majority of colleges and universities now offer, usually on an interdisciplinary basis, environmental programs and courses, which are concerned with governmental policies and their adminis- tration. However, the field of environmental policy and administration is a relatively new one, emerging in the late 1960s; thus, it lacks a body of theory and knowledge. It is my hope that the present volume will supply some of this much-needed theory and knowl- edge.

With leading scientists predicting imminent environmental crises in the near future, with environmental destruction and deterioration everywhere, and with the increasingly powerful and permanent political and governmental forces concerned with the environ- ment, it is timely to study this relatively unexplored, but important, area, which will affect the survival and quality of our lives and the lives of those who may come after us. For an in-depth understanding of such problems, however, it is necessary to acquire a theoretical basis for critical analysis; this has been the major orientation of my research, and throughout the book I have attempted to treat the subject in general terms, emphasizing its interdisciplinary aspects.

The policies of the U. S. federal government have been emphasized throughout, but the discussion is also relevant to governmental and environmental relationships of other nations, particularly Canada, as well as to state and local policy and government. Although this book is primarily addressed to upper-division undergraduate and graduate students in political science, public administration, and interdisciplinary environmental courses and seminars, it is also addressed to the general reader who has an interest in environmental affairs.

Thus, a basic purpose of the book is to help the student and reader understand the complex overt and covert processes and institutions which underlie and shape environ- mental policy and its administration. Too often policy-makers (including public officials) fall into these processes in a manner not unlike that of Alice, of Wonderland fame, falling into the rabbit hole. In essence, then, the book seeks to provide some meaning and a conceptual framework for understanding the "mysteries" of these processes. Critical, in-depth analysis, consequently, becomes an important element of this approach; little understanding comes from platitudes and descriptions of the status quo. The approach further recognizes that environmental policy and administration does not exist in a vacuum and, hence, requires interdisciplinary considerations and orientations, particularly from the social sciences, in order to have a realistic perspective. Environmental intangibles (e.g., scenic beauty, open space, etc.), quality, and change, are also considered throughout the discussion.

A central theme of the book is that environmental policy and administration is basically concerned with human considerations and values pertaining to environmental interaction. Governmental policy and administration essentially involves the management and control of people and environmental relationships, rather than management of the environment per se. As a result, the decision-making processes are highly political with strong attention being given to values and value conflicts. Politics is defined as "the conflict between competing values through human interaction in the struggle for power to attain a legal governmental decision which will determine an environmental action or nonaction, or degrees thereof." The values may represent a variety of political, economic, ideological, ecological, and sociological interests with positive or negative results for the environmental public interest. Yet, much of governmental dogma in this area has emphasized the technoscientific, professional, and economic criteria, with little consideration being given to other values and political judgments. Moreover, it is recognized that many environmental problems cannot be resolved by technoscientific solutions. In such cases, realistic solutions call for effective and wise human management and control on a sound ecological basis through value input and the political processes of environmental policy and administration.

Because of the complexity, vastness, and dynamic nature of the relationships which exist between the government, the public, and the environment, I have attempted to explore and analyze the interrelationships between a given policy and its administration, particularly emphasizing the politics and values which are inherent in the policy-making process. It now appears that governmental *management* of the environment through technoscientific professionalism, based on *nonecological* values, is not working. Effective governmental stewardship of the environment calls for value judgments and, changes, increases, and a sound ecological basis. Consequently, it is imperative that a realistic approach to the understanding of a given environmental policy and its administration should center on values and politics.

Since the research and writing of this book extended over a period of several years, it is an almost impossible task to acknowledge the numerous individuals who have assisted and contributed to the gathering of data and the preparation of the manuscript. Those who have helped me include the undergraduate and graduate students in my seminars on environmental policy and administration, my past professors (including the late Dr. Roscoe Martin of Syracuse University), governmental officials (many of whom were also enrolled in my seminars), conservationists, environmentalists, Montana congressmen, colleagues, industrialists, ranchers, lawyers, and lumber executives, among others. Many of the above individuals offered healthy criticism, which forced me to study, reanalyze, and enlarge my explanation of the underlying reasons for these processes. A special acknowledgement is extended to a major advisor, the environmental scholar Professor Lynton K. Caldwell from the Department of Political Science of Indiana University, and to Dr. Asit K. Biswas, in the Policy and Planning Directorate of Environment Canada, for his very helpful editorial comments which were incorporated throughout. Also, two Montana environmentalists, Ellen Bloedel and Dewey Cronk, supplied valuable editorial assistance. Finally, I wish to thank Robert Goodman, Director of the College Department of the American Elsevier Publishing Company, Inc., for his patience and unfailing cooperation.

Acknowledgement is also due to The National Wildlife Federation whose Ernest Swift Memorial Fellowship enabled me to complete much of my research and writing. I am also grateful for the help I received in compiling the Bibliography from the libraries of Eastern Montana College, Rocky Mountain College, particularly through Mrs. Lidie Miller, and the University of New Mexico, as well as from the Environmental Policy Division of the Library of Congress, through Wallace Bowman. The Program for Advanced Study in Public Science Policy and Administration, University of New Mexico, where the author served as a visiting associate professor of public administration during the 1970–1971 academic year, provided a challenging and creative atmosphere for research. The Council on Environmental Quality supplied valuable data as did numerous other federal agencies; my special appreciation is extended to the U. S. Forest Service. Typists too numerous to name shared faithfully in the task of preparing the manuscript. I also wish to thank those heretofore unnamed people and organizations whose various contributions enabled me to write this book.

Finally, I want to acknowledge the help of my family who gave up many hiking and fishing vacations while I worked on the manuscript: my wife Dorothy, who was awakened early on countless mornings to provide coffee, patience, environmental data, and inspiration, and my daughter Tundra Dawn, who was told all too often, "not to bother Daddy when he is working." In time, it is hoped that they and others will think that it was worth it.

Billings, Montana   Daniel H. Henning

LIST OF FEDERAL AGENCIES APPEARING IN THE TEXT

Reference to these agencies is made frequently in the text. For the reader's convenience, the name of each agency is given, with the abbreviated version of that name following in parentheses. The type of agency, i.e., whether it is an independent organization or part of another, is specified. For more detailed descriptions of the agencies, consult the *U.S. Government Organization Manual*, 1971–1972.

Atomic Energy Commission (AEC)
    (Independent Agency)
Bureau of Land Management (BLM)
    (U.S. Department of the Interior)
Bureau of Outdoor Recreation (BOR)
    (U.S. Department of the Interior)
Bureau of Reclamation (BR)
    (U.S. Department of the Interior)
Bureau of Sport Fisheries and Wildlife (BSFW)
    (U.S. Department of the Interior)
Corps of Engineers (CE)

Council on Environmental Quality (CEQ)
    (Executive Office of the President)
Environmental Protection Agency (EPA)
    (Independent Agency)
Forest Service (FS)
    (U.S. Department of Agriculture)
National Aeronautics and Space Administration (NASA)
    (Independent Agency)
National Parks Service (NPS)
    (U.S. Department of the Interior)
Public Land Law Review Commission (PLLRC)
    (Independent Agency)
Soil Conservation Service (SCS)
    (U.S. Department of Agriculture)

Chapter 1

ENVIRONMENTAL ADMINISTRATION: SOME CONSIDERATIONS

In essence, public administration is the process of directing and managing governmental policies and affairs under broad legislative guidelines that protect the public interest. It is a human group process, in which individuals interact and work toward the achievement of certain objectives—a process involving both conflict and cooperation. Politics and public administration are intertwined in the struggle for power to effect legal governmental decisions. In the final analysis, every public administration decision is a human decision and a direct or indirect product of the political process. Regardless of its area of responsibility or clientele, each public administration agency must operate within the framework and influence of the ecosystem as well as within a given culture and government.

As a unique field within public administration, environmental administration on the federal level involves numerous governmental departments and agencies as well as independent agencies associated with environmental or natural resource concerns. Besides the regulatory roles of such organizations, many of them are directly charged with the administration of the 771 million acres of public lands in the United States (about one-third of the total geographic area). With the myriad congressional legislative and organizational policies, and with the variety of natural resources and environmental concerns, an all-embracing public administration policy for the environment does not appear to exist. In the discussion that follows, we shall elaborate on those considerations that apply uniquely to the environmental administration.

GENERAL CONSIDERATIONS

Ecological Complexities

The term ecology is derived from the Greek term *oikos,* which means "home." The addition of *logy,* or "study," gives us a term signifying study of the home or environment. Ecology includes man and all living things, and their interrelationships with each other and with the environment. The ecological concept of interrelations provides a central theme for environmental administration. With the administration and management of a specific natural resource at a given time and place, a complex of interrelations and interdependencies is established that will influence the environment in the present and possibly in the future. For example, the manipulation or administration of water resources cannot occur without affecting wildlife, plantlife, and other natural resources,

1

while also affecting a host of ecological subsystems. Currently, many resource agencies are subscribing to an ecological approach. In reality, however, this orientation is largely confined to superficial treatment and short-range planning. When serious decisions are to be made through the political and administrative processes, old values and the vested interests of agencies and clientele groups usually assume paramount importance.

Environmental Crises

Many leading scientists have expressed deep concern over serious environmental problems that have resulted from neglect of ecological considerations. Through mass communications, including such books as Rachel Carson's *Silent Spring*, Stewart Udall's *The Quiet Crisis*, and Paul Ehrlich's *The Population Bomb*, a virtual tidal wave of public opinion has sprung up, and is affecting political processes relating to the environment. Urgent and strong pressures are now being exerted upon the environmental administration in both governmental and private sectors.

Future Generations

All public administration is supposedly oriented toward the public interest. In the case of environmental administration, this concern must extend to future, as well as present, generations. Although many natural resources are replaceable or renewable, others are susceptible to removal or reduction in quality in the future. It is very difficult, however, to predict the value systems and protect the resources of future generations.[1]

NATURAL RESOURCES CHARACTERISTICS

According to traditional classification, natural resources are directly produced by nature. Renewable natural resources are those that create or sustain life, such as forests and wildlife. They can either renew themselves by reproduction, or can be continued by natural processes, although man can aid or interfere with these processes. Under a utilitarian philosophy, a natural resource must be used, or have the potential for use, by man. However, uses and needs, as well as values and attitudes toward natural resources, may change greatly over time, and with location and culture. Thus, an isolated mountain peak may be a natural resource, depending upon man's perception of it. Urban values may indicate appreciative, or nonutilitarian, attitudes toward some natural resources. These contrast with the utilitarian attitudes of more rural communities, which depend upon occupations that exploit natural resources.[2] Because of attitudinal time-lag, many environmental agencies are primarily concerned with the utilitarian aspects of natural resources, for example, the U.S. Forest Service (FS) and Soil Conservation Service (SCS).

Although natural resources and the environment are highly susceptible to and influenced by public administration, governmental manipulation actually represents a small proportion of the environmental administration in the United States. "Management" is a myth. In reference to their functions and application to the tasks before them, the majority of resource managers are actually administrators who spend a large part of their time in offices. They are basically concerned with management of people's behavior relative to natural resources, rather than with natural resources per se. Management usually implies some manipulation of natural resources and the environment, whereas the main function of resource managers is to interpret or to decide upon the various uses or degrees of use (e.g., grazing, logging, etc.) to be granted to private nongovernmental individuals and organizations. Actual management by the government is relatively slight here, as contrasted to forestry in Germany, for example, where intensive management and manipulation are practiced by governmental foresters and their staffs.

Natural resource administrators usually recognize that the great preponderance of their time is spent on problems affecting the population at large. Hence, their *human* decisions involve value determinations and perceptions that are further complicated by the changing complexities of ecology, science, technology, economics, and the population explosion, and also by resource availability. In this decisional process, environmental resource administrators must make value judgments within the political environment of competing interests and powers. Further, these judgments are complicated by the decision-maker's limited mental picture of the world, which, in turn, is influenced by his personality, past education and experience, and by his field of specialization and the agency's ideology. The entire decisional process hinges upon value perceptions.

Management implies control, but a general understanding of the present environmental situation is that man cannot control a complex ecosystem with the giant hand of technology. Ecologists acknowledge the complexities and fallacies of man's role in changing and influencing the Earth and its life with the term *noosphere.* This term, from the Greek word *noos,* meaning "mind," implies a world dominated by the mind of man, rather than a biosphere or a naturally evolving world. Ecologists caution us about the philosophy of the noosphere, and most (ecologists) agree that man is not wise enough to understand the results of his actions. The noosphere is also referred to as the *anthrosphere,* which generally means the part of the global environment under influence of the human mind. Both terms can be related to the cornucopian philosophy that man, through management by science and technology, will be able to produce the type of controlled environment or world which will do nothing but serve his needs and wishes. Yet, there is the implication that man, as the dominant animal of the Earth's ecology, is a responsible creature with respect and values for other men (including future generations) and for other forms of life.[3]

Given the value emphasis of environmental administration, there are numerous elements that comprise natural resources. They vary greatly in physical and geographical distribution and are widely dispersed. Often, their distribution exceeds political and agency boundaries, as in the case of a watershed. Thus, a major task of environmental administration is to relate the administrative process to natural resource distributions, needs, and jurisdictions on an ecological basis. Natural resources, moreover, differ in utility and accessibility. Thus, a *potential* natural resource may not be an *actual* natural resource. Many developing nations, for example, claim rich natural resources, but the value of the resources is unredeemable under a given technology, economy, or location.

Qualitative and quantitative definitions of both natural resources and environment may change in response to various needs, and in different time periods, according to population, value bases, ecological awareness, and levels of science, technology, and economics. Although ecological processes are constantly in operation, man, through administration and management, becomes the determining factor affecting the quality and quantity of natural resources. For example, an economic situation may dictate substituting the logging of "lower" quality trees near a sawmill with the stoppage of logging operations on "higher" quality trees in a mountain forest owing to transportation problems.

Although natural resources are highly elastic and flexible in terms of management and administration, they are also destructible and exhaustible. Renewable natural resources, as forms of life, supposedly renew themselves through reproduction and other natural processes, which can be aided or hampered by man. Yet, there is the danger that management, as much as man's interference with the ecosystem, can produce negative effects on the renewing process. The effects of man's interference can be seen in the dying ponderosa pines in San Bernardino National Forest, poisoned by air pollution from Los Angeles. When resource management is based on strong economic and political factors, it is possible to deplete a natural resource to the point where it will not be able to recover in terms of its former quality or quantity. In extreme cases, this may result in a particular natural resource becoming seriously endangered or even extinct.

From the viewpoint of man, however, natural resources are replaceable and, in many cases, other natural resources or artificial products can be substituted for them. With modern science and technology it is possible even to improve upon natural resources as is illustrated by forest genetics. Consequently, environmental administration is highly oriented to change and to unpredictability. The fact remains, however, that certain natural resources are irreplaceable or have very limited replacement potential in their essential life-sustaining characteristics. A good example is water. Moreover, associations and interdependencies exist which preclude the administration and manipulation of a single natural resource without influencing and affecting other related natural resources. In ecological terms, some resources may not be substitutive or replaceable if associated natural resources in the ecosystem are negatively affected. In Florida, for example, diversion or drainage of water from marsh land may adversely affect plants and wildlife. History and conservation books contain numerous illustrations of such catastrophes, which result in serious problems for man as well as for other forms of life.

Given the determination of natural resources in terms of location, substance, and time in a constantly changing pattern, appreciative or nonutilitarian value structures appear to be exerting a powerful influence on current environmental administration. While some define natural resources in terms of use or potential use by man, others employ definitions that are of a qualitative and intangible nature. These qualitative definitions and attendant demands have always been present in some form throughout history; they now appear to be much more prevalent in the environmental concerns of an educated citizenry. This has resulted in the recognition that a natural resource should be administered for its own sake, with nonutilitarian benefits for man. As a specific illustration of this trend, the FS has recently classified the wilderness as a natural resource and various water development agencies are legally required to make provision in their activities for wildlife and scenery resources.

AMERICAN CULTURAL FACTORS

As a mirror of the American culture, environmental administration does not operate in a vacuum. It reflects the cultural forces that have interacted with it. To understand the processes of environmental policy that operate within the framework of the American culture, it is necessary to consider these cultural forces. Although many of these considerations are applicable to Canada and other Western democracies, emphasis will be given to the culture of the United States.

Democracy: Our form of democracy has important positive and negative implications for environmental administration. With concepts of majority rule, representation, and individual dignity, it is obvious that democracy exerts strong pressures for the responsiveness of environmental administration to public opinion, politics, and the public interest. Under majority rule, the growing force of public awareness of environmental issues will obviously contribute positive pressures for responsive governmental action. On the other hand, democracy may interfere with long-range policies and planning for future generations. A totalitarian form of government does not have the obligation to recognize and satisfy diverse and fragmented interests when determining its policies for the environment. There is also the complication that a democracy, in an effort to solve problems and to be relevant, may not be able to make rapid and necessary changes in environmental administration. Charles E. Lindblom notes: "Democracies change their policies almost entirely through incremental adjustments. Policy does not move in leaps and bounds."[4]

Science and Technology: There is a cornucopian belief prevalent in the American culture that science and technology can solve all problems, including those of the environment. However, Garrett Hardin notes that some problems simply have no scientific or technical solution, despite the tendency to seek such solutions without consideration of human values or morality.[5] Within the last 50 years, science and technology have had dynamic and profound influences on the American life style and economy. These influences defy assessment or predictions concerning their effect on the environment. The federal government, moreover, has a strong commitment to scientific research and

5

development representing about $16 billion in annual expenditures. Allowing for the benefits that accrue from this commitment, unpredictable change, rapid consumption, and other ecological complications should still be important considerations for science and technology. It should also be recognized that in the postatomic era science and technology can no longer claim neutrality in the realms of values, politics, and environmental administration.

Progress, Industrialization, and Materialism: In many areas of American culture, the value of progress in any form is unquestioned. This premise, however, sometimes involves a short-range orientation with major concern for quantity, economic benefits, "newness," and expediency, without consideration of long-range quality. Development, innovation, and improvement are criteria applied to natural resources as well as to other areas, including the government itself. Such attitudes appear to be confined to a materialistic culture; unfortunately, considerations of ecological balance, quality, aesthetics, and other intangibles may be sacrificed to the desire for progress. An important aspect of progress is the emphasis given to materialism in goods, services, and *things*, which naturally creates demands upon environmental administration. Many resource agencies are administered with a view to obtaining certain material products. With a history of a rich frontier and unlimited opportunities, progress and materialism have emerged as essential elements of the American Dream, which affects environmental administration. Demands on private and governmental environmental administration may, in many cases, be directed toward a standard of living rather than toward quality of life.

Pragmatism: As discussed by John Dewey and others, pragmatism appears as a major philosophic orientation of the American culture. Given this orientation, great emphasis is placed upon the practicality of environmental administration. Although practical solutions and results may appear to be realistic and concrete for many resource problems on a short-term basis, in long-range terms, they may yield fragmented and inadequate programs that have not taken into consideration values essential to an integrated approach. Also, with the concern for valid or practical results, many long-range considerations do not lend themselves to immediate or quantitative evaluation, which places further emphasis on the short-range pragmatic solution within the political framework of environmental administration.

Gabriel Almond notes a tendency for Americans to be optimistic toward ends ("things can be done") but improvising toward means ("know-how"). He states, "In complicated questions of social and public policy there is a genuine distrust of complex and subtle reasoning and a preference for earthy 'common sense.' " Under this orientation, he feels that Americans, despite advantages of new technical approaches to problems, fail to reap the net advantages of thoughtful policy planning, achievable through greater intellectual discipline.[6]

Middle Class: Although the American culture is not considered class conscious, the majority of Americans identify strongly with the middle class. Major factors in this identification are competition, materialism, and conformity, with positive orientation to

6

innovation, accomplishment, and improvement. This orientation obviously creates growing needs, wants, and demands on environmental administration. Almond states that many cultures provide various forms of religious, social, and institutional support and stability that reward the individual for committing himself to materialism.[7] A cultural paradox appears to be present here in that much of the support for nonmaterialistic conservation of the environment comes from the American upper-middle class.[8]

Urbanization: In the United States about 75 percent of the population is now concentrated in metropolitan areas, with less than 7 percent involved in agricultural production. This is in contrast to other nations where high percentages of the populations are in agricultural situations. Today's urban values and needs naturally place different pressures upon environmental administration than did those of the agrarian economy of earlier days. As previously indicated, urban attitudes may be appreciative, nonutilitarian, and recreational, as contrasted with utilitarian attitudes toward nature that reflect the occupational roles of rural communities.[9] Yet, Wilson Clark notes the inconsistency of many urban people in ". . . wanting the fruits of industrial and agricultural exploitation, yet fighting that exploitation."[10]

From a sociological viewpoint, the urban situation produces secondary relationships that are impersonally and manipulatively oriented, and privately concerned, which contrast with the primary relationships of rural societies. Thus, the urban situation dictates a lack of corporate concern and a tendency toward centralized government; this naturally departs from the grassroots representation of rural communities upon which many resource agencies place a high value. Moreover, under the "one man—one vote" principle, the urban population has caused a shift in political power from the rural base, which now permits the urban population to exert a strong influence upon environmental administration.

Mixed Economy: As with many other national economies, the American economy is a blend of conditions and policies, a complexity of free enterprise, service, welfare, and totalitarian elements, with great emphasis on growth, industry, and profit considerations. Governmental influence upon, and interference with, the economy is taken for granted today, yet little attention is paid to the social and environmental costs of such manipulation. Much attention, however, is paid to increasing the Gross National Product (GNP) and the standard of living, both in real terms. Under natural resource limitations and environmental pressures, this attitudinal circumstance may undergo a reorientation toward quality and survival, e.g., energy crises. This is particularly true with the scarcity concept in operation, where several economic institutions are in competition for the allocation of environmental *segments.* Ecological interdependencies and the environmental cost of negative influences may then complicate the economic—environmental system. H. T. Odum cited a study based on a soil analysis in a Denmark farming community, which indicated that the agricultural and plant capacity and productivity had been reduced approximately 30 percent due to pollution from surrounding industry.[11]

Communications Revolution: As conceptualized by McLuhan, the relatively recent

7

"communications revolution" now exposes practically everyone to various media on a current and changing basis.[12] The impact of this revolution appears to be a paradox for environmental administration. On the one hand, exposure to mass media creates increasing "needs," and wants for affluence among all segments of the public. This naturally results in increased demands for goods and services, with a consequent depletion of natural resources and the deterioration of the environment in many cases. On the other hand, the various media also present information on environmental issues and problems which results in an informed citizenry and in organizations which are increasingly, and aggressively, modifying and influencing environmental policy decisions through their expression of concern for environmental quality survival.

Big Government: With the emergence of big business and big labor organizations, big government has also become a way of life for America. A vast complex of autonomous bureaucracies with specific ends and murky centralization inevitably has great difficulties in developing an integrated environmental approach. There are more than 60 federal agencies, several major departments (the State Department has recently added an Environmental Affairs Section to its organization), and about a dozen independent agencies involved, directly and indirectly, in environmental matters within the framework of the federal government alone. This array does not take into consideration their environmental counterparts on the state and local levels or the bulk of the total government, which has more indirect influence on environmental administration. On the federal level, there are more than 150 agencies handling more than a thousand different programs. Although big-government considerations are a very important factor in environmental decisions, irresponsiveness—exemplified by agency selfishness and impotency within the mass of the bureaucracy—prevents the solution of many real and urgent problems. Yet, in a big-government-oriented society, there is the assumption that government will solve all problems, including environmental ones.

Social and Psychological Aspects: We are becoming aware, through the social sciences, of various factors and forces that influence modern man, and, hence, directly and indirectly, the environmental administration.

1. *Alienation and anomie.* With high mobility (about 20 percent of the population moves each year), urbanization, and other complexities, many Americans today lack a realistic identity with governmental and environmental concerns. The consequences of this are apathy and irresponsibility, which are characteristics of a secondary society.

2. *Constant change.* Under the tremendous social and scientific changes within the last 50 years, value systems are constantly undergoing great stages of flux. Rapid change and ambivalence appear to be normal for contemporary American life. Yet, Milgram notes an overload concept of change: "Overload refers to a system's inability to process inputs from the environment because there are too many inputs for the system to cope with or because successive inputs come so fast that input A can not be processed when input B is presented."[13] The end result is usually a confusion of values for long-range governmental and environmental planning.

3. *Crisis orientation.* Public attention and governmental actions appear, in many ways, to follow a pattern of reactions to crisis situations. This results in large inputs over short terms, rather than continuous inputs on a given problem or issue over the long range. Some individuals have observed that this may be the response pattern on environmental issues.

4. *Organizational orientation.* According to de Tocqueville, America is a nation of joiners of organizations.[14] Pressure groups and organizations exert strong influences upon the government and the environment. Action by individuals is slight compared to that of the organization or outer-directed man who is oriented to group values, rather than to inner values. Organization values, of their own particular collective nature, can thus become determining values for environmental administration.

Christianity: Although America may be a conglomeration of religions, it is still strongly influenced by Christianity and certain misconceptions of it. Lynn White, Jr. states, "Especially in its Western form, Christianity is the most anthropocentric religion the world has seen." He comments that some Christian assumptions provide man with the justification for technological exploitation of the earth and its living things without recognition of responsibility toward other forms of life.[15] Obviously, exploitative values and actions are sometimes based on such misconceptions, and exert considerable pressure on environmental administration.

Western Characteristics: Given that the great majority of public lands and natural resources is located west of the Mississippi, it would be wise to note general characteristics of the western subculture as identified by both Donnally and Jonas: (*1*) the emphasis on development of natural resources, particularly water; (*2*) strong natural resource pressure groups, especially in the areas of water, power, ranching, and mining; (*3*) an acute awareness of the federal government and the strong influence of westerners on federal natural resource agencies; and (*4*) the weight given to an individual's independence and personality.[16,17] Independent economic exploitation of natural resources is highly valued in many cases. Many western attitudes and values center around the traditional frontier exploitation, with little recognition of environmental problems and considerations. New Mexico ranchers, for example, recently used a harmful pesticide on caterpillars, disregarding its environmental effects. Many westerners tend to view public lands as provincially owned. Also, federal administrators, under the concept of multiple use, are subject to pressure for economic development from local communities.

Frontier Tradition: In terms of "progress" and other considerations discussed above, the frontier tradition is still somewhat operative in America regardless of time and value lags. F. J. Turner, in his classic paper *The Frontier in American History,* considered American Democracy to be the outcome of experiences of people in dealing with the West. He considered the frontier interaction to have had profound influences on American values. America has had the richest frontier in the history of the world (large rivers, deep soil, relative absence of danger, etc.). Although Turner documented the disappearance of the American frontier in 1890,[18] symbolic frontier concepts and values still

9

permeate American life, and hence, affect environmental administration. Some of these exploitative and negative attitudes remain in both the public and private sectors, affording a danger to present and future environmental conditions.

Population Explosion: As a paramount problem confronting environmental survival, quality, and administration, the population explosion has been, and is being, discussed through various media. It is obvious that through geometric growth, averaging 2 percent or more each year with death controls and persistent birth rates, the carrying capacity of the world environment will soon be exceeded. Under the impact of what Ehrlich describes as "too many people," there will be serious repercussions for environmental administration, including pressures from domestic and external sources, such as world famines. Ehrlich notes that an American child, as a member of the largest consumer nation of the world, consumes many times the amount of resources that a child from an underdeveloped nation would consume.[19]

From a governmental viewpoint, a decrease in democracy, and in the personal dignity, quality of life, and welfare of the individual, occurs with a large increase in numbers. This usually involves expanded governmental controls through bureaucracy and centralization. In short, if the population explosion is not controlled, a proliferation in totalitarian and authoritarian patterns of government is bound to result. As part of the governmental process the environmental administration—because of the increasing pressures caused by the population explosion—will inevitably be forced to control and regulate the behavior of individuals for their collective survival. A minor indication of this process is an alternative which has recently been proposed for the future of Yellowstone National Park; this alternative would consist of a computerized reservation system which would dictate if, when, and how long an individual could visit the park over a several-year period. Although this is a relatively minor intrusion on individual freedom, with a continued population explosion it is obvious that the government would be forced into severe restrictions based on overpopulation.

CONSERVATION AND ENVIRONMENTAL MOVEMENTS

As major influences on environmental policy and administration, the conservation and environmental movements can be contrasted and compared. Literature on these movements is more than abundant in the communications media; thus, only a brief conceptual treatment will be given. Gusfield defines social movements as "socially shared demands for change in some aspect of the social order." He notes that movements, with growth and recognition, tend to generate public controversy.[20] For all practical purposes the environmental movement can be viewed as an extension and elaboration of the conservation movement. Yet the former, which essentially emerged as a mass ideology in the late 1960s, is a much more powerful force. Simplified, the conservation movement is oriented to the "wise" use of natural resources for present and future generations, which may sometimes mean preserving the status quo. As a concept, conservation is highly valued in America; few politicians or administrators would publically oppose this ideology.

Although not specifically called conservation, various measures and regulations were introduced to promote wise use of natural resources in America as early as the colonial period. Regulation on the number of deer one could take, forest reservations for timber for the Royal Navy, land reserved for town parks, etc., were examples of these early conservation activities. Officially, however, the conservation movement in America is attributed to the 1908 White House Conference on Conservation, which was comprised of state governors and conservation leaders who were called together by President Theodore Roosevelt. Gifford Pinchot, the chief of the Forest Service from 1899 to 1908, was a powerful force behind conservation and the conference.

Pinchot is credited with proposing the direction for early conservation efforts, that is, the use and management of natural resources for the greatest good of the greatest number of people over the longest time. This goal, however, was borrowed from the utilitarian ideal of the English philosopher Bentham, who was referring to concepts of law when he made the original statement. Given the broad concepts of wise use, numerous different interpretations, approaches, and philosophies were introduced into the conservation movement by individuals, agencies, and organizations. Hendee, Gale, and Harry note that in the conservation movement of the mid-twentieth century a schism exists between individuals promoting conservation for wise use and development and those promoting conservation for purposes of preservation and appreciation. They consider the latter to be associated with the more educated and middle-class segments of society.[21] This schism within the conservation movement has had a considerable impact on pressure directed at natural resource agencies, which are, in many cases, concerned with wise use of a single resource or area of concern.

Although the conservation movement has usually subscribed to management of natural resources on an ecological basis, a total ecological approach did not come into play until relatively recently. Individuals, agencies, organizations, and industries were previously operating within comfortable definitions and limits of their responsibilities relative to specific natural resources. W. F. Clark identifies three major forces which recently changed the narrow and specific orientation of the conservation movement: (*1*) the population explosion; (*2*) the urban movement with voting reapportionment; and (*3*) the cumulative and indiscriminate effects of manipulation and contamination. Regarding the latter, he notes:

> Each small action, each shovel of dirt, each ounce of pesticide, each car exhaust, each jet plane, each backyard incinerator, each cow in the feedlot, each yard of asphalt or concrete covering the water-absorbing earth, each beer can in the barrow pit, each mile of interstate, each acre of block-filled land, each building on a flood plain, each pound of garbage, each acre of overgrazed land, each factory or refinery, and, yes, even each rocket shot into space has little effect. But cumulatively the effect is staggering and catastrophic.[22]

11

Under the impact of these forces, ecological gaps were not being covered by the conservation movement, or by government and society at large. The impact of the environmental movement emerged with the growing awareness of conservationists and other segments of the population. Where the conservation movement encompassed ecology, the environmental movement is based on ecology, with emphasis on population and pollution problems. Many of the leaders of the conservation movement were government scientists and individuals from various professions. But the spokesmen of the environmental movement are largely professional ecologists and biologists, such as Eugene Odum, Barry Commoner, and Paul Ehrlich. In the role of modern Jeremiahs, they are warning the public and government about imminent environmental problems from man's abuses and interventions in a complex and interrelated ecosystem.[23]

Although the conservation movement contained relatively small segments of the total population on an organized basis, it could count on hazy and fluctuating support from the general public. With the ecological inputs bombarding the public through various media, however, the environmental movement appears to have taken on the nature of a mass ideology, with strong and active public support. A certain amount of this might be explained by man's intuitive recognition that he is a dependent part of the complex biosphere, with responsibilities for both *Homo sapiens* and other forms of life. Surrounded by examples and cumulative effects of environmental deterioration, it is obvious that the general public has become responsive to the ecological message. As an experienced conservationist, Doris Leonard, notes, "We are frustrated by what is happening around us, as is everyone else, but at least the song we have been singing all our adult lives is now being hummed by a great many people.[24]

Although the conservation movement was involved in political–administrative processes, it did not have the political and public force that the environmental movement now appears to have. While conservation issues were involved in politics, and while limited political activities were undertaken by conservationists, the recent environmental movement has politicized conservation. Environmental administration and its associated agencies, and also private industry, are greatly influenced by this political–environmental movement as contrasted with past conservation activities, the environmental movement— much more than the conservation movement—has embraced the law as an effective means for attaining its objectives.

Like all movements, however, conservation and environmentalism are subject to numerous interpretations, and are beset with controversies over their broad philosophic concepts. Differing degrees of emphasis on values, priorities, and perceptions, the relative importance of crises, and the appropriateness of uses, actions for preservation, etc., result in a somewhat disorganized and discordant internal situation. All movements, moreover, usually have to face an antimovement; the antienvironmental movement or ecology backlash contains various organizations that feel threatened by having public attention diverted from their movements, or in having their vested interests attacked. Regardless of this, the environmental movement appears to be a powerful unifying force for America. There are some 150 national organizations with thousands of state and local groups, which may reflect the tip of the iceberg of public concern. There are also numerous ad hoc environmental groups formed to deal with specific problems, and environmental committees within diverse organizations.

The conservation movement was mainly concerned with a program of wise use of natural resources with ecological considerations. The central message of the environmental movement is change based upon ecology, for survival and quality; social, economic, political, and institutional changes will have to occur in order to meet growing environmental problems and crises. Relatively few conservationists advocated drastic changes on a doomsday basis. Yet, the very basis for the changes advocated by ecologists and environmentalists is the prediction of imminent environmental disaster. Commoner notes, "Every one of the ecological changes needed for the sake of preserving our environment is going to place added stresses within the social [and governmental] structure. We really can't solve the environmental crisis without solving the resulting social crisis." Commoner feels that once Americans recognize the problems, they will arrive at proper answers through the democratic process.[25]

On the assumption that environmental policy should be strongly oriented to ecological concerns, recognition of the social, cultural, political, and economic considerations, is a first step toward wise decision making for the public interest. Limitations of government associated with a narrow agency ideology and vested interests will obviously be subjected to the impact of the environmental movement. Given that environmentalism is an extension of the conservation movement, with a broader and more urgent ecological and political decision-making process, which can, in turn, result in the conservation of the government and society.

Scientific and technological management of the environment without ecological consideration is not working. Environmental policy and administration cannot operate in a vacuum. Interaction of science with positive ecological values can strongly influence the political decision-making process, which, can in turn, result in the conservation of the environment for man and other forms of life. Administrative stewardship of the environment calls for value recognition and change on a sound ecological basis.

REFERENCES

1. Daniel H. Henning, "Natural Resources Administration and the Public Interest," *Public Administration Review* 30, no. 2 (March–April 1970) pp. 134–140.
2. John C. Hendee, Richard P. Gale, and Joseph Harry, "Conservation, Politics and Democracy," *Journal of Soil and Water Conservation* 24, no. 6 (November–December 1969) pp. 212–215.
3. Daniel H. Henning, "Comments on an Interdisciplinary Social Science Approach for Conservation Administration," *BioScience* 20, no. 1 (January 1, 1970) pp. 11–12.
4. Charles E. Lindblom, "The Science of Muddling Through," *Public Administration Review* 29 (Spring 1959) p. 84.

5. Garrett Hardin, "The Tragedy of the Commons," *Science* 162, no. 3859 (1968) p. 1243.
6. Gabriel A. Almond, "The General Value Orientations of the American People," in *Readings in the American Political System,* eds. D. L. Shaw and John C. Pierce (Lexington, Mass.: Heath, 1970) pp. 24–27.
7. *Ibid.,* pp. 25–27.
8. John C. Hendee, Richard P. Gale, and Joseph Harry, "Conservation, Politics and Democracy," *Journal of Soil and Water Conservation* 24 no. 6 (November–December 1969) pp. 212–215.
9. *Ibid.,* p. 214.
10. Wilson F. Clark, "The Technician's Role in Public Conservation Education" (Paper delivered at the Soil Conservation Service District Conservation meeting, Boise, Idaho, September 1969) p. 2.
11. H. T. Odum, Comments following a paper delivered at the Interdisciplinary Natural Resource Biologists' Conference of the American Institute of Biological Sciences, University of Wyoming, June 31, 1970.
12. Marshall McLuhan, *The Medium is the Message* (New York: Bantam, 1970).
13. Stanley Milgram, "The Experience of Living in Cities," *Science* 167 (March 13, 1970) p. 1461.
14. Alexis de Tocqueville, *Democracy in America* (New York: New American Library, 1965) pp. 196–200.
15. Lynn White, Jr., "The Historical Roots of Our Ecological Crisis," *Science* 155, no. 3767 (March 10, 1967) pp. 1203–1207.
16. Thomas C. Donnally, *Rocky Mountain Politics* (Albuquerque: University of New Mexico Press, 1940) pp. 1–30.
17. Frank Jonas, *Western Politics* (Salt Lake City: University of Utah Press, 1961) pp. 357–373.
18. Frederic Jackson Turner, *The Frontier in American History* (New York: Holt, Rinehart & Winston, 1947).
19. Paul R. Ehrlich, *The Population Bomb* (New York: Ballantine, 1968).
20. Joseph R. Gusfield, "The Study of Social Movements," in *International Encyclopedia of the Social Sciences,* ed. David Sills (New York: Macmillan, 1968) p. 1.
21. John C. Hendee, Richard P. Gale, and Joseph Harry, "Conservation, Politics and Democracy," *Journal of Soil and Water Conservation* 24, no. 6 (November–December 1969) p. 3.
22. Wilson F. Clark, "The Technician's Role in Public Conservation Education" (Paper delivered at the Soil Conservation Service District Conservation meeting, Boise, Idaho, September 1969) p. 2.
23. *Time* August 15, 1969, p. 38.
24. Doris Leonard, personal communication, February 27, 1970.
25. *Time* August 3, 1970, p. 42.

Chapter 2

ENVIRONMENTAL POLICY AND POLITICS

VALUE AND POWER CONTEXT

Decisions affecting environmental policies grow out of a political process. This process involves the *values* of individuals, groups, and organizations in the struggle for *power* through human interaction relative to the decisions. Basically, it is a process of human interaction relating to the political ecology. The technologies and sciences of environmental administration cannot supply the value base for governmental decisions, considered means rather than ends. Although resource management sciences and technologies of environmental administration have attained a relatively high level, present problems and political realities call for emphasis on values, power conflicts, and human interaction in determining environmental policy.

In the framework of this text, values will be approached within a broad, encompassing definition. Thus, "values" include ends, goals, interests, beliefs, ethics, biases, attitudes, traditions, morals and objectives that change with human perception and with time, and that have a significant influence on power conflicts relating to policy. Money and power are encompassed in this definition as are such intangibles as quality and aesthetics. The definition encompasses value systems of individuals and of groups, agencies, organizations, and professions. It is recognized that organizational values may differ somewhat from an individual's, in that the organization has a life of its own; it is an organism in symbolic sense. Adjustments and interactions of individuals and organizations will, however, result in interrelated value systems.

A central characteristic of our age is ambiguity and confusion of values. America appears to have difficulty with values and goals while attaining near perfection in science and technology. Values, moreover, are constantly changing. Phillip Abelson notes that social goals become moving targets for science and technology. With the targets coming and going in short periods, an impossible mismatch occurs relative to research and application.[1] The priorities and tenacities of values may also vary over time, particularly as they are affected by power conflicts. By their very nature, values are difficult to describe and analyze in realistic terms relative to power and policy.

Gordon Allport considers values to be unattainable goals, projected criteria, social consciences, and internalized images that exert creative pressure when applicable.[2] Numerous educators agree that values cannot be taught, but that they must be learned by

15

the individual through experience and inspiration or both. Philosophers note that some values may not consciously emerge until one becomes angry at a particular negative discussion, decision, or action. With the foregoing complexities, it is probably safe to say that values pertain to something of worth and conscience on both an individual and collective basis. This worth or conscience would have to be sufficient to influence individual or organizational activity in the power struggle surrounding a given policy decision.

Among the complex value systems in politics, environmental administration also encompasses dimensions of values unique to ecology: future generations, other forms of life, quality, and other intangibles. Some of them are eloquently described by Aldo Leopold in "The Land Ethic."

The Ethical Sequence

This extension of ethics, so far studied only by philosophers, is actually a process in ecological evolution. Its sequences may be described in ecological as well as in philosophical terms.

An ethic, ecologically, is a limitation on freedom of action in the struggle for existence. An ethic, philosophically, is a differentiation of social from anti-social conduct. These are two definitions of one thing. The thing has its origin in the tendency of interdependent individuals or groups to evolve modes of cooperation. The ecologist calls these symbioses. Politics and economics are advanced symbioses in which the original free-for-all competition has been replaced, in part, by cooperative mechanisms with an ethical content.

The first ethics dealt with the relation between individuals; the Mosaic Decalogue is an example. Later accretions dealt with the relation between the individual and society. The Golden Rule tries to integrate the individual to society; democracy to integrate social organization to the individual.

There is as yet no ethic dealing with man's relation to land and to the animals and plants which grow upon it. . . . The land-relation is still strictly economic, entailing privileges but not obligations.

An ethic may be regarded as a mode of guidance for meeting ecological situations so new or intricate, or involving such deferred reactions, that the path of social expediency is not discernible to the average individual. Animal instincts are modes of guidance for the individual in meeting such situations. Ethics are possibly a kind of community instinct in-the-making.

The Community Concept

All ethics so far evolved rest upon a single premise: that the individual is a member of a community of interdependent parts. His instincts prompt him to compete for his place in that community, but his ethics prompt him also to cooperate (perhaps in order that there may be a place to compete for).

The land ethic simply enlarges the boundaries of the community to include soils, waters, plants, and animals, or collectively: the land.

In short, a land ethic changes the role of *Homo sapiens* from conqueror of the land-community to plain member and citizen of it. It implies respect for his fellow-members, and also respect for the community as such.[3]

Given the general environmental value placed on harmony between man and nature, it is appropriate to recognize the complexities, intensities, and varieties of individual interpretations given as they relate to environmental policy. On the assumption that there is not a transcendental ecological value, specific situations, conflicts, and compromises may dictate combinations of value interpretations. In fact, with the intense popularity of the environmental "game" in public, political, and governmental spheres, sound ecological values may become platitudes supporting nonrelated values, interests, and opportunities. With more than 80 federal agencies involved in the environmental issue, and with environment as a risk-free political issue, value appeals may not prove to be actualities because of interagency power struggles.

In the political administrative process of environmental policy, it is thus appropriate to recognize that actual ecological values (or interpretations thereof) may be of limited significance in the power struggle preceding decision making. On a realistic basis, values pertaining to agency survival and expansion, to clientele, industry, and interested individuals, are a definite part of the process. In this sense, power itself can become a value. Given a particular value orientation, it becomes automatic to categorize the "good guys" and the "bad guys" in a given power struggle. With the environmental movement, this categorization becomes increasingly complex and difficult. Under the environmental umbrella a multitude of individuals, groups, and organizations compete for limited power.

Logical positivists and scientific individuals argue for the application of empirical and behavioral sciences in administration, rather than for value considerations. David Hume, an eighteenth-century Scots empiricist, noted that the use of reason is definitely limited. Although reason can be used to show logical relationships, it cannot determine values, which are the products of passion. Thus, reason, according to Hume, is helpful in directing action toward the attainment of values, but it is only an instrument, and cannot discover values. Further, he states, reason is the "slave of passions."[4] Simon, Smithburg, and Thompson also note:

> Close examination of the premises that underlie any administrative choice will show that they involve two distinct kinds of elements: value elements and factual elements. Speaking very, very roughly, the distinction between value elements and factual elements corresponds to the distinction between ends and means, respectively. Before an individual can rationally choose between several courses of action, he must ask himself: (1) what is my objective—my goal [value]? and (2) which of these courses of action is best suited to that goal? . . .[5]

> Almost every value premise has some factual element in it—an element that cannot be completely removed—because most ends or goals [values] are at least partly means to more final ends than ends in themselves.[6]

In order to influence a policy decision, a particular value must have power over other values. This political process occurs through human interaction. Howard Lasswell considers the study of politics to involve the relationship between the influenced and the influential. The latter are those who get the most of what there is to get. They are the elite who make governmental decisions.[7] Lasswell also notes that political life is a life of conflict and competition for scarce power resources.[8] In the *Federalist Papers,* Madison said: "The latent causes of factions are thus sown in the nature of man; and we see them everywhere brought into different degrees of activity, according to the different circumstances of civil society"; and, "The regulation of these various and interfering interests forms the principal task of modern legislation and involves the spirit of party and faction in the necessary and ordinary operation of government."[9] Madison thought that factions of interest were bound to emerge in governmental problems that would cause conflicts. Many of the factions he anticipated were based on poverty (or symbolic territory).

In a pluralistic society, the group basis of politics is stressed. Various groups, including governmental agencies, representing disparate values, constantly compete for power, and for decisions favorable to their particular vested interests. Politics affect environmental policy when: (*1*) segments of the public are affected in a positive or negative manner; (*2*) a particular natural resource (including, on occasion, public land) has possibilities for utilization, with alignments being created automatically; and (*3*) economic, social, and ideological impacts occur or are possible. According to Norman Wengert, however, many policy decisions for the environment are made privately, by nongovernmental means.[10] Nevertheless, public concerns and, hence, the government, are increasingly involved. With the involvement of government, political considerations become the dominant force in decision making, especially in a society that relies heavily on government.

A major aspect of politics in government, including environmental administration, is the informal exercise of power. Livingston and Thompson note that bureaucracies frequently rely on brokerage politics to solve problems.[11] By brokerage politics, they mean the process of resolving conflicts in democracy without reference to "the consent of the governed." This process involves informal bargaining, compromise, and dealing with interest groups involved in value conflicts. Griffith describes this brokerage process with his whirlpool theory, which includes informal and formal associations and conferences among various people (including governmental officials) who are interested in common objectives or problems. These individuals are often acquainted on a first-name basis with counterparts representing other interests. People are "whirlpooled" into the decision-making process through bargaining. According to Giffith, much of governmental policy is matured in this process.[12]

GENERAL POLICY

Policy is a reflection of the culture in which it is formulated and operates. In the American culture, pragmatic and pluralistic characteristics are dominant in general policy areas. Wengert notes that this orientation results in an absence of an overall, ideological policy for the environment. He recognizes only one common ideological basis for all environmental programs; this is the involvement of government with social goals and

18

problems relating to natural resources.[13] Without a general ideological base, various values are reflected in policy adopted at every level. The end result is a collection of fragmented, short-range policies throughout the spectrum of environmental policy.

Modern public administration appears to operate on a crisis basis, oriented to immediate problem solving. Today, the political climate and changing conditions do not appear to allow much stability in policy. Given the thousands of legislative acts pertaining to the environment, and given the more than 80 federal environmental agencies with their respective policies in constant flux, macro and micro policies have a tendency to reflect a quest for pragmatic, short-term solutions. Regarding this approach, Wengert notes:

> A critic once wrote that a major characteristic of pragmatic philosophy was that it was no philosophy. Although this judgment is perhaps unduly harsh, it points to a lack of interest in the formulation of general principles or ideological systems among those pragmatically oriented. Pragmatism is pluralistic and eclectic, focusing on problems and performance rather than principles, upon action rather than upon ideas. The pragmatic test of "will it work" or "how does it work" deemphasizes ideology in the sense of a developed synthetic system of beliefs and values to govern action.[14]

In the pragmatic and pluralistic approach to environmental policies, the one unifying ideological theme is ecology. Although this concept has been present in varying forms since the early conservation days, it has only recently attained actual legislative authority. During the last several years, legislation and policy have greatly expanded the theme. A central piece of legislation was the U.S. National Environmental Policy Act of 1969. The purposes of the Act were: "To declare a national policy which will encourage productive and enjoyable harmony between man and his environment; to promote efforts which will prevent or eliminate damage to the environment and biosphere and stimulate the health and welfare of man; to enrich the understanding of the ecological systems and natural resources important to the Nation; and to establish a Council on Environmental Quality."[15]

The National Environmental Policy Act stipulates that a systematic, interdisciplinary, and interagency approach to environmental quality be followed by the more than 80 agencies concerned; this and other environmental requirements are considered as supplemental to the original agency legislation and policy. The agencies are also to report any inconsistencies and deficiencies of legislation, policies, or procedures that interfere with compliance with the purposes and provisions of the Act.[16] It is obvious that the great majority of the agencies must be mission policy organizations with vested interest areas. Under broad congressional mandates over the years, agencies have evolved policies, procedures, programs, philosophies, and clienteles that limit their responsiveness to broad environmental needs. In a sense, the limitations and definitions of policy responsibility have served to protect agencies from complexities and demands. But with the environmental movement and its inherent problems the agencies are forced, through legislation, into change and into neglected problem areas, as well as into consideration of the total environment. Although outward conformance to changes in policy is required, this does not necessarily mean that the dominant influences of the past will not retain a key role in the actual direction of each agency.

At the same time, under the constant crisis situation faced by modern public administrators, executives are making policy on a regular basis and are drafting the majority of legislation for policy. Thus, the American Society for Public Administration's Task Force on Society Goals notes:

> The jamming together of policy and administration raised an eyebrow a generation and a half ago; now it is so much the case that the administrators make up a very high proportion of the policy makers.

> Today's crisis exceeds all historical crises in public administration. Due to the complexity of government, the intricate interrelationships between policy and administration, the public executive of today and tomorrow has a newly recognized role and responsibility, whether he or she is on a public or private payroll. Public executives, taken as a group, have not yet awakened to the fact that they are in charge. They are responsible for the operation of our society; they cannot wait around for somebody to tell them what to do. If they don't know the answers, we're lost.[17]

Because there are definite indications of an increasing tendency for environmental policy to be formulated and implemented by public executives, their individual value systems are becoming crucial.

In essence, policy itself is a statement of principles, intentions, values, and objectives that serves as a guide for operation and limitation of an agency. While policy is largely based on legislation, this usually involves broad, idealistic guidelines that are themselves highly subject to interpretations by the administrator. Ambiguity naturally enters the picture, particularly with changes in time, individuals, problems, and institutions. This is particularly true of crisis-type administrative policy making, in which the overall policy appears to be less than stable or permanent. Policy itself is an expression of objectives which, in conflict situations, compete for dominancy.

Given the value emphasis of policy, Lindblom notes that values are always a problem of adjustments at a margin, and that there is no practical way to state marginal objectives without reference to particular situations. Relative to the individual administrator's value system, he notes that shifts in values occur according to the situation. Hence, it is impossible to establish a rank order of values that would apply to different situations. Lindblom states that: (*1*) "... one chooses among values and among policies at one and the same time"; and (*2*) "... the administrator focuses his attention on marginal or incremental values." Lindblom considers policy making to be incremental. It is a process of adding to existing precedent in a relevant and simplistic fashion. He notes that although policy is formulated through a group process, the decision makers cannot explain the theories or values behind their policy decisions.[18]

On the other hand, Biswas observes that policy decisions, particularly in water resources management, are rarely of a "once-off," or final, nature. He states that ". . . the problem initially started with usually gives rise to new problems which necessitate new techniques of solution, which, in turn, make decision making a dynamic process. Hence, in general, water resources decisions are not once-off decisions; they are a series of successive decisions, somewhat similar to the dynamic programing type of approach."[19]

MULTIPLE USE

The ambiguity of marginal values, suggested in Lindblom's approach, automatically lends itself to multiple use, a major policy orientation in many resource management agencies. Although multiple use will be considered in other sections, it will be treated briefly here in relation to general policy goals. In essence, multiple use provides a concept for dealing with two or more uses of a given area or resource. But, like any other concept, multiple use is highly subject to individual interpretation. The U.S. Forest Service (FS) is particularly noted for having utilized the concept of multiple use over the years in handling conflicting interests. Through actual or implied authorization, other resource agencies, for example, the Bureau of Reclamation (BR), and Bureau of Land Management (BLM), have operated under the policy concept for some time. In 1960, Congress made it official policy for the FS and other agencies.

There appear to be two schools of thought on multiple-use policy. The first, specialization, advocates assigning a particular area or resource to a dominant use, and then permitting complementary, nonconflicting uses (and excluding some possible uses that might conflict) to form around the dominant use.[20] The other, generalization, permits as many uses of a given area or resource as possible, with the understanding that some conflicts will occur. However, demands for the use of a particular resource are not mutually exclusive. Often contributions to one can be made at the expense of another. A former chief of the FS and strong advocate of generalization, Richard E. McArdle, feels that the multiple-use policy should follow the middle of the road and that a key principle should be "the greatest good to the greatest number in the long run." McArdle further suggests that multiple use serves as a "buffer" in a democracy by not permitting a given interest to have its way. Thus, he notes that dissatisfaction expressed by various interests and organizations is actually a healthy sign that the multiple-use system is operating satisfactorily.[21]

Through brokerage politics, and because of marginal value ambiguity, the multiple-use concept can serve as a smokescreen for the favored interests and commercial satellites of a given agency. For example: (*1*) FS–lumber industry; (*2*) BLM–grazing industry; (*3*) National Park Service (NPS)–mass recreation; (*4*) Soil Conservation Service (SCS)–family-sized farms; (*5*) BR–irrigation; and (*6*) Corps of Engineers (CE)–flood control. Although recent legislation, as well as administrative arrangements, prescribe other environmental quality criteria, tradition and legislation establishing dominant use and interest may preclude agency responsiveness under a multiple-use concept. Thus, policy decisions may sound good in marginal value areas when they favor an interest that is interwoven into the agency fabric. Although multiple use can often be a valuable working concept, it does provide a smokescreen where favored interests can operate outside environmental considerations.

PRESSURE GROUPS

In all aspects of environmental policy, including the multiple-use concept, pressure groups exert powerful and continuous forces upon policy formulation and its implementation. This has been true from the nation's earliest days, particularly as concerns distribution or retention of federally controlled public lands. Wengert notes that a major characteristic of resource (i.e., environmental) politics is extensive pressure group activity and associated diversity, intensity, and inflexibility.[22] As in other areas of public policy making, thousands of pressure groups are involved in the environmental policy-making process; they have a great influence upon decisions made by the federal executive and legislative branches, as well as at the state and local levels. The general concern of pressure groups is to gain access to the governmental decision-making process whenever and wherever policy is being formulated that affects their special interests.[23]

Commenting on the activities of pressure groups, Wengert notes:

> In simplest terms, the struggle is for power—power to influence and control factors of major, even vital, importance to the group and to its members. The political struggle is more often for something than against other groups. It is a struggle for advantage and position rather than a fight with specific adversaries. It may also involve the protection of status quo and a desire to veto change. At the same time, the success of one group may mean the failure of another, so conflict and hostility among groups may exist, although it is not often an immediate goal and end in itself. . . .
>
> More often, however, the struggle is based upon winning friends, alliances, and alignments as a means of influencing the course of governmental decisions. Typical weapons are discussion and debate, persuasion and education, propaganda and advertising and decisions are usually reached by conference negotiation and ballot, rather than by means of the blackjack or tommy gun.[24]

With the billions of dollars involved in environmental resource policies, many of the pressure groups are economically oriented. A broad generalization can be made concerning environmental pressure groups. They are divided into two categories: (*1*) those associated with the economic interests of a particular clientele, e.g., the National Woolgrowers' Association (grazing) and the National Reclamation Association (water); and (*2*) those associated with ideological interests of private citizens, e.g., the Sierra Club (wilderness) and the National Wildlife Federation (wildlife). As a result of the environmental movement many of the ideologically based groups are now oriented toward broader environmental concerns. Generally speaking, those associated with specific economic interests are registered lobbyist citizen organizations, while ideologically motivated groups are considered educational, even though they, too, seek to influence policy in various spheres. Both categories of pressure group are, however, engaged in creating a public and political force favorable to their particular interests. And both types usually maintain professional staffs to handle many of their activities.

The above-mentioned classification is based upon the formal definition of pressure groups, with their obvious connotation of specialized interest. A more realistic and comprehensive picture would encompass all organizations that influence, or are influenced by, the complexities of environmental policy. In the private and public spheres, large organizations make a majority of the decisions that influence environmental policy at the governmental level. At the same time, it becomes increasingly difficult to identify various aspects of the decision-making process within the large governmental agencies and private industries that have a stake in the environment.

All organizations, whether the BLM or General Motors, are intrinsically dedicated to survival and expansion. Don Kash identifies modern organizations as technological complexes and syntheses of managerial and specialized skills and ideas.[26] He notes that modern organizations are capable of developing new technologies and, hence, of dictating and changing governmental policies. Underlying their concern for survival, there is also a force within such organizations to create new functions and policies to permit their continued operation and expansion. As an example of this, witness the present efforts by National Aeronautics and Space Administration (NASA) and the Atomic Energy Commission (AEC). In many instances, technology becomes the instrument for survival of organizational goals. Managerial and specialized skills become the complex force behind this instrument for sustaining life. Kash also notes that when an organization attains a particular goal, program, or task, it has accumulated skills and tools which, in turn, force it to develop new goals, programs, and tasks.

Thus, Kash considers that organizations are necessarily forced to expand into all spheres, including that of the government, with the result being the further growth of a technological society. Yet he notes that much of this growth is oriented at first-order consequences that are of a tangible, quantitative, materialistic, and progressive nature. Second-order consequences, according to Kash, are ecological considerations of quality and other intangibles, which large technological organizations tend to ignore. He further suggests that the value orientation of modern organizations toward innovation and growth dictates the ideology of our present society.[27] With this emphasis, technological organizations become pressure groups that influence environmental policy. Given that the decision-making process is difficult to identify, political and economic actions, as well as the force of technological innovations, permeate the entire spectrum of institutions and power bases (e.g., the executive and legislative branches) involved in determination of environmental affairs.

It should also be recognized that governmental agencies are operating as environmental policy pressure groups in the informal sense. With the existent broad legislative directives regarding the establishment and missions of the more than 80 federal agencies involved in environmental affairs, it is obvious that many environmental and natural resource policy decisions are products of pressure exerted by the individual agencies. Legislative liaison sections and federal agency personnel contribute a large percentage of congressional legislation. Through informal operations of the whirlpool theory and brokerage politics, agency personnel influence environmental policies and programs at various levels.

Agencies, at the same time, are clientele-oriented organizations that serve special interests through their mission orientations. Thus, they give a high priority to a favored interest and its commercial satellites in their pressure group activities (e.g., the FS and the lumber industry, the BR and irrigation programs). Symbiotic relationships are sometimes maintained between an agency and its clientele by means of behind-the-scenes political operations and support for specific policies, programs, and budgets (e.g., the relationship existing between the BR and the National Reclamation Association). Many agency–client relationships are economically oriented and, hence, are given first-order consideration; this results in little attention to second-order considerations concerned with the public interest. Complex informal associations are formed between personnel of the agency and the client, which have a pragmatic effect on policy making. Specialized and compatible dominant interests within agencies and organizations form the basis for these associations.

A major offshoot of such shared interests has been the growth and intensity of pressure groups associated with conservation and environmental matters. Because of the public's recent interest in the environmental movement, the membership of these thousands of organizations now numbers in the millions. The groups are organized through existing affiliations or independently along national, state, and local lines. Although their interests and objectives may reflect diverse ideologies centered around a particular resource or cause, there is a growing tendency for various organizations to unify in support of a specific environmental program. Many of the conservation and environmental pressure groups are primarily concerned about the dominant, or specialized, objectives pertaining to their establishment; for example, the Wilderness Society–wilderness; the National Audobon Society–birds; the National Wildlife Federation–wildlife, etc. Some of the more recently formed environmental action groups, e.g., the Friends of the Earth, are, however, concerned with general ecological matters.

Given the diversity of the conservation and environmental groups, a common characteristic is their growing involvement in politics, seeking action on environmental problems. Although the organizations are based on voluntary citizen memberships and contributions, an executive director with a professional staff usually handles the everyday operations and directs each organization. Newsletters and other releases from the professional staff bring matters for action—contributions, public hearings, studies, projects, letters to congressmen and administrators, etc.—to the membership's attention. Much of this action is centered on influencing the legislature and the administration to adopt a policy decision or to take action in line with the objectives of the organization. Through formal (committee reports, testimony, statements, budget hearings) and informal (whirlpool, watchdog activities, and brokerage politics) methods, the organizations' professional staffs and elected officials carry on complex interactions with congressmen and administrators in an effort to influence environmental policy.

With the growing political involvement of conservation and environmental pressure groups, in contrast to their previous educational roles and minor political activity, complexities have been introduced regarding the legal status of these organizations under The Federal Regulation of Lobbying Act of 1946. This Act prescribes that anyone engaged in lobbying must report his expenditures and activities. It also requires that lobbying organizations cannot be tax exempt and, hence, contributors to an organization of this nature cannot claim charitable tax deductions for income tax purposes. Although the Act is notorious for its loopholes and superficial compliance regulations, economic pressure groups—in order to curtail environmental pressure groups—have called upon the Internal Revenue Service (IRS) to investigate such groups, enforcing the Act's various regulations. In the late 1960s such a challenge resulted in the IRS's revocation of the tax-exempt status of the Sierra Club; the organization is no longer exempt from federal income tax and contributions to it are no longer deductible.[28] Under this pattern, other environmental pressure groups have been intimidated.

It should be noted that environmental pressure groups are citizen-oriented, nonprofit organizations with meager budgets based on volunteer contributions. In many cases they come under the same classification as church and educational pressure groups which the IRS has not investigated regardless of their political activities. Harry, Gale, and Hendee note that the membership of conservation and environmental organizations is largely comprised of upper-middle-class citizens who are well educated and articulate, with an urban base, and long-term commitments to difficult causes.[29] Although many of the conservation organizations were originally formulated with educational objectives (including the education of politicians and officials), it is obvious that present environmental organizations lean more toward political activity. Some organizations, such as Friends of the Earth and Zero Population Growth, have waived all tax-exemption considerations so that they may engage directly in political and lobbying activities (including contributions to political candidates). Perhaps this exemplifies a growing recognition that pressure groups, including agencies, are strong formulators of governmental policy. Yet, severe IRS interpretation and enforcement of the Lobbying Act could result in serious loss of financial support to most environmental pressure groups.

The National Wildlife Federation notes:

> Non-profit organizations representing the public interest depend on tax exemptions for survival. Through intent or circumstance, the vague tax laws and IRS rulings (or lack of them) make for a tenuous existence.
>
> The tax laws and rulings for tax-exempt organizations legitimately representing the public

interest are plainly inequitable. A private company can lobby in Congress, take out newspaper ads, pay attorney fees, and largely write off the cost as a business expense. A tax-exempt organization representing the public interest, however, exists at the whim of the IRS and engages in similar activities at its own peril.

The classic case in point, of course, was the debacle wherein the Sierra Club took out newspaper advertisements supporting conservation issues such as the Redwoods National Park and IRS promptly revoked the Club's tax exemption. Of course, the private companies on the other side of the issues wrote off their ads as business expense.[30]

In contrast to the ambiguous position of environmental pressure groups under the Lobbying Act of 1946, economic pressure groups, as representatives of the special interests of industrial and profit-oriented organizations, are usually registered as lobbyists under the Act (e.g., the American Mining Congress, the National Association of Manufacturers, the National Woolgrowers' Association, the Chamber of Commerce, etc.). Although a single industrial organization may have its own pressure group, many economic pressure groups are representatives of several organizations or of various segments of a given industry. With large amounts of money available (although seldom fully declared under the Act's regulations) through industry, economic pressure groups are able to employ outstanding professional staffs, including top legal aides and specialized services. They are also able to engage in a full spectrum of lobbying and public relations activities (sometimes contracted to public relations firms), to create public pressures upon legislators and administrators.

As in the case of environmental pressure groups, economic pressure groups are concerned with protection or expansion of specialized environmental interests. An obvious pattern in economic pressure groups is emphasis on defending the status quo, and delaying legislative and administrative actions that would regulate industry. Obviously, many environmental measures would involve cost increase and profit loss for many segments of industry. Economic pressure groups are naturally concerned with opposing or diluting governmental measures that would harm their organizations or coalition industries. Although it has been a form of political suicide to oppose conservation per se, the intense politicization of the environment has placed economic pressure groups in a complicated and unpopular position in a short period of time.

In essence, much of the struggle facing economic and environmental pressure groups hinges on an ideological polarization, with first-order considerations (profit, materialism, unrestricted free enterprise) at one pole and second-order considerations (ecology, quality, and other intangibles) at the other. To this conflict are added the broad interpretations of modern technological organizations, including governmental agencies. Given this complex array of formal and informal pressure groups, power struggles emerge which have produced, or will produce, an ever-changing environmental policy. Much of this struggle occurs on the informal level. One official from the Nature Conservancy described it as "dealing under the sheets where we punish our enemies and reward our friends as in any political situation."

An emerging pattern is that of environmental pressure groups, particularly local ones, challenging and appealing micro policy decisions made by governmental agencies. Growing public awareness of environmental matters is reflected in the recent trend toward an informed citizenry aggressively modifying and influencing policy decisions through expressions of their values and opinions. It is obvious that resource managers and administrators in a democratic society must be sensitive and responsive to this trend. Perhaps a part of the public's new activism may be ascribed to what McLuhan describes as the "communications revolution" which exposes everyone to resource problems and benefits through various media.[31] Reflecting these local watchdog activities, Edward Cliff, chief of the FS, notes in a special memorandum, "The public is increasingly unhappy with us. This will continue until we get balance and quality into our programs, as well as public involvement in our decisions. Until we do this, the course of the public entering into our fairly routine decisions through protests, appeals, and court cases will have the effect of reducing our ability to put timber on the market to help meet housing goals."[32]

Reflecting further on the FS concern for public involvement in micro policy, at the request of Sen. Lee Metcalf (Democrat, Montana), a special study was made by a select committee of the University of Montana faculty. The study was published in the *Congressional Record* and received national publicity. Among other findings, the committee noted:

> The Forest Service as an effective and efficient bureaucracy needs to be reconstructed so that substantial, responsible, local public participation in the processes of policy formation and decision making can naturally take place.

> The problem arises from public dissatisfaction with the Bitterroot National Forest's overriding concern for sawtimber production. It is compounded by an apparent insensitivity to the related forest uses and to the local public's interest in environmental values. . . .

> It is a federal agency which measures success primarily by the quantity of timber produced weekly, monthly and annually; the staff of the Bitterroot National Forest finds itself unable to change its course, to give anything but token recognition to related values, or to involve most of the local public in any way but as antagonists.[33]

Currently the FS and other resource and environmental agencies are taking drastic steps to ensure public participation in and responsiveness to their policy making. In a pluralistic society, the far greater influence comes through the representatives of pressure groups. It should be recognized that many environmental pressure groups are urban based and, hence, must act from a distance on local policy decisions. With emphasis on local input and official recognition, environmental and economic pressure groups will have an even greater involvement in local environmental policy. Yet a great deal of any pressure group's effectiveness depends upon the local administrator's value system, and his perception of and responsiveness to interests of given pressure groups.

Most environmental agencies are staffed by local administrators with various technological specializations. Ehrmann notes: "A merely technical education, however excellent, does not prepare one sufficiently for the task of developing long-range policies. Pressure of time, always particularly great in these administrations, is added to the pressure of special interests. The shorter the perspective and the narrower the field, the more the civil servant will be inclined to be swayed by the persuasive, pragmatic [argument] profferred by his counterpart speaking for the private sector of the economy."[34]

An unreleased FS study of foresters' perceptions of local pressure groups has revealed that a high percentage of foresters attributed legitimacy to the pragmatic expectations of economic pressure groups, while only a low percentage of foresters considered the intangible expectations of environmental pressure groups to be legitimate. The same study noted the high percentage of foresters committed to utilitarian values (e.g., logging, grazing, mining) associated with local economic pressure groups and communities as contrasted with the appreciative values of urban communities and environmental pressure groups. In many cases, environmental pressure groups, encountering serious frustrations in dealing with bureaucracies to attain their objectives, turn to the law for help.

Environmental Law

Pressure groups, agencies, special legal organizations, and individuals are increasingly turning to the law as a means of attaining particular objectives in the environmental field. In many cases, merely by implying that a given policy will be subjected to legal proceedings, an environmental group can exert enough pressure upon a particular agency or industry to correct the violation, thus avoiding costly and lengthy court proceedings. Nevertheless, with bureaucratic and industrial resistance or apathy to certain objectives of environmental pressure groups, there is increasing recourse to the courts. It is not unusual, for example, to have a given national forest involved in several legal suits with court cases pending. In fact, the growing number of environmental cases, particularly those involving pollution, has caused serious consideration of the establishment of environmental courts.

The recourse of environmentalists to the law can influence environmental policy on an interactional basis. Precedents and legal interpretations relating to the environment forge much of actual environmental policy. With the thousands of federal, state, and local laws pertaining to the environment, as well as numerous administrative laws and agency procedures, it is obvious that the fields of environmental policy and law are complex and interwoven. Moreover, much of environmental policy and law is oriented along ambiguous idealistic lines. Recent environmental legislation and policy are often concerned with quality, but, according to the *Environmental Law Handbook,* this concept is difficult to determine or to define; thus, it is subject to interpretations and manipulations by individuals and organizations.[35] Further, complex and negative ecological influences are not specifically covered in many situations and so must be decided through administrative and legal processes.

The *Environmental Law Handbook* notes that the burden of proof for determining social and ecological costs and damages is usually placed upon the lawyer representing the conservation group. It notes, "This explains why the advocate of environmental quality is almost invariably the plaintiff, complainant, or intervenor in law suits or administrative proceedings and has the attendant heavy burden of showing that the status quo is unreasonable." Continuing, the *Handbook* acknowledges that, "The structure of government contains built-in resistance to change. Officials tend to be victims of bureaucratic inertia. In addition, the present legal and statutory structure is often based on the outmoded concept of unlimited growth."[36]

At the same time, much of environmental law represents the public interest on an equity basis. Bowler notes that the law of equity, which is sometimes known as the law of conscience, is a well recognized part of the legal system under the doctrine "that which should be done shall be done." He further notes that the law of equity is sufficiently powerful legally to overrule statutes, contracts, and other legal forms when demanded by the common right and public benefit.[37] In this sense, the National Environmental Policy Act, requiring government and industry to be responsible to the environmental public interest, might be considered a stated equity law. However, environmental law and pressure groups will be important factors in determining actual policy decisions made under this Act (i.e., regulation) until such time as institutional changes occur.

According to the *Environmental Law Handbook,* a shortage of funds is the most severe problem faced by environmental quality advocates; this is in contrast to the huge resources available to industrial and government lawyers engaged in judicial or administrative proceedings. Although valuable *pro bono publico* services are provided free by many private lawyers, clashes of interest with their fee-paying clients and losses of time and income require that the burden of litigation be transferred to public interest firms, environmental pressure groups, and government lawyers. Public interest law firms are wholly or partially supported by foundation grants such as the Environmental Defense Fund and Natural Resources Defense Council. Precluded from participation in direct legislative activities representing the public interest, environmental advocates operate in gray and uncertain areas where tax-deductible contributions are involved. As in the case of environmental pressure groups, environmental advocates representing the public interest are under scrutiny by the Internal Revenue Service.[38]

The *Environmental Law Handbook* recommends that environmental lawyers align themselves only with serious and established conservation organizations whose status enables them to sue on environmental matters since *ad hoc* groups and individuals often have serious problems in this area. Such established environmental pressure groups also have (*1*) adequate funding, (*2*) the ability to organize public pressure, (*3*) sources of factual data, (*4*) expert and scientific witnesses for testimony, and (*5*) a professional staff and lawyers who are trained in negotiation and advocacy techniques.[39] Given the variety and scope of conservationist and environmental objectives in these organizations, an emerging force appears to be the alliance of environmental pressure groups and environmental law as an influence on environmental policy making and the creation of new legislation.

Various authorities have noted that numerous laws advocating environmental quality already exist, and that government lawyers have an important potential role in the struggle to enforce protection of environmental quality. For example, one of the strictest water pollution laws, the Refuge Act of 1899 (33 U.S. C 407), prohibits dumping "any refuge matter of any kind or description whatever other than that flowing from streets and sewers and passing therefrom in a liquid state, into any navigable water of the United States. . . ." However, the Justice Department has since ruled to adopt lesser standards.[40] Regardless of legal justificiation for enforcement of antipollution standards, political and agency considerations inhibit many government lawyers from taking aggressive positions for the environmental public interest, as well as encouraging negative representation for vested interests. Thus, much of the work of environmental advocates and pressure groups is that of seeking enforcement, and adequate interpretation, of existing legislation. They also observe governmental agencies to assure that the agencies follow proper procedures under administrative law, including injunctions against those who violate the law. The end result of such watchdog activities is that environmental pressure groups are able to influence environmental policy.

Public Land Policy

The 771 million acres of federal public lands are an important part of environmental policy, in that they comprise about one-third of the entire United States (2.3 billion acres). These lands are administered by various federal civil and defense agencies. Major public land administration agencies are the BLM (administering 60 percent of the public land, half of it in Alaska); the FS, which manages 24 percent; NPS; Bureau of Sport Fisheries and Wildlife (BSFW); and the BR.[41] It is estimated that there are some 10,000 or more federal laws applying to public lands, which are mainly under control of the U.S. Department of the Interior. The public land policy has changed from one of almost complete disposal to one of almost complete reservation. The federal government once owned some 1.5 billion acres or more than three-fourths of the continental United States, which was acquired through cession, treaty, and by purchase. For many years, Congress followed the policy of disposal of the public domain by various methods, such as sales and grants to individuals, grants to states, and grants to corporations. By the late 1800s, most of the good farmlands and large areas of the better forest and range lands had passed into private ownership. Since 1891, with the passage of the first Forest Reserve Act, the public land policy has been one of retention of practically all lands, with the reservation or withdrawal of these lands for various purposes (e.g., for national forests, national parks, fish and wildlife refuges, national defense, etc.)[42]

It is significant that the great majority of public land is located in the West, which retains many elements of a traditional frontier culture, emphasizing independence from governmental control and the economic exploitation of natural resources. Many westerners view public lands as provincial or state owned. Western congressmen dominate the Committees on Interior and Insular Affairs in both houses of Congress, consequently influencing legislation, policy, and agency decision making that affects the West. Also, federal administrators, under the concept of multiple use, are subject to intense pressure from pressure groups, local communities, and individuals for economic development of public lands. FS officials are currently receiving considerable pressure from local chambers of commerce and other sources to develop a road through a scenic wilderness area between Cooks City and Big Timber, Montana. Although western attitudes toward conservation are changing, a great deal of support for environmental quality, recreational use, and intangible benefits comes from urban areas in the East.[43]

The Public Land Law Review Commission (PLLRC) and its predecessors were established by Congress to aid in learning more about the West and its problems. Public land commissions before the current one (which submitted its report to Congress on June 31, 1970) were primarily concerned with land inventory rather than with policy and legislation. The previous five major land survey commissions included the Lewis and Clark expedition, and four geological inventory commissions, one of which was led by John Wesley Powell in the late 1870s. The congressional act of September 19, 1964, which established the present PLLRC stated: "... policy of Congress [is] that the public lands of the United States shall be: (a) retained and managed or, (b) disposed of, all in a manner to provide the maximum benefit for the general public."[44]

A study by the author revealed that the PLLRC should be considered a political body due to the makeup and orientation of its top personnel and their biases toward economic development of public lands. At the time, Congressman Wayne Aspinall (Democrat, Colorado), chairman of the Interior and Insular Affairs Committee of the House of Representatives, was the major sponsor of the Commission Act and was the chairman of the PLLRC. Numerous conservationists are of the opinion that Congressman Aspinall has definite convictions favoring extensive and intensive economic development of public lands, and the transfer of portions of public lands to state and private ownership. Congressman Aspinall was opposed to the passage of the Wilderness Act (1964) because he believed that the Act would "tie up" portions of public lands, keeping them from economic development. He was also instrumental in introducing mining provisions into the Wilderness Act which are currently delaying and complicating wilderness classifications.[45] Congressman Aspinall was defeated in 1972 when running for reelection.

Milton Pearl, who was associated with Congressman Aspinall in legislative work and who is a former official of the CE, was appointed executive director of the PLLRC, and Harry L. Moffett, an ex-official of the American Mining Congress, was appointed assistant director of administrative matters of the PLLRC. A council without voting powers was appointed to advise the PLLRC. The council of the PLLRC is partially composed of 25 members of major citizens' organizations concerned with public lands, with commercial interests, such as livestock, mining, oil, lumber, etc., having substantial representation. With important aspects of the PLLRC's report hinging on interpretation of policy and law, values associated with economic interests of the large number of individuals on the PLLRC caused concern over the Commission's responsibility for the general and national public interest. Moreover, the PLLRC's public hearings drew data mainly from western political ecology, which is highly oriented toward local economic interests.[46]

It is not surprising that many of the 137 recommendations contained in the PLLRC's final report to Congress are under severe attack by conservationist and environmental organizations and by private citizens. Although some sound environmental quality recommendations were made, many recommendations were against multiple use, and were primarily concerned with creating advantages or benefits for special interests associated with economic development and industry. For example, rather than being concerned in the general and national public interest, the report recommended that large tracts of public lands be used exclusively for the logging industry.[47] The PLLRC was specifically charged with developing new recommendations for legislation and policy pertaining to public land minerals which, under the General Mining Law of 1872, were being badly abused by private industry to the detriment of environmental quality. Yet, for all practical purposes, the PLLRC recommended the continuation of the General Mining Law of 1872 with some amendments, although the archaic Act severely hampers wise management by agencies that administer public lands. The 1872 Act is generally criticized by land managers and users with the exception of those mining interests benefiting directly from its perpetuation.

Recommendations of this nature by the PLLRC, which obviously reflect vested values and biases, have not only resulted in severe criticism from responsible authorities, but have also led to the growing realization that the report may not be taken seriously by Congress, despite some of the Commission's good and necessary recommendations for environmental policy and quality. A professional conference called by the Commission in Denver in 1970 resulted in very negative feedback. The Bolle report, in considering multiple-use recommendations, states:

> It appears inconceivable and incongruous to us that at this time, with the great emphasis upon a broad multiple use approach to our natural resources,—especially those remaining in public ownership—that any representative group or institution in our society would advocate a dominant use philosophy with respect to our natural resources. Yet it is our judgment that this is precisely what is occurring through the federal appropriation process, via executive order and in the Public Land Review Commission's Report. It would appear to us that at this time any approach to public land management which would de-emphasize a broad multiple use philosophy, a broad environmental approach, a broad open-access approach, or which would reduce the production of our public land resources in the long run is completely out of step with the interests and desires of the American people. What is needed is a fully funded program of action for quality management of all public lands.[48]

The *Environmental Law Handbook* notes that the basic policy question on public lands is that of classification relative to the general use to which they should be put. In this sense, classification limits the range of uses to which public land may be subject. Federal departments and agencies are under various directives concerning this classification process, for example, the U.S. Department of the Interior and the BLM are classified under the Multiple Use Act of 1964; U.S. Department of Agriculture and the FS are under a general and wilderness classification. Both public and private interests are associated with classification processes, particularly with the permanent nature of public land policy implications.[49]

As an important part of environmental policy, public lands are naturally covered under the National Environmental Policy Act of 1969 and by other environmental policy legislation that applies to federal agencies involved in land ownership and related activities, including mineral leasing. Yet the PLLRC notes:

> As studies prepared for the Commission have revealed, land management agencies have little, if any, statutory guidance, but have developed administratively a plethora of objectives and directives to promote consideration of aesthetics, wildlife, and related values. Even so, definitions, criteria, and standards for environmental quality lack operational meaning. Air and water quality standards, where applicable, appear to be the only standards that have been defined specifically enough to be reviewed and monitored. Others often must be identified and defined at the lowest level of management and applied on an ad hoc basis.[50]

The PLLRC further notes that the National Environmental Policy Act of 1969 establishes highly desirable goals for environmental quality, but that the Act does not get down to goals that are sufficiently specific for actual management.[51] At the same time, the PLLRC provides ample evidence and illustrations of obvious abuses to environmental quality permitted on public lands, which range from improper logging practices to strip-mining.[52]

Under the National Environmental Policy Act of 1969, federal agencies involved in public lands are required to clear various programs through the Council on Environmental Quality (CEQ) as well as to have their present operations meet environmental quality criteria. At the same time, broad and idealistic environmental goals leave much to interpretation by each agency and its personnel. Moreover, as previously noted, environmental quality is ambiguous and hard to define in specific situations. On the other hand, abuses and deterioration of environmental quality arising from various sources, ranging from recreation to mining, are obvious in most situations even to the lay person. With the lack of actual statutory guidance, agencies and their personnel make environmental policy for public lands based upon interpretations of the public interest. Given the further complexity of agency procedure, administrative law, and the influence of vested interests and values, many of the final policy decisions are achieved through the administrative process.

REFERENCES

1. Phillip H. Abelson, "Science and Immediate Social Goals," *Science* 169, no. 3947 (August 21, 1970) p. 722.
2. Gordon Allport, "Various Readings in Social Psychology," in *Personality and Social Encounters: Selected Essays* (Boston: Beacon Press, 1960) pp. 1–386.
3. Aldo Leopold, *A Sand County Almanac* (New York: Oxford University Press, 1966) pp. 217–220.
4. M. Judd Harmon, *Political Thought: From Plato to Present* (New York: McGraw-Hill, 1964) p. 319.
5. Herbert Simon, Donald W. Smithburg, Victor A. Thompson, *Public Administration* (New York: Knopf, 1962) p. 58.
6. *Ibid.,* p. 59.
7. Howard Lasswell, *Politics, Who Gets What, When, and How* (New York: McGraw-Hill, 1963) p. 1.
8. *Ibid.,* p. 182.
9. Alexander Hamilton, James Madison, and John Jay, *The Federalist Papers* (New York: Mentor Book, New American Library, 1964) p. 79.
10. Norman Wengert, *Natural Resources and the Political Struggle* (New York: Doubleday, 1955) pp. 6–9.
11. John C. Livingston and Robert C. Thompson, *The Consent of the Governed* (New York: Macmillan, 1966) pp. 238–241.
12. Ernest S. Griffith, *Congress: Its Contemporary Role* (New York: New York University Press, 1956) p. 127.
13. Norman Wengert, "The Ideological Basis of Conservation and Natural Resources Policies and Programs," *The Annals of the American Academy of Political and Social Sciences* 344 (November 1962) p. 65.
14. *Ibid.,* p. 69.
15. Council on Environmental Quality, *First Annual Report* (Washington, D.C.: U.S. Gov't Printing Office, 1970) pp. 243–253.
16. *Ibid.*
17. American Society for Public Administration Task Force on Society Goals, "The Future of ASPA–A Super Everest or a Higher Hill," *News and Views* 20, no. 4 (October 1970) pp. 5–6.
18. Charles E. Lindblom, "The Science of Muddling Through," *Public Administration Review* 20 (Spring 1959) pp. 79–88.
19. Asit K. Biswas, "Mathematical Models and Their Use in Water Resources Decision-making," *Proceedings,* Fourteenth Congress of International Association of Hydraulic Research, Paris, vol. 5, p. 246.
20. S. A. Pearson, "Multiple Use in Forestry," *Journal of Forestry* 42, no. 4 (April 1944) p. 243.
21. Richard E. McArdle, "Multiple Use–Multiple Benefits" (Paper presented at the Eighteenth North American Wildlife Conference, Washington, D.C., March 10, 1953) p. 5.
22. Norman Wengert, *Natural Resources and the Power Struggle* (New York: Doubleday, 1955) p. 708.
23. Daniel H. Henning, "The Politics of Natural Resources Administration," *The Annals of Regional Science* 1, no. 2 (December 1968) p. 245.
24. Norman Wengert, *Natural Resources and the Power Struggle* (New York: Doubleday, 1955) p. 11.
25. Daniel H. Henning, "The Politics of Natural Resources Administration," *The Annals of Regional Science* 1, no. 2 (December 1968) pp. 245–246.
26. Don Kash, Seminar presented to the Public Science Policy and Administration Program, University of New Mexico, Albuquerque, October 26, 1970.
27. *Ibid.*
28. Irving M. Grant, "The Sierra Club: The Procedural Aspects of the Revocation of its Tax Exemption," *UCLA Law Review* 13(1968) pp. 200–216.

29. Joseph Harry, Richard Gale, and John Hendee, "Conservation: An Upper-middle Class Social Movement," *Journal of Leisure Research* 1, no. 3 (Summer 1969) pp. 246–254.
30. National Wildlife Federation, *Conservation News* (December 1, 1970) p. 15.
31. Daniel H. Henning, "Natural Resources Administration and Public Interest," *Public Administration Review* 30, no. 2 (March/April, 1970) p. 139.
32. Edward Cliff, "The Forest Service in the Seventies," Memorandum, U.S. Forest Service, Washington, D.C., October, 1970.
33. Arnold Bolle and Committee, "A University View of the Forest Service," *Congressional Record* S-18401-08 (November 18, 1970) p. 1.
34. Henry W. Ehrmann, "French Bureaucracy and Organized Interests," *Administrative Science Quarterly* 5 (March 1961) p. 539.
35. Joseph J. Brecher and Manuel E. Nestle, *Environmental Law Handbook* (Berkeley: California Continuing Education for the Bar, 1970) p. 204.
36. *Ibid.,* p. 24.
37. Bruce Bowler, "Socio-Legal Aspects of Environmental Management" (Paper presented to the Winter Chapter Meeting of the Society of American Foresters and American Society of Range Management, Boise, Idaho, March 19, 1970) pp. 3–4.
38. Joseph J. Brecher and Manuel E. Nestle, *Environmental Law Handbook* (Berkeley: California Continuing Education for the Bar, 1970) pp. 70–71.
39. *Ibid.,* pp. 75–76.
40. *Ibid.,* pp. 89–91.
41. Bureau of Land Management, *Public Land Statistics* (Washington, D.C.: U.S. Gov't Printing Office, 1969) p. 1.
42. Study Committee on Natural Resources and Conservation, *Report* (Washington, D.C.: Commission on Intergovernmental Relations, 1955) pp. 14–17.
43. Daniel H. Henning, "The Public Land Law Review Commission: A Political and Western Analysis," *Idaho Law Review* 7 (April 1970) p. 83.
44. *Ibid.,* p. 77.
45. *Ibid.,* pp. 78–82.
46. *Ibid.,* pp. 80–85.
47. Public Land Law Review Commission, *One Third of the Nation's Land* (Washington, D.C.: U.S. Gov't Printing Office, 1970) pp. 1–317.
48. Arnold Bolle and Committee, "A University View of the Forest Service," *Congressional Record* S-18401-08 (November 18, 1970) p. 1.
49. Joseph J. Brecher and Manuel E. Nestle, *Environmental Law Handbook* (Berkeley: California Continuing Education for the Bar, 1970) pp. 276–277.
50. Public Land Law Review Commission, *One Third of the Nation's Land* (Washington, D.C.: U.S. Gov't Printing Office, 1970) p. 68.
51. *Ibid.,* pp. 67–68.
52. *Ibid.,* pp. 67–88.

Chapter 3

THE ENVIRONMENTAL ADMINISTRATIVE PROCESS

With considerations of ecological complexities, environmental problems and crises, a politically powerful environmental movement, and concern for future generations and for present quality of life, the process of environmental administration is conducted in an atmosphere of severe responsibility and challenge. A central mandate is that the process should be attuned to a total ecosystem. Yet the manifestations of government in areas of environment and natural resources indicate that this has not usually been the case. Given the relatively recent impact of environmental awareness, government has responded minimally to demands for ecological considerations in the administrative process. It should, however, be recognized that an administrative process is a continuing operation involving many changes. There are lags, but the trend, with public and legislative pressures, is toward considerations of ecological and environmental quality.

Nevertheless, there is definite resistance to ecological considerations among the federal agencies involved in public management of environmental affairs. By their very nature, these agencies are social and political institutions with their own sets of values and vested interests. Nadel notes: "Institutions, by virtue of internal growth, internal need, internal habit, and external defense, grow into bureaucracies. Bureaucracies, whether efficient or not, reach a level of organization that settles into equilibrium. Therefore, ideas of projects which disturb that equilibrium may initially be resisted, since they may call for internal adjustments of the status quo, or challenge the propriety of the bureaucracy."[1] Bureaucratic ideology, moreover, is basically concerned with survival and expansion of a given organization, with concern for the latter contributing to the former. Consequently, the degree of administrative acceptance or resistance of environmental quality considerations becomes dependent upon bureaucratic ideology.

With pressures from clientele groups, and with policy limited by considerations involving the agency's security and expansion (although some limitations result from past congressional direction), a total environmental orientation is seldom attained in the administrative process. As an institution or symbolic organism, a bureaucracy is concerned with its own welfare first, with the result that individual, ecological, and public interests are secondary considerations in its operational process. On the other hand, much of agency policy as well as recent environmental legislation stipulates environmental quality goals for governmental organizations. According to Parsons, goal attainment or effectiveness is an organization's most important condition for survival. An organization actually is a product of its goals, with the achievement of its goals having dominance over all other organizational problems.[2] In the administrative process of an organization, Reidel notes, "Goals are those services or products that an organization sets out to produce. An effective organization is an organization whose outputs coincide with those stated goals."[3]

Yet Reidel also observes that many organizations do not follow goals in their actual administrative process. He indicates: "They [organizations] have found a substitute for goals, a reasonable facsimile for real goals, that satisfy the system's need for goal attainment to survive. One would think that these pseudo-goals would be easy to detect and identify. Unfortunately, these 'other' goals are also part of the organization's normal processes. They, too, are part of the organization's life but have taken first place when they should be secondary."[4] Thus, a goal displacement occurs with secondary goals being substituted for primary, or real, goals. Reidel notes that the organization is basically living on a substitute relative to goal requirements and that this is further complicated by other values demanding a place in the primary goal structure.[5] In the case of a governmental organization, political and social pressures (including the demands of economic clientele groups) may become more important considerations than primary goals, while means and procedures may become more important than ends. A consequence of such value displacement is neglect of ecological considerations and environmental quality.

Various complexities are naturally involved in the goal-selection process. Goals are seldom specified, and change with time. Some of the complexities involve identification and analysis of who defines the goals, and by what processes, and how priorities are to be determined, a difficult task in the modern organization. In respect to their eventual resolution, problems such as those involving environmental quality are presented to a given organization in terms relative to that organization's nonspecific goals. The very nature of this ambiguity creates a vacuum that permits the organization, consciously or unconsciously, to substitute secondary goals more oriented toward its vested and political interests than toward those of society or the environment.

The preoccupation of agencies with secondary objectives through goal displacement, regardless of the political and social considerations, can result in a lack of responsiveness toward environmental goals. A budget can become an end rather than a tool for achieving real organizational goals, and it can serve to limit expenditures for environmental quality programs. A resource management plan can become a dogma rather than a flexible guide for changing needs and environmental considerations. Under a utilitarian and pragmatic orientation, concrete quantitative outputs of secondary and substitute goals are, in many cases, given preference over intangible and qualitative outputs of primary and ecological goals. The end result may be serious resistance to environmental quality considerations, regardless of efforts of agency personnel, the general public, and Congress.

This resistance might be questioned in terms of the rationality of governmental organizations. Douglas Price notes:

An organization is not only a means for achieving division of labor and allocations of authority, it is also a coordinative system that makes decisions (including some wrong ones) and solves (or tries to solve) problems. In doing so, most organizations do not function completely rationally: inaction is favored over action, the status quo program is favored over a proposed alternative, dissatisfaction must build up before there is serious search for alternative programs, and patterns of communication lead to considerable decentralization of effective—as distinguished from nominal—decision-making.[6]

At the same time, it should be recognized that a governmental organization may have its own sense of rationality, and of morality, which can differ sharply from an outsider's views. Thus, resistance to ecological criteria and standards can be a natural product of the organizational process. Price notes, however, that sufficient dissatisfaction will cause the organization to search for alternatives, and to change its policies.

In the environmental administrative process, a great deal of dissatisfaction occurs at all levels, particularly in the more traditional federal resource agencies. Externally, with the communications revolution and growing public awareness of the problems, environmental abuses are being brought to the attention of the official in the field as well as the agency head. Public dissatisfaction eventually creates organizational dissatisfaction. Internally, many resource agencies are definitely recognizing a generation gap between younger personnel (oriented toward second-order considerations of environmental quality and ecology) and older personnel (oriented toward first-order considerations of materialism and economics). Although chronological age may sometimes have little to do with this dichotomy, it is realistic to recognize that internal value conflicts of this nature can create dissatisfaction sufficient to lessen organizational resistance to change.

Unfortunately, much of organizational change occurs through crisis-type situations with public "explosions." A case in point was the Lincoln Back Country Wilderness hearing conducted by the Senate Subcommittee on Public Lands of the Interior and Insular Affairs Committee in Great Falls, Montana, on September 23, 1968. Severe public attacks on the Forest Service (FS) led to the abandonment of an economic and mass recreation development plan for the area, as well as changes in general procedures and attitudes involving the public in planning for other such areas.[7] Under provisions of the National Environmental Policy Act of 1969, agencies are now required to make ecological surveys and furnish appraisals for all developments and programs which affect the environment. Attention is now being focused on the possible negative impact on ecological harmony of a planned development or program. The plan or program, with the ecological survey and appraisal, must then be approved by the Council on Environmental Quality (CEQ) through interagency arrangements.[8]

Although numerous questions have been raised about how effective the new procedure will be, it is obvious that it will have an influence on the environmental administrative process. With constant environmental and ecological accountability required at various stages and levels, organizational goals of a secondary, as well as a primary, nature will have to be evaluated in terms of their impact upon the environment. Given the built-in resistance of organizational systems, the input of legitimate criteria could very well create some influence for change and reorientation. The extent of this influence will naturally depend on how adamant the CEQ is regarding enforcement of the procedure, and how much support it will receive from public and governmental agencies. But the very demands of justifying and evaluating decisions, programs, plans, and developments on the basis of environmental quality and ecological standards will cause some adjustments in the entire administrative process. This is particularly true when one considers that environmental abuses and deterioration generally could be prevented if each governmental agency were dedicated to environmental considerations rather than to its own needs and interests.

At the same time, it should be recognized that we now have insufficient knowledge for predicting complex variables in future ecological consequences of present-day developments. In many cases, our decisions are based upon differing opinions supplied by so-called experts, with the "right" opinion being the one that reflects the hierarchical power and vested interests of the agency. Even with the requirement of environmental impact statements for proposed developments, the influence of vested interests may still be felt despite interagency and public review. An environmental impact statement does not preclude an opinion favorable to a given agency's interests. Further, the courts and other institutions have difficulty challenging administrative discretion on the acceptance of an opinion once the legal requirements of a procedure have been met.

DECENTRALIZATION

With environmental demands being made at all levels of administration, considerations are naturally focused on decentralization. Regarding this concept, Price notes: "Decentralization of effective decision making results from subordinates communicating to superiors the inferences they draw from a body of evidence instead of the evidence itself. The decision is then based on the subordinate's analysis which in part circumscribes the decision. This Simon and Marsh call 'uncertainty absorption,' i.e., the uncertainty concerning an answer is absorbed by the subordinate though the superior appears to make the decision."[9] Price compares this process to a book review in which the reviewer draws inferences and then communicates his conclusions to the reader who does not read the book.[10]

Decentralization implies a process away from the consolidation of decision making in a central headquarters, that is, toward decisions made in the field rather than in Washington, D.C. Decentralization, by its very closeness to the local situation, also implies more responsiveness to and perception of environmental implications and the local political, economic, and social conditions involved. However, this very closeness permits situations where local political and economic interests can influence and manipulate decisions toward nonecological values and away from the environmental public interest. On the other hand, agency objectives and interests are among the most important value premises that enter into the decentralized administrative process. Many controls of the agency are incorporated through a *preformed* decision process which Kaufman aptly describes in his study of the forest ranger. Thus, Kaufman notes, ". . . events and conditions in the field are anticipated as fully as possible and courses of action to be taken for designated categories of such events and conditions are described. The field officer then need determine only into what category a particular circumstance falls; once this determination is made, then he simply follows the series of steps available to that category. Within each category, therefore, the decisions are preformed."[11] In describing the FS *Administrative Manual* (with its similarities to other agency manuals), he states: "The provisions describe what is to be done, who is to do it, how (and how well) it should be performed, when (or in what sequence) each step should be taken, where the action should take place, and even explain the 'why' of the policies—the reasons for their adoption, the objectives they are expected to attain."[12] Thus, many ranger-level decisions are made for the rangers.

Obviously, some changes and innovations will be made in this process as a result of recent environmental legislation. For example, stipulations of the National Environmental Policy Act of 1969 require agencies to review and change various policies and procedures that conflict with standards and requirements of the Act. Yet, one should recognize that procedures, manuals, and informal ways of doing things are slow to change, particularly at the field level. Change, as well as decentralized decision making, is further complicated by ineffective communication among levels of organizations. Thus, Argyris notes that dysfunctional activities and elaborate defenses result in a reduction of the probability that accurate information will flow through an organization. Because of lack of trust and a desire not to "make waves," important aspects of information and truth are withheld, on a self-fulfilling prophecy basis, from communication between upper and lower levels of an organizational hierarchy.[13] The end result of this may be superficial treatment of environmental problems in decentralized decisions; the whole truth will not be told because of possible negative connotations. Consequently, a great many headquarters—field communications appear to emphasize the positive, conservative, technical, and superficial, without covering real problems and issues.[14]

The fieldman's (fieldmen are defined as officials operating at the district level with some time allocated to field and outdoor activities in a given district) individual mental picture is of importance in the decentralization process in that his values will naturally be reflected in the decisions made. With professional and organizational socialization that indoctrinates him to be responsive and sympathetic to local economic interests, it is obvious that a fieldman may incorporate community values into his official actions. The location of administrative offices in small towns places fieldmen in continuous professional and personal contact with individuals and organizations that are strongly committed to economic uses of natural resources. This is in contrast to transitory contacts with recreationists and environmentalists concerned with noneconomic uses. Although frequent rotation in job assignments may retard ties to local political and economic interests, in the case of forestry (as well as other resource professions), such local interests may be a definite part of the fieldman's mental picture, based on his background, training, and personality.[15] He may have a value bias toward economic considerations regardless of location.

In their study of the perceptions of foresters (GS–9 and above, middle-management positions) in field situations, Bultena and Hendee concluded:

> The foresters included in this study almost unanimously aligned themselves with commercial interests on the issue of timber cutting and, in addition, interpreted the Forest Service (via their perception of their superiors) as sympathetic to these interests. These data support the accusation that local foresters favor commercial over social interests in forest management....[16]

> It must be recognized that favoring certain clientele groups over others, of which the Forest Service has been accused, is characteristic of resource agencies generally. Studies of state conservation departments, the Soil Conservation Service, the Army Corps of Engineers, the Bureau of Reclamation, and other agencies similarly reveal philosophies and programs which are slanted toward subgroups of their clientele.... From a collective viewpoint, however, they may be dysfunctional by restricting the ability of public agencies to respond to newly felt needs and emergent values in the population except as these come to be articulated through influential pressure groups.[17]

THE ENVIRONMENTAL PUBLIC INTEREST

Given the influence of the individual's mental picture, it is recognized that the administrative or decentralized process is charged with carrying out the environmental public interests of the general public and that of the nation as a whole. Given values or biases favoring local economic groups, administrative personnel may be susceptible to making decisions that favor economic, over environmental and natural resource, considerations. These possibilities are particularly prevalent in the case of public lands, which are mainly located in the West away from urban centers. On a professional, personal, and social basis, much of the daily contact of agency personnel is with individuals and organizations in small communities who are concerned with economic and commercial use of public lands. Many resource agencies, moreover, have policies, procedures, and guidelines that require responsiveness and special attention to local economic interests. Thus, the *Forest Service Objectives and Policy Guides* states:

Generate Forestry Opportunities to Accelerate Rural Community Growth

Work with all appropriate public and private agencies to provide public services, income, jobs, and amenities in rural areas through planning, resource management, economic development, and manpower programs.

Seek opportunities for development of forest based enterprises which will contribute to rural growth rates at least equal to the national average.

Identify and promote opportunities for community development, including new towns, and ensure that Forest Service programs contribute fully to their growth.[18]

Yet, a major point of the environmental movement and legislation is that environmental administration should be based on ecological considerations and environmental quality rather than on economic developments per se. This is not to say that economic interests and developments are not an essential and necessary concern of the environmental administrative process, but it is to say that they obviously are not the primary considerations. In essence, environmental administration involves the *management* of natural resources based on what is best for the environmental, societal, and ecological public interests. With little intensive management being practiced by government, however, environmental management mainly consists of deciding on the use or manipulation by nongovernmental or private individuals and organizations of public lands and other resources. Thus, public personnel in environmental administration are basically concerned with people management and the majority of their time is taken up by "human problems." Modern requirements, however, dictate that this people management be directed toward environmental public interest.

S. A. Cain notes that, "Environment is the aggregate of surrounding things, conditions, and influences to which an organism is sensitive and capable of reacting, man included."[19] Nevertheless, environment, like the public interest, is subject to various interpretations based upon the values and perceptions of a given individual or organization. Some confusion naturally occurs when these differing conceptions collide in the decision-making process. Environmentalism implies a new holistic view or core philosophy involving social, political, and economic implications as well as physical and ecological considerations. The concept of public interest has been around a long time. Regardless of area of responsibility or clientele, governmental administrators usually claim that their decisions are in the public interest. This vague concept is often associated with assumed public benefits or needs. But like any other concept, public interest is highly subject to individual opinions. Supposedly, public *opinion* becomes public *interest* in the process of governmental decisions. But such decisions usually occur through the subjective interpretations of administrators operating within a broad legal framework. Moreover, public opinion is seldom fully expressed or understood as a determining influence within any given period.[20]

In actuality, much of the administrative process is devoted to determining the public interest in a given environmental decision. R. W. Behan, in his article "The Myth of the Omnipotent Forester," notes the tendency of professional foresters to assume that they know what is best for the land, and that they can tell the public how lands should be managed. Behan states, "It is when the professional forester arbitrarily determines those ends, or even clumsily tries to, that he most seriously violates our classless society and democratic politics." Behan also feels that environmental pressure groups are properly

42

most hostile and challenging when foresters involve themselves and their agencies in problems by attempting to determine the social ends of natural resources. He indicates that "It is when we invoke this rationale by judging, in its terms, 'goodness' and 'badness,' that pressure groups properly challenge our leadership. 'Goodness' and 'badness' in our society are collective value judgments, and land expertise is no better a qualification than many others for making them."[21]

But it is realistic to assume that administrators play an important role in the process of determining the social ends of an abstract public interest. It is also realistic to recognize that pressure groups (including agencies acting as pressure groups) forge their values and vested interests into administrative policy and make decisions in the power struggle of brokerage politics. Bruce Bowler notes that many decisions are thus made for private, rather than the public, interest. Yet, under the law of equity, he believes that there is sufficient legal backing to make decisions for the environmental public interest. Bowler states:

> ...and the leading case in the U.S. Supreme Court of Udall v. Federal Power Commission recognizing the public interest test in the Middle Snake as paramount including fish and wildlife and wild river values. The great rule of this case is that *the test is not private benefit, but public benefit* where the use of a public resource is involved. Tested in this light you all would know examples of resource use that could not meet this criterion. This is basic equity precedent we now have as a matter of law from our highest courts, and all future environmental decisions should be made in conformity where public resources (and public officials) are involved.[22]

Elaborating the principle of equity, Bowler notes:

> In the American system of law we have what is known as the law of equity. This is a very old system of law brought to this country by its founders from England. Equity was there developed because some of the king's laws were unjust, and the development of the law of equity was known as the law of conscience and had its beginning with the ecclesiastical courts. In this day it is a well recognized part of our law the doctrine of which is that which should be done shall be done. Equity has the power to overrule statutes, contracts and other legal situations which common right demands.... Equity and administrative law go together. The statutes set broad policy and purpose, and it is the responsibility of administrators to make the rules which govern the application of that law to serve the equitable results desired.

Bowler further considers that the equity principle permits administrators to make decisions for the environmental public interest and to place economic interests in their proper modern context, that is, away from the domination of private interest over public interests in the environment.[23]

Much of this requires that the environmental public interest be considered in the administrative process. At various levels of policy and decision making, many environmental agencies do involve committees and consultants in environmental problems. Although specialists may very well qualify in the resource field under study, it does not automatically follow that they are qualified to determine the public interest as it relates to that particular resource. This would naturally depend to a great extent upon the individual involved, but it is reasonable to assume that one of the most important functions of resource consultants should lie in the articulation of, and recommendations for, the public interest in a given environmental problem. Consequently, a valid requirement in selecting a consultant might be that the individual have competence in social and value analyses, as well as expertise in the area of concern.

The employment of nontechnical experts as advisers on the relationship of society to a particular resource or environmental problem is an approach that remains generally unexplored in either general or specific decision making. In many situations, agency personnel consider only the narrowest and most limited values of the environmental public interest, for example, the mass recreation orientation of the National Park Service (NPS). Boards of nontechnical experts, with grassroots representation, could make contributions to the value bases for decisions, provided they were legally sanctioned by agencies. Individuals with vision, sensitivity, and broad knowledge, coupled with some familiarity with environmental resources, could reflect the spirit of the public interest by articulating various social ends (value bases) that could be implemented by the personnel of an environmental agency.

In many cases, advisory committee memberships include representatives of various pressure groups with obvious biases and values (not to mention the members and consultants chosen for their sympathy with agency objectives). Hence, the major operation of these committees involves compromises and power struggles reflecting the bias of various members with respect to the data and problems at hand. Thus, little emphasis can be given to the articulation of the public interest. Members of juries are usually examined to determine the presence of any possible bias; similar examinations might be made of potential members of committees concerned with the objective study of a given environmental plan as it relates to the public interest.

With the constantly changing complexities of society and the environment, values do not remain static. Consequently, interdisciplinary committees of consultants, with environmental perspective and wisdom, are needed for an adequate articulation, identification, and judgment of the changing complexities of the environmental public interest. Given that specialists have a necessary and essential position in natural resources, this should not preclude the use of nontechnical individuals with social training and some familiarity with the environmental situation, such as social scientists, psychiatrists, lawyers, philosophers, human ecologists, and so forth. A particular function of such nontechnical individuals could be to make value decisions and recommendations in nontechnical language on the selection of various alternatives prescribed by administrators and specialists. The combination of technical and nontechnical individuals on a committee could remove some obvious conflicts inherent in separate committees. This arrangement could also contribute to an integrated and comprehensive approach to public interest and the total environment.

PUBLIC HEARINGS

Under the Administrative Procedure Act of 1946, agencies arrange public hearings for two types of agency processes: *adjudication* and *rule making*. With the stipulation that the public hearings should not interfere with the orderly conduct of public business, the Act indicates that interested persons may appear and present their views to any agency on any issue. Charles Reich notes that there would be a substantial increase in public participation if the agencies conformed to the Act and if there were less ambiguity in it. Reich further notes that judicial review is barred on any agency action that is "by law committed to agency discretion." Although many agencies may voluntarily subject themselves to the Act, Reich believes that the public can look for little help from the Administrative Procedure Act.[24]

On the other hand, under the Wilderness Act of 1964, public hearings are required on wilderness classification and are a definite part of the administrative process. Nevertheless, in a typical public hearing on wilderness, agency personnel actually sit in judgment of their own interests with a hearing officer merely conducting the meeting and officially recording such public data as individual and organizational testimony and statements, alternate proposals, etc. Public hearings are not called until the agency has formulated its own plan for the particular wilderness area. Although the agency proposal for the wilderness classification may contain alternatives, it is obvious that the agency has formulated its views based on its own study and vested interests. It cannot claim to be objective or disinterested in judging at public hearings. The same administrators who initiate and argue in support of a particular proposal are not good evaluators of public criticism or alternative opinions. Reich comments, "Lawyers know from long experience that disinterested, well considered decisions are most frequently reached by clear-cut separation between those who advocated and those who decide."[25] The problem is not with unfairness or intentional biases, but with human weakness and minds closed as a result of past involvements.

Due to geographical factors (the greater numbers of hearings are held in small western communities near the proposed wilderness areas under study), a great deal of public input is lost through the absence of oral testimony. Much of the support for appreciative values and protection of wilderness areas comes from the urban East, but because of transportation problems, little of this organizational or individual support is physically present. With the advantages of location and obvious economic motivation, adequate local representation is seldom a problem for individuals and organizations associated with economic development. Local interests, with immediate personal and professional contacts with agency personnel, are also able to ensure adequate input throughout the study process. This is not to say that agency personnel do not receive inputs from other sources during their study process. But the utilitarian and economic value orientation of many resource administrators and managers tends to make them more responsive to economic inputs from the local community.

After a public hearing, agency personnel evaluate the oral and written testimony as a part of the total framework for future decisions and recommendations. The public testimony becomes one block in a flow chart upon which final recommendations to headquarters are based. Testimonies are categorized quantitatively, according to location, pro and con considerations, organization, etc. This is followed by qualitative interpretations, involving the values of agency personnel as well as the vested interests of the agency. With values sympathetic toward the economic interests of small communities, there are possibilities for bias in the agency evaluation. Moreover, there seems to be an ingrained belief on the part of many agency personnel that the total of local interests and those of the clientele organization actually represents the national interest in a given situation. But the sum of local interests may *not* add up to a general or national public interest, particularly with environmental quality, geographic, and urban considerations.

PUBLIC RELATIONS

Under the guise of supplying information, environmental agencies carry out extensive public relations programs with the obvious objective of building public support and gaining congressional and departmental influence. These programs are oriented toward describing, explaining, and justifying the specific policies, missions, and activities of the agencies. However, complications arise when an agency, through such programs, dictates social ends to the public, and implements them with public relations techniques. Public relations programs can then be used as a tool for the agency ideology and the vested interests of its clientele. An administrator can, for example, articulate a value decision, and then defend and sell it to the public. Many agencies, moreover, are committed to first-order considerations (progress, economic and materialistic values) rather than to second-order considerations (ecology, quality, and intangibles).

A biased premise with data selected to back it up will do little to enlighten public opinion. In fact, it may be repugnant to thinking people who like to consider the alternatives rather than to be "sold" a position. Many agencies neglect their responsibilities to inform people objectively of the facts, and of alternative solutions to environmental problems, and offer instead a *closed* system. For example, much of the public literature from agencies is confined to platitudes and "niceties" on a low educational level. Through privately funded media associated with the communications revolution, however, the public *is* being informed on environmental concerns. As a result, there is a recent trend toward an informed citizenry, aggressively influencing policy decisions through expressions of values and opinions. It is obvious that, in a democracy, environmental administrators must be sensitive and responsive to such a trend.

Barry Commoner notes that the new duty of scientists (and administrators) during the environmental crisis is to furnish information that will enable their fellow men to use judgment in the humane use of science. Without this, Commoner states, "We will have deprived humanity of the right to sit in judgment of its own fate."[26] Moreover, Clark notes that the public now insists on a voice in this judgment; he states; "Now, more than ever before, the public will poke, pry, criticize, and influence individual, corporate, and governmental agency resource extraction and use decisions. The previously sleeping giant of public opinion is awakening, and the more it awakens, the less it likes what it sees. . . . The political power lies with urban and city people, and no amount of ranting will change that."[27]

Reidel also notes that much of the aroused public in the environmental picture consists of youth who are willing to make a more total commitment, and who are strongly motivated toward change.[28] Nevertheless, in public relations programs as in other areas of operation, government has been relatively slow to respond to the growing public force that might be compared to a social and cultural movement.

This lack of responsiveness might be largely attributed to agency tendencies to define areas of responsibility in terms of a rural nation. But environmental pressures call for a broader perspective, including truth in public relations. For example, new public participation guidelines by the CEQ state, "The public for the first time has a ringside seat as federal decisions affecting the environment are slugged out among executive agencies, and a chance to have its voice in the outcome. Federal agencies will have to disclose the environmental impact of their proposals (draft statements) at least 90 days before putting them into effect under the new guidelines."[29] Given pressures of this nature, agency public relations programs are still obligated to make the agency look good, and to protect its vested interests.

On the other hand, public relations implies a two-way communication process between the agency and the public, with strong influences from both. In our massive bureaucracy, many individuals and citizens' organizations become disillusioned through their frustrated efforts to obtain accurate and complete information, and their inability to influence agencies' environmental decisions. Thus the Bolle report, which was commissioned by Sen. Lee Metcalf (Democrat, Montana), notes:

> The problem arises from public dissatisfaction with the Bitterroot National Forest's overriding concern for sawtimber production. It is compounded by an apparent insensitivity to the related forest uses and to the local public's interest in environmental matters . . . is completely out of step with the interests and desires of the American people. . . .
>
> They feel left out of any policy formation or decision making and so resort to protest as the only available means of being heard. Many of the employees of the Forest Service are aware of the problem and are dissatisfied with the position of the agency, but they find it impossible to change, or at least to change fast enough.[30]

McDonald considers that the present democratic processes may be too slow and unresponsive, and that new channels must be created for effecting public participation in environmental programs. He notes that appeals to congressmen or state legislators result in long delays with little result. In an age of rapidly expanding technology and bureaucracy, an agency may originate and implement a particular environmental program before either the public or Congress has time to consider its consequences or to influence it. McDonald concludes that communication bodies should be developed between agencies and citizens (including environmental organizations) at the grassroots level, with efforts directed toward an exchange of real information and the actual participation of citizens in the decision-making process; in other words, an *open* system should be developed.[31]

There appears to be a growing recognition among agencies of the public's demands for involvement in governmental decision making, and a consequent effort to implement citizen participation. This might involve a transition from the management-type agency to the people-oriented agency. The management-type agency is basically a closed system with its decisions based on the needs and interests of the organization and its clientele groups; the management activities are then carried out and "explained" to the public with little public input into the process. The people-type agency, on the other hand, involves public inputs throughout the decision-making process with constant and true feedback; activities of the agency are referred to the public for review and further input. Given the professional and technical nature of many environmental agencies, this should not preclude public participation in value and alternative decisions throughout the entire process. At present, the environmental agencies appear to be of the management type, on a closed-system basis. Yet, true public relations, besides representing the agency's present concern for political image, should involve open two-way communications and public contributions to the decision-making process.

INTERAGENCY RELATIONS

L. K. Caldwell considers that previous ideologies (economy and efficiency) and other motivations for coordinating interagency relations have not worked, particularly in the field of natural resources. He states:

> The dissimilarities in the specific economic problems of management among specific natural resources made their coordination somewhat like an effort to coordinate the varieties of goods on supermarket shelves. In contrast, the environmental issue, especially in its Spaceship Earth context, provides a more coherent view of life and society from which public policies might be deduced and around which governmental organization might be construed.[32]

The National Environmental Policy Act of 1969 contains numerous provisions calling for interagency coordination and review in terms of environmental quality. Thus, environment, with its ecological considerations, provides a new focus and potential for meaningful and effective interagency relations. According to the Library of Congress, some 80 federal agencies are involved in environmental matters. With the addition of numerous state and local government agencies, it is obvious that interagency relations need a central theme for unity of action and programs.

Wengert, however, concludes that an environmental focus will not put an end to perennial political conflicts of agencies. He believes that an environmental context will subject incompatible objectives to fuller consideration in terms of issues and values. But he notes:

> The environment is a unity, but resources are discrete—hence a problem of coordination arises when an effort is made to reconcile resource-centered programs and agencies with comprehensive environmental goals. . . .
>
> Coordination of public programs dealing with or affecting many different facets of the environment superficially, at least, would seem to leave much to be desired. In many cases, little or no coordination is apparent, separate programs going their separate ways. In other cases coordination is only *pro forma* and superficial. Given those planning and conducting particular programs with obvious interrelationships have not consulted together, and in many cases programs dealing with similar or related problems may be seeking different and even conflicting goals or objectives, the pluralism of our society has been projected to government activities.[33]

On the other hand, Morton Grodzins argues for this very pluralism. He believes that a lack of neatness, and a fragmentation of responsibility among many governments (e.g., federal, state, and municipal) in outdoor recreation, for example, disperses initiative and releases energies. In presenting his case for "the virtues of chaos," Grodzins considers the following advantages: (1) overlapping concern of many governments promotes the establishment of general goals (this centers around his "marble cake" concept of federalism with various levels of government influencing and making decisions on national, state, and local issues; (2) free operation of many governments in an area promotes an openness in the system with many initiatives; (3) many power centers of agencies are responsive to the infinite variety of expressed needs; and (4) duplication permits agencies to meet and relieve growing pressures. Grodzins feels that charges of inefficiency and wastefulness in multigovernment situations have been ineffectively demonstrated and that ambiguity should be tolerated in healthy institutions.[34]

However, in the past, the toleration of pluralism in the actions of governments has led to serious environmental deterioration. Despite resistance to centralization, many look toward government at the national level to provide direction and focus based on a total environment; this would not permit a given agency to operate as an autonomous agent without consideration for environmental effects or for interagency coordination related to these effects. For example, this arrangement would not tolerate the disregard of the Corps of Engineers (CE) for environmental concerns and interagency cooperation. Yet, with tolerance of pluralism, environmental agencies have evolved policies, programs, and missions that automatically resist coordination of environmental responsibility. This resistance is very much involved in the political process through clientele pressures for survival of the specific agency and expansion of its role.

Resistance also takes the form of an agency's static adherence to lines of responsibility in given environmental situations. Under restrictive guidelines (stated or implied), personnel are frustrated and kept from effective interagency cooperation in a total approach to the environment. In this sense, overlapping and duplication may not be so much the problem as is the lack of authorization to take unified action, or "underlapping." Informal cooperation may occur among specialists, particularly at field levels, but it may also lack the sanction of the agencies involved. Hence, such informal activity may lack real power for concentrated action on a long-term basis. Although "memorandum(s) of understandings" are made between agencies for cooperative arrangements, this type of arrangement usually ends up like a treaty between nations, with each agency concerned about defining its responsibilities and limiting any policy innovations or other commitments. A case in point is the Interagency Wildlife Committee, which was established to handle overpopulation of elk (and their migration) at Rocky Mountain National Park, Colorado. Wildlife specialists from five agencies were involved, but the committee soon found that it could really not make any policy or even policy recommendations for a flow resource on a regional basis. Hence, its duties consisted of a superficial exchange of information and research.[35]

Resistance to interagency coordination often exists within a given department. An example is the U.S. Department of the Interior's BR and NPS conflict in the Echo Park Dam controversy. Cain notes, "There was truth in the description of Interior [Department of] as a 'loose confederation of sovereign agencies often at war with each other.' "[36] Much of this interagency conflict might be attributed to historical time lapse regarding the narrow value bases for mission agencies, which has taken on political connotations. Thus, White notes: "Almost each of the 80-odd agencies which shared management of the American environment had a history of its own, crusted over with an entrenched bureaucracy, each ferociously defending its own prerogatives. Such bureaus had been born variously of a national crisis, a public outrage, a scientist's insight or a President's dream—but all reflected that hoary first principle of American government: when something itches, scratch it."[37]

Another underlying cause of interagency conflict may be a territorial compulsion that results in defensiveness and empire building. Operating as a symbolic organism, with its supporting clientele and pressure groups, an agency may operate to defend or extend its symbolic or actual territory. Competition cannot form a basis for interagency cooperation under this territorial dictum: witness the long-standing feud between the NPS and FS over public lands and recreation. Territorial jealousy is particularly true of resource agencies that offer a fragmented approach to their particular responsibilities, without consideration of environmental unity; thus, a total environmental orientation is seldom attained. The territorial compulsion of specific agencies, along with their political orientation, might also raise questions as to how effective the interagency review will be relative to requirements by the CEQ.

Wengert notes several factors that contribute to political conflicts in interagency coordination: (1) ideology and values (differing within a unit as well as between units); (2) costs and benefits; (3) time; (4) bureaucratic self preservation; (5) technological biases (with technicians adhering to programmatic values and with conflicts over the best type of technicians); and (6) leadership and personality factors.[38] Given this potential for conflict, there appears to be a growing effort on the part of many agency personnel toward interagency relations based on environmental considerations. But this effort must be supported with sufficient political power to transcend the biases of a given agency. It also involves some drastic changes within the administrative hierarchy, with emphasis on the establishment of real and improved communications among and within agencies to achieve a common environmental focus.

REFERENCES

1. Michael Nadel, "Comments on Attitudes and Reactions of the Executive Branch as Reflected in the National Park Service" (Paper delivered at the Regional Conservation Leaders' Conference of the Wilderness Society, Denver, Colorado June 23, 1969) pp. 1–4.
2. Talcott Parsons, *Structure and Process of Modern Organizations* (New York: Free Press, 1969) pp. 1–15.
3. Carl H. Reidel, "Wasteful Organizational Practices," in *Organizational Management in Forestry,* ed. R. Rodney Foil (Baton Rouge: Louisiana State University Press, 1969) p. 71.
4. *Ibid.,* p. 72.
5. *Ibid.,* p. 73.
6. Douglas Price, "Organizations: A Social Scientist's View," *Public Administration Review* 19, no. 2 (Spring 1959) p. 127.
7. U.S., Congress, Senate, Subcommittee on Public Lands, Committee on Interior and Insular Affairs, *Lincoln Back Country Wilderness Area, Montana* (September 23, 1968) 90th Cong. 2nd sess. (Washington, D.C.: U.S. Gov't Printing Office, 1968).
8. U.S., Congress, House Subcommittee of the Committee on Government Operations, Quality Council, 91st Cong. 1st sess. *Transferring Environmental Evaluation Functions to the Environmental Quality Council* (Washington, D.C.: U.S. Gov't Printing Office, July 9, 1969).
9. Douglas Price, "Organizations: A Social Scientist's View," *Public Administration Review* 19, no. 2 (Spring 1959) p. 127.
10. *Ibid.,* p. 128.
11. Herbert Kaufman, *The Forest Ranger: A Study in Administrative Behavior* (Baltimore: Johns Hopkins Press, 1960) p. 91.
12. *Ibid.,* p. 96.
13. Chris Argyris, "Understanding and Increasing Organizational Effectiveness," *Commercial Letter* (October 1968) pp. 1–4.
14. Daniel H. Henning, "National Park Wildlife Management Policy: A Field Administration and Political Study at Rocky Mountain National Park," Ph.D. Dissertation, Syracuse University, 1965.
15. Gordon L. Bultena and John C. Hendee, "Conflict and Accommodation: Forester's Perception of Interest Group Positions on Forest Policy" (Manuscript, Seattle, Washington: University of Washington, 1969) pp. 10–15.
16. *Ibid.,* p. 17.
17. *Ibid.,* p. 18.
18. U.S. Forest Service, *Framework for the Future: Forest Service Objectives and Guides* (Washington, D.C.: U.S. Gov't Printing Office, 1970) p. 6.

19. Stanley A. Cain, "Environmental Management and the Department of Interior," *Public Administration Review* 28, no. 4 (July/August, 1968) p. 321.
20. Daniel H. Henning, "Natural Resources Administration and the Public Interest," *Public Administration Review* 30, no. 2 (March/April, 1970) pp. 134–140.
21. R. W. Behan, "The Myth of the Omnipotent Forester," *Journal of Forestry* 64 (June 1966) p. 400.
22. Bruce Bowler, "Socio-legal Aspects of Environmental Management" (Paper delivered at the Winter Chapter Meeting of the Society of American Foresters and American Society of Range Management, Boise, Idaho, March 19, 1970) p. 10.
23. *Ibid.,* pp. 3–4.
24. Charles A. Reich, *Bureaucracy and the Forests* (Santa Barbara, Calif.: Center for the Study of Democratic Institutions, 1962) pp. 7–8.
25. *Ibid.,* p. 6.
26. Barry Commoner, "Informing the Public: The Duty of the Scientist in the Environmental Crisis" (Paper delivered to the Secrecy, Privacy, and Public Information Symposium, Annual Meeting of the American Association for the Advancement of Science, New York, December 29, 1967) p. 13.
27. Wilson Clark, "The Role of the Bureau of Land Management in Public Conservation Education" (Paper delivered to the South Dakota Section Meeting of the Society of Range Management, Lemmon, South Dakota, November 23, 1970) p. 6.
28. Carl H. Reidel, "Environment: New Imperatives for Forest Policy" (Paper delivered to the Division of Economic and Policy Meetings, Society of American Foresters, October 13, 1970) pp. 4–6.
29. *Albuquerque Journal,* 24 January 1971, p. 7.
30. U.S., Congress, Senate, Committee on Interior and Insular Affairs, Select Committee of the University of Montana, *A University View of the Forest Service* (Washington, D.C.: U.S. Gov't Printing Office, 1970) pp. 14–15.
31. Correy McDonald, vice president, New Mexico Wilderness Study Committee, Albuquerque, N. M. Personal interview, March 3, 1971.
32. Lynton K. Caldwell, "Environmental Management as a Public Function" (Paper delivered to the School of Community Services and Public Affairs Conference, University of Oregon, May 16, 1968) p. 11.
33. Norman Wengert, "Perennial Problems of Federal Coordination," in *Political Dynamics of Environmental Control,* ed. Lynton K. Caldwell (Bloomington: Indiana University Institute of Public Administration, 1967) p. 42.
34. Morton Grodzins, "Sharing of Functions: The National Recreation System," in *The American System,* ed. Daniel J. Elazar (Chicago: Rand McNally, 1966) pp. 125–153.
35. Daniel H. Henning, "National Park Wildlife Management Policy: A Field Administration and Political Study at Rocky Mountain National Park," Ph.D. Dissertation, Syracuse University, 1965.
36. Stanley A. Cain, "Environmental Management and the Department of Interior," *Public Administration Review* 28, no. 4 (July/August 1970) p. 321.
37. Theodore H. White, "How Do We Get From Here to There," *Life Magazine,* June 26, 1970.
38. Norman Wengert, "Perennial Problems of Federal Coordination," in *Political Dynamics of Environmental Control,* ed. Lynton K. Caldwell (Bloomington: Indiana University Institute of Public Administration, 1967) p. 42.

Chapter 4

ENVIRONMENTAL PERSONNEL

An obvious but realistic generalization concerning environmental administration is that it will be a product of the type and quality of personnel involved. Practically all of the professional and administrative personnel in this field have had formal training in a scientific or technological specialty such as forestry, engineering, biology, or wildlife management. The predominance of specialized training is characteristic of other areas of the federal government. W. L. Warner notes: "Government at the higher levels is a world dominated by professionally trained men, showing in common the perspectives and attitudes of a long period of specialization."[1] Pfiffner and Prestus further observe that about 20 percent of those in the federal government are classified as general administrators, and about 80 percent in specialist classifications involving program tasks and scientific–technical activities.[2]

In environmental administration particularly, specialized personnel tend, through upward mobility, to find themselves serving as generalists with responsibilities involving more "people management" than environmental considerations. Yet, competency in a technoscientific field does not automatically assure success in such a generalized administrative role. With many generalists operating as "specialists" on the handling of other specialists, the conflict of generalist versus specialist, or authority versus ability, is recognized as one of the problems of modern organizations. Thus, Victor Thompson notes: ". . . in addition to the right to be consulted and the desire for enhanced influence, excessive insistence upon joint decision reflects the insecurity which is inherent in the position of the modern executive. This insecurity is a result of the increasing dependence which increases generally as specialization advances and in any particular organization as one rises to higher position."[3]

Given the complexities of managing specialists, a generalist, with a specialized background, is expected to attain certain understandings as he rises in an organizational hierarchy. John J. Corson considers these understandings to be: "(a) of the substantive field in which he works, (b) of ways and means of directing the work of others, (c) of the functions of other units within the organization and of related governmental entities, (d) of the society, economy, and the citizens he serves, and (e) of ways and means of projecting the policies and programs throughout an enterprise and seeing to it that they are carried out." Corson further indicates that these understandings require continuing expansion of knowledge after expertise in a particular field is achieved. He believes that understanding one's social, political, and cultural setting is essential for the higher positions in government.[4]

A valid questioning of the capacity of general administrators to achieve these understandings is illustrated in the *Peter Principle*. After observing that many generalists appear to be incompetent in executing their duties, Peter and Hull postulated the following principle: "In a hierarchy every employee tends to rise to his level of incompetency," with corollaries, "In time, every post tends to be occupied by an employee who is incompetent to carry out his duties," and, "Work is accomplished by those employees who have not yet reached their levels of incompetence."[5] Although the principle and its corollaries might be considered satirical, there nevertheless appears to be some validity to this assessment of generalists in their hierarchial roles in modern organizations. This is particularly true with changes and complexities in science, technology, and society. Further complications arise with current environmental considerations, which add new dimensions to the generalist's role. Full competence would require analysis of these complex forces and influences relative to each specific decision, and their effect on the interrelationships among the various segments of the organization. This might well be beyond the competence of many generalists, particularly those with a specialized background; they cannot be expected to have superhuman comprehensiveness.

Thus, the generalist, with his specialized background, is dealing with complex forces within his organization. Although no longer specialists, many general administrators still make the claim of professionalism based on earlier specialization. A characteristic of American environmental–natural resources administration is the emphasis placed on professionalism and specialization. With the high regard for and responsiveness to scientific and technological expertise in America, environmental personnel are respected for their specialization. However, complications emerge when such environmental personnel reach administrative levels where policy is increasingly made, and are expected to participate in determinations of the public interest in various general decisions. On the one hand, their decisions are no longer professional, technological, or specialized, but have become value decisions. On the other hand, they can take part in brokerage politics with other interest groups while, because of their given specialization, they may still claim professional detachment and the respect that attends it.

Professionalism, with agency support, may well be the dominant force in justifying environmental decisions. Under the claim of professionalism and objectivity, a "halo" effect is sought to convey that the agency is not involved in brokerage politics or value decisions. However, a paradox exists in that administrator–generalists are actually determining and acting upon environmental problems through their professional, specialist image. Thus the generalist makes a claim, based on professionalism, for political objectivity. He may want to make value decisions claiming the neutrality of his former professional specialization, but actually colored by his own definitions of the ends of society. At the same time, he may want to avoid political involvement with other interests and values. W. R. Pierce expressed this desire at a recent Senate hearing on wilderness when he stated, "It is a request for the necessary freedom that the professional forester needs to do his job in forest preservation."[6] Yet the Senate hearing on the issue basically called for a value decision on whether the area should be legally designated a wilderness, or devoted to economic development and mass recreation.

Many environmental agencies operate under this orientation toward professionalism. The U.S. Forest Service (FS), for example, with its emphasis on the profession of forestry, has strong features of solidarity and an intense *esprit de corps* combined with high motivation toward increasing professional status. National Park Service (NPS) personnel also have a professional approach, although their training may be in a variety of fields. Under the guise of professionalism an agency enjoys the halo effect, despite political involvements and manipulations. Moreover, many agency personnel actually function in political roles within their professional orientation. Janowitz indicates:

> Professionalization can be defined as a process by which the members of an occupation develop a training procedure, a body of expert knowledge, and a set of operating standards. To speak of overprofessionalization implies that concern with the forms of professional status outweigh concern with functional performance. . . .
>
> Overprofessionalism leads to an exaggerated concern with the specification of missions and roles and to organizational morale based on parochialism rather than on a sense of competence.[7]

Yet, the upper ranges of the administrative hierarchy, as well as the agency itself, may be quite devoid of professional specialization. Past experience in a given specialty may not equip a generalist for an entirely new range of administrative responsibilities in terms of perspective, values, and training. Nevertheless, many generalists operate under the guise of professional expertise, particularly in the determination of the environmental public interest. Concerning foresters Frome notes: "The day when 'the forester knows best' is over. The sooner this is recognized the better off we all shall be. Foresters, with all credit to them, rarely have the depth and breadth of vision to make ecological and environmental judgments; but if they did, they are wise to seek broader views."[8] Referring to Frome's comments, Reidel notes: "Frome is not criticizing our science. I'm sure that he would defend the scientific competency of foresters. It is our 'judgments' on the use of that science that he questions—our policy making—not what we know how to do."[9]

One role of a generalist is to make judgments that involve values. Although Lindblom notes that many of these value determinations are in marginal areas,[10] a generalist's role, by its very nature, would imply enough perspective to bring broad and general value considerations into environmental decisions. Under the political—administrative process, however, a paradox exists in that the reverse may occur, with only narrow and specific values being involved, and with the value base being restricted accordingly. This restriction involves pressures and constraints of traditional vested interests, missions, and goals of an agency and its satellite clientele groups under political dictates, and also involves the limited scope and biased perspective of many generalists. Such limitations may preclude consideration of environmental quality and other intangibles comprising the public interest. The domination of specialization and technology creates a power image for many generalists, but does not necessarily increase their value base or enrich the basis of their judgments on environmental matters.

SPECIALISTS

Although the majority of environmental personnel were trained as specialists, their actual roles place them in quasi-general administrative roles. While their specialties may involve a particular natural resource, environmental concern, or a subfield thereof, much of their actual time is spent dealing with human aspects of those specialties. This is particularly true of the specialist–manager who decides on or interprets the use, manipulation, or regulation of the environment for private individuals or organizations, but who in fact practices little of his specialization on intensive environmental management. Consequently, many of these persons are specialists only in the sense of being information administrators in a technoscientific segment of the private sector dealing with the environment. Technological competence is required for such a position, but the associated human problems make value judgments a major consideration, as they are for general administrators. Human and value judgments are increasingly significant with upward mobility in the hierarchy.

On the one hand, specialists operate with commitments to their particular professions; on the other, they operate as government officials with commitments to their respective agencies. Political considerations are naturally involved. Conflicts are bound to emerge concerning their divided interests and loyalties. Nevertheless, specialists may emphasize commitments to their professions. An FS specialist notes: "Specialists in different agencies do cooperate better than their administrators, but I believe this [is] mainly because specialists are more concerned about what *needs* to be done, rather than *who* should do it. In other words, specialists are more mission-conscious than agency-conscious."[11]

Wengert further suggests: "At the point where programs affect the environment, specialists can more readily comprehend how their several interests are related. They can see the consequences of their actions and often feel the need for supportive efforts by others whose authority and responsibility complement their own."[12]

Yet a claim made by many generalists and "specialists on specialists" is that they have the responsibility for placing a given area in the proper perspective within the whole operating picture of the organization. The overriding requirement for both generalists and specialists is the exercise of judgment. The degree of judgment required in the political and social realms increases in the upper levels of the agency hierarchy. Judgment, in this sense, may be the highest function of management.[13] In the final analysis, every governmental decision by environmental personnel involves some type of value judgment with one individual making decisions concerning the environment. With the technoscientific backgrounds of both generalist and specialist, coupled with political complexities, the question arises whether administrative judgments reflect a broad value base and environmental considerations. Today many agencies and their personnel are under attack because of negative or narrow judgments (e.g., the Corps of Engineers (CE), Soil Conservation Service (SCS), and FS).

Technoscientific training can be considered in terms of a particular field of specialization, for example, forestry, engineering, or wildlife management. Subdivisions within these applied sciences introduce complications, as do research orientations of some personnel in basic sciences. But the major point is that specialists develop a conceptual framework for viewing their disciplines and the world, based on the methodologies, techniques, and models of each *particular* discipline. This assumes no general technoscientific approach, but a variety of technical approaches related to each discipline (just as there is no single scientific or philosophical approach). A specialist would have one conceptual structure under a given technoscientific discipline, and another conceptual structure based on individual human considerations. The latter could be called a value or ethical system relative to his personal view of the world. Values or ethics automatically imply a judgment for good or bad in the way one conceptualizes the world. Through interaction a specialist, like all human beings, is constantly making value judgments of the world. The world is not seen in isolation, but from a particular perspective relative to outside things that produces an ethical judgment (that is, a mental picture of the world).[14]

With the complexities of ethical description, it is probably safe to say that values pertain to perceptions of worth that react on an individual basis with something in the environment to produce a judgment. From a political and administrative viewpoint, this worth would have to be sufficient to affect an individual's activity in the power struggle concerning a particular environmental decision. Many specialists and generalists refute the importance of values with the observation that they are highly subjective (i.e., not empirical or quantitative). Halo images and concern for professionalism are naturally threatened by realistic recognition of ethics in judgments of environmental personnel. Given the objective nature of a technoscientific conceptual structure within a particular area of specialization, however, the individual's ethical conceptual structure is also a valid projection relative to the environment. Technoscientific and ethical conceptual structures may come into conflict when a particular decision has a potential for positive or negative effects on a given environmental situation, and when it is one of several possible alternatives available.

On the other hand, organizational and professional pressure for conformity may dictate that the specialist not give way to his personal ethic, although this may prove dysfunctional in environmental considerations. This is particularly true in the case of specialist—managers. Herbert Kaufman notes two processes for insuring conformity of personnel of the FS in possible conflict situations: (1) internalization of values by indoctrination, with informal and formal training programs; and (2) a preformed decision process with agency manuals, handbooks, and reports.[15] However, an FS official engaged in research states: "There certainly is a determined effort by the Forest Service to ensure that employees 'keep the faith.' Although it would be difficult to describe in specific terms, this effort reaches insidiously well into the research branch and tends to restrict freedom in research in certain areas. If one wanted to examine where keeping the faith currently is most restrictive to study freedom, I suggest he would do best to look into the matters of water pollution by pulp mill wastes and air pollution by slash burning."[16]

Forces for conformity are, in many cases, based on an organization's vested interests and political dicta, suggesting that values do affect the operations of specialists. In this sense, questions might be raised as to what is completely objective and professional, in that ethical interpretations usually permeate scientific and quantitative data in the very selection of the problems studied and in the inferences, conclusions, and recommendations that result. It is also common knowledge that scientific, statistical, or quantitative data can be manipulated in light of a given bias, or under political constraints. Environmental decisions require a great deal of technical and scientific data, but the data do not necessarily yield decisions based on value considerations. The value bias of individual environmental personnel is further complicated by: (1) the specialist who is concerned with his field and its programs; and (2) the general administrator (usually a former specialist with a lapse of time in his given field) who is concerned with correlating a special program with other agency programs and with considerations of brokerage politics.

RELATIONSHIPS BETWEEN GENERALISTS AND SPECIALISTS

The conflict between the specialist and the generalist is usually recognized as a major problem of modern public administration. Weidner believes that the main clash or conflict of values occurs within a unit of government rather than between units. He indicates that professionalism (i.e., specialization) creates powerful programatic values that influence the behavior of personnel. Weidner notes, "The technicians themselves have become attached to and encourage the creation of programmatic values."[17] Power struggles by environmental personnel naturally emerge among various programs and organizations. Further complications result when many specialized programs involve a single resource such as water or soil, with pet causes and different value orientations represented within a given organization. Nevertheless, a generalist with responsibilities for a range of programs, and the specialists involved, must resolve conflicts and competing demands in order to utilize effectively the organizational resources allocated. The values of specialists thus become involved in a human power struggle for a governmental decision. With the high governmental regard for the technoscientific, the generalist may

58

be in a position of less regard, and at a disadvantage in the crisis type of administration characteristic of much contemporary public administration. Yet, attention to expedient and pragmatic solutions to technoscientific conflicts may not yield a total environmental approach. Further complications naturally emerge with the political interaction of the organization with outside interests, or among clientele groups associated with given programs.

A certain amount of the specialist's power hinges on the concept that information is power. Staff or specialist positions are actually power spheres for value decisions in many cases. Further, generalists become somewhat dependent on specialists for supplying the latest information and recommendations or quasi-decisions. The traditional organizational categories of line and staff are less clearly defined than formerly relative to power and decision making. This is particularly true on the basis of informal complexities involved in decision making. Although staff specialists may be studying, advising, and recommending, they also make value inputs and engage in power struggles relating to a given decision. At Rocky Mountain National Park, for example, national and regional headquarters wildlife specialists of the NPS were instrumental in making the decision to have park rangers directly reduce the overpopulation of elk and deer after the problem had been identified for more than 12 years. To do this, several specialists engaged in informal activity over the years to provide a power base for the decision as well as writing strong reports colored by value considerations.[18]

Position in the organizational hierarchy also influences the decision-making powers of specialists. A headquarters specialist on a visit or in written communications conveys to the field personnel the image and prestige of the headquarters office. His advisory functions effectively place the specialist in a quasi-line position in terms of his dealings with field personnel. Specialists thus project to their counterparts at the field level an image of power within the institution. Moreover, many headquarters specialists have government service ratings (GS rating pertaining to salary schedule and agency status) that are higher than those of line and staff personnel in the field. Also, because of close contact with headquarters line personnel, the headquarters specialist is in a position to gain support for his decisions affecting the field. The end result is that the headquarters specialist, given variables of personality and situation, has the potential for operating as a line administrator in field operations, with emphasis on the informal power base.

In headquarters administrative operations, specialists occupy key positions for making value judgments. In constant contact with line administrators, they have access to formal and informal decision points, particularly with their technoscientific insights on many of the issues at hand. Many decisions, moreover, are made through group processes at staff meetings or conferences where specialists are included. Concerning these processes, Thompson notes: "What appears to be a frank, open, rational, group problem-solving process is very often a bargaining or political process. The outcome is likely to be determined by power, even though on the surface it seems to be a result of rational analysis."[19] In the case of the wildlife reduction decision at Rocky Mountain National Park, a specialist encouraged the park superintendent to call the conference that actually gave official sanction to the specialist's position.[20]

The institutional context may be a very important factor in influencing the specialist himself relative to environmental value inputs. Harold Woodward noted a tendency on the part of many specialists in the Colorado Game and Fish Department to ask for more time for study whenever an answer was needed. He noted that they were reluctant to commit themselves or to prescribe recommendations or alternatives.[21] Among other factors, the reward systems of agencies and professional societies may not encourage specialists to advocate environmental values openly and officially. Job security and the survival and expansion of a given government agency through its limited agency objectives can become more important to some specialists than is the commitment to total ecological considerations. In other words, the political ecology rather than the natural ecology can become the important real concern of many specialists.

There are also inferences, values, interests, and biases associated with any given discipline that may interfere with a total environmental perspective. These are further complicated by management functions involved in some specializations. A trained forester, hydrologist, soil conservationist, or range manager will tend to be selective in terms of his specialization, thus limiting his mental framework. A specialist may observe, study, and recommend in terms of his own specialty, rather than considering the total system. Moreover, many specialties are traditionally strongly identified with a utilitarian, economic use (e.g., forestry–lumber industry). Professional societies may reinforce such identification, as in the case of the Society of American Foresters or the American Society of Civil Engineers. A given discipline may influence individuals to think in certain ways not conducive to environmental protection. In considering environmental values, Lawrence Halprin notes that engineers think mostly in straight lines about efficient solutions (in economic terms this translates into least costs, benefits–costs ratios, and engineering feasibility) to clearcut problems threatening to the environment. He indicates that: "... the problem is that they don't understand the impact of what they are doing—or aren't interested in the impact. . . . I don't think any one specialized field is a hazard as long as the people in it are thoughtful and creative. . . . But I find the engineers I deal with are so specialized—the ones I know—that they have no relationship to anything else. This is where the problems come."[22]

There is also a tendency among many specialists in government to be conservative. In concert with conservative tendencies of organizations, specialists themselves are generally prone to lean toward the safe side in estimates, recommendations, or projections. D. H. Ogden, in his case study, "The Struggle for a Redwood National Park," notes that the NPS Projection Study by specialists was a definite underestimate.[23] Martin, in *From Forest to Front Page,* considers that FS estimates on board feet in one controversial area were very low while timber surveys conducted by TVA foresters in the same area were considerably higher.[24] In Rocky Mountain National Park wildlife studies by wildlife rangers from 1931 to 1941, projections, estimates, and recommendations, although fluctuating, tended to be of a safe and conservative nature.[25] The important point here is that many governmental specialists may tend toward conservativism, while many environmental quality matters call for a more liberal approach to achieve positive action on problem areas.

With the trend toward electronic data processing (EDP) current in most organizations, there is an emphasis on increasing the growth of specialist staff in general and administrative hierarchies. Some scholars speculate that organizations under the influence of EDP will move toward a bell-shaped form rather than the traditional pyramidal hierarchy, with personnel increases occurring in top staff positions, and with a reduction of middle-management positions. At the same time, the increasing reliance of generalists on staff specialists and EDP support may place the specialist in even a stronger position to supply value judgments along with his information.[26] Given that computers cannot think, but that the specialists working closely with them can, specialists are in a position to make an even greater value input with the growing dependence of the generalist on EDP staffs. Yet, under an EDP orientation, with a somewhat mechanistic view of man and the environment, many intangible, quality values pertaining to the environment may be excluded. In the face of the "computer revolution," many organizations have formulated objectives relative to the effect or contribution of EDP in their total programs.[27] It is obvious that the role of specialists will be more significant in the decision-making process.

Given the complexities of categorizing specialists, particularly those involved in managerial roles, it is safe to say that they are involved in many value judgments and many quasi-generalist roles concerning environmental matters. Moreover, Oganovic and Leich note that most specialists recognize that advancement up the organizational ladder usually means assuming some type of administrative role.[28] On the assumption that many will eventually gravitate from point of organizational entry, as specialists, to generalist or quasi-generalist roles, it can be recognized that virtually all generalist personnel in environmental administration are former specialists. At the same time, the far greater majority of environmental personnel are limited by their technical, scientific, or resource management training, which may not be applicable, relevant, or even valuable, in various aspects of their actual responsibilities pertaining to the environment.

PROFESSIONAL EDUCATION

In commenting about the shortcomings of specialist training for a generalist's role in forestry, Reidel identifies a "white-shirt crisis" which takes place when a forester becomes an administrator. He notes:

> Now a desk has become his principal place of work. The forest is a place to be visited occasionally on a hurried inspection trip or on a weekend picnic with the family. . . . His

days are spent with people—all kinds of people who seem to generate questions much faster than answers. In a very short span of time he finds himself armed with the wrong weapons—the tools and concepts learned at school. The time-honored weapons of the traditional forester are too often useless, for now he is surrounded by people, not trees. Between him and the forest are a host of people. The standards and models that provided the keys to decisions in the past are largely meaningless in his new role. The decisions he is called upon to make cannot be decided on the basis of growth and sustention. The variables are many and the goals are vague.[29]

In many cases, specialists, as well as quasi-generalists, find themselves lacking formal education, beyond their specialized training, that prepares them to handle people and deal with environmental concerns.

While technoscientific competency is required of specialists, and of specialists who later become generalists, little attention is directed by professional schools toward education in areas of values, people, and environment, all relative to actual roles that the specialists and generalists will be performing. In the Society of American Foresters' study of forestry schools, for example, Olaus Murie comments, "Our world today needs fully educated men, and we can no longer be satisfied with only technicians skilled along certain lines."[30] Murie also notes that there is too much specialization too early in the forestry curriculum. Clark observes the "closed ring" of forestry curricula that involves technically trained forestry professors who are training students for governmental positions where the job requirements are devised by professional foresters.[31] Forestry schools are noted for their emphasis on timber management and similar technical subjects despite public pressures for environmental and recreational areas. Wildlife management curricula as well as other resource management and engineering curricula reflect this technical emphasis. Yet, many members of the resource management professions will readily admit that their technical training has little to do with their actual functional responsibilities, particularly as administrators and generalists.

In specifying the entrance requirements for forestry agencies, the U.S. Civil Service

Table 4–1. Course Work Required at the College of Forestry of Syracuse University

Freshman	

First semester	Hours	Second semester	Hours
Forest botany	3	Forest botany	3
General inorganic chemistry	3	Organic chemistry	3
Technical drawing	3	Technical drawing	3
Freshman English	3	Freshman English	3
Forest resources and their uses	3	Freshman mathematics	3
Freshman mathematics	3	Public address and public speaking	2
Physical training or ROTC	0	Physical training or ROTC	0
	18		17

Table 4–1. (Continued)

	Summer camp	Hours
	Adirondacks Forest–A case study in	3
	forest management (mensuration	
	and surveying)	7
		10

Sophomore

First semester	Hours	Second semester	Hours
Dendrology	2	Dendrology	2
Plant physiology	2	Technical writing	2
Geology for foresters	2	Elementary forest	
Plane surveying	3	entomology	3
General physics	3	General physics	3
Forest zoology	3	Forest zoology	3
	15	Optional–program course	3
			16

Junior

First semester	Hours	Second semester	Hours
Introduction to economics		Forest pathology	2
for foresters	3	Principles of forest	
Harvesting	2	economics	2
Forest mensuration	3	Forest mensuration	2
Foundations of silviculture	3	Forest soils	2
Introduction to forest products	2	Seeding and planting	2
Elementary wood technology	2	Practice of silviculture	6
Optional–program course	3	(summer camp)	16
	18		

Senior

First semester	Hours	Second semester	Hours
Principles of forest		Resource management	2
economics	3	Forest management and	
Advanced literature and		operation	3
composition	3	Optional–program courses	
Forest administration		and electives	12
and policy	3		17
Optional–program courses			
and electives	8		
	17		

From the College of Forestry, *General Catalog 1963–1965* (Syracuse: State University of New York, 1965), pp. 54–55.

A total of 141–144 semester hours is required for graduation.

Commission generally requires four years of formal training experience or equivalent education, with the completion of at least 24 semester hours or 36 quarter hours of course work in forestry. The 24 semester hours of forestry must fall in at least four of the following areas: (1) silviculture, (2) forest management, (3) forest protection, (4) forest economics, (5) forest utilization, and (6) forest-related areas of a technical nature, e.g., forest mensuration, forest pathology, etc.[32] Professional forestry school curricula, however, are strongly oriented toward technical and scientific courses with little room for electives in the liberal arts. Although it has been suggested that there be more offerings from the social science, humanities, and environmental areas, there is resistance toward these alternatives from professional foresters who want to maintain a timber-management oriented technoscientific curriculum. Many forestry professors, moreover, encourage their students to take their electives in scientific and technical subjects, Although the Civil Service Commission requirements are minimal, forestry schools usually exceed technoscientific requirements, paying little attention to the social sciences and humanities.

A typical curriculum in general forestry from the College of Forestry at the State University of New York at Syracuse is presented in Table 4–1 to illustrate the emphasis on technoscientific subjects.

Bernard Rosen, Executive Director of the U.S. Civil Service Commission, notes federal administrators of forestry programs recommend that 24 semester hours (36 quarter hours) of forestry are the bare minimum of professional training requirements. Rosen further states:

> The technical forestry requirement is typically much less than that required by schools of forestry. For example, the forest resources management curriculum at the University of Montana requires a total of 195 quarter hours, including 84 quarter hours in forestry and 20 in botany. Thus we feel that the forestry curriculum could be greatly changed without affecting the 36 quarter hours required for eligibility for Federal Civil Service positions. . . .
>
> We agree with your observations that foresters need to be broadly trained so that those so inclined have opportunities to advance to managerial positions. Courses in liberal arts provide an important base of education. Of course, there is still an additional need for on-the-job and other broadening and development of managerial skills.[33]

Under Civil Service Commission requirements for in-service training, various programs are conducted by agencies. For example, the FS operates a Continental Divide Regional Training Center for its personnel; in its program for new personnel, however, the majority of its offerings emphasize the technical and procedural aspects of forestry and the FS.[34] A recent trend of in-service training by many agencies is to conduct various programs called *grid seminars* that emphasize organizational and management skills. These programs involve environmental personnel; one of them, developed by Scientific Methods Inc., specializes "in the application of behavioral science principles to increase corporate excellence through Grid Organizational Development."[35] Management skills in this framework tend to emphasize technoscientific group decision making, organizational efficiency, and role orientations that may not increase the value base or perspective of the personnel since quantitative measurements are often assigned to various types of human interaction.

Several intensive surveys conducted by students investigating environmental personnel of the FS, BLM, and SCS revealed various problems associated with the technoscientific training of those interviewed. Personnel, both in specialist and generalist categories, indicated that they were mainly dealing with people, problems, and considerations on an organizational basis, and that their past academic training did not really prepare them for their actual roles in many situations. In answer to the question about courses they would take if they had an opportunity for future university education, the great majority of them indicated a preference for training in the humanities and social sciences. Some of their comments on this question are included.

> As an administrator, I feel inadequate in handling people, both inside and outside my office. Therefore, I would take classes in the social sciences which would help [me] to understand and work with people.

> The social sciences to aid in handling the public. Less of the technical and more of the liberal arts. I need more knowledge in the management of people.

> In the field of psychology, guidance counseling, and other social sciences.

> Environmental management, which is my specialty, and social management, which as an administrator I am dealing with—how to manage people.

It is interesting to note that only a few of those interviewed indicated they would select more technoscientific courses.[36]

There also seems to be a need for further environmental and ecological training among such personnel. For instance, the Wilderness Society notes:

> A distinction needs to be drawn between managers who take an ecological, public interest outlook and those whose perspective overemphasizes economic values. A forester, after all, is not a purely objective "professional." Unfortunately, a major segment of forestry education—and an overwhelming part of on-the-job forestry experience—is economics—production oriented. It has only shallow ecological roots. It is also highly compartmentalized into specialities. Thus the seeds of conflict are sown. The fundamental need to start on an ecological base, to work with nature, is submerged. All the emphasis is on how man and his machines can manipulate the forest, its flora and fauna.[37]

The Wilderness Society also notes the need for a distinction between the forest as a biological and ecological entity and as a treasury of economic resources.[38] Although foresters and other resource personnel usually have had several college hours of ecology in their professional training, this does not necessarily become the foundation for their future operations. In the student surveys, many of the personnel recognized the need for additional ecological and environmental training.[39] Thus, advanced courses and seminars pertaining to the total environment might be of service to personnel. Reidel defines forestry as applied ecology, with an environmental perspective.[40]

Much of this environmental perspective hinges on a broad value base, since personnel are basically dealing with the relationships of people to the environment. However, in specialized technoscientific curricula, little attention is given to value-oriented courses. As a result, many personnel are limited to mass ideologies and utilitarian platitudes in their value considerations, resulting in a strong emphasis on first-order considerations. The introduction of humanities and social science courses into environmental curricula would at least provide the opportunity for exposure to second-order considerations. More exposure to liberal arts subjects could enlarge the intellectual horizons and perspectives of technoscientific students, and might contribute to their judgmental processes by offering them an opportunity to observe different value systems. This could lead to a better understanding of intangible, qualitative values involved in human and environmental interaction.

Relative to this, George Maslach notes:

> When society commands the means to do almost everything it wants, value judgments of ends are crucial. . . . It is not nearly so easy to explain why the study of philosophy, history, and literature prepares one for making discriminating judgments about the significance and beauty of life as it is to point out what physics and chemistry have to do with the practice of engineering. To an embarrassingly great extent, advocates of the liberal arts as preparation for life in the real world find it hard to go much beyond Matthew Arnold's view that it is good to know the best that has been thought and said in the world and that somehow this will contribute to sweetness and light. In a rapidly industrializing society bent on supplying the means of subsistence and creature comforts for all and dominated by the austerities of remnant puritanism, there often seems to be something a bit irrelevant, if not actually frivolous, about a preoccupation with sweetness and light.
>
> By an interesting paradox, the progress of science and technology has now demonstrated that it is not inevitable and certainly not desirable that we do everything we can do, that the choice of what to do is, in fact, our most important problem, and that the ultimate basis of choice is aesthetic. We must have faith that the soundest base for aesthetic judgment is the cultivation of the best that has been known and thought.[41]

Reidel notes that an environmental curriculum should have a synthesis orientation as well as an analytical one. He considers that many curricula are fragmented into specialized courses to meet the interests and abilities of highly specialized and research-oriented professors. In order to present an education that permits students to synthesize their understanding of the environment, Reidel advocates regrouping some courses and consolidating or eliminating others, to provide a course of study stressing quality rather than quantity. He also recommends a series of core courses with a philosophical nucleus that gives a student, "an ecological insight into the interdependencies, interconnectedness, and symbiotic relationships of his education."[42] On both undergraduate and graduate levels, particularly for midcareer enrichment programs, sound curricula should be oriented toward an ecological synthesis for true environmental awareness, with a broad liberal arts influence. Yet many technoscientific curricula for environmental personnel continue to produce individuals technically competent for governmental careers, but lacking the value base and ecological perspective for making judgments on human and environmental concerns. Adding a course or two on environment may not alter the situation; instead, attention must be paid to the total curriculum and its emphasis on long-range considerations of the individual and the environment.

Rosen recently wrote that the Civil Service Commission shows its ambiguity regarding environmental personnel in terms of professional training, definition, and classification.[43] Agencies are now in the process of defining environmental personnel positions and training requirements, and acknowledging that a technoscientific degree may not qualify one relative to the environmental judgments required. The National Environmental Policy Act stipulates an interdisciplinary ecological approach. Perhaps professional training for environmental personnel should be oriented toward this goal. A true environmental curriculum, whether for an engineer, forester, or some new category of professional, could synthesize the liberal arts, as well as ecological and technoscientific courses. Similarly, the education of the social scientist in environmental and governmental fields should encompass exposure to courses in relevant technoscientific and resource-management areas, in conjunction with an interdisciplinary ecological program. Throughout their careers, the generalist and specialist will be making value judgments and determining ends for human and environmental interaction. It would appear reasonable to assume that a professional education should help to supply the value base and environmental perspective necessary for this very important governmental responsibility.

REFERENCES

1. W. L. Warner, *The American Federal Executive* (New Haven, Conn.: Yale University Press, 1963) p. 155.
2. John M. Pfiffner and Howard Prestus, *Public Administration* (New York: Ronald Press, 1967) p. 127.
3. Victor A. Thompson, *Modern Organizations: A General Theory* (New York: Knopf, 1963) p. 87.
4. John J. Corson, "Equipping Men for Career Growth in the Public Service," *Public Administration Review* 23, no. 1 (March 1963) pp. 1–10.
5. Lawrence J. Peter and Raymond Hull, *The Peter Principle* (New York: Bantam, 1970) pp. 1–10.
6. W. R. Pierce, Prepared Statement at the United States Senate Hearings on the Lincoln Back Country, Great Falls, Montana, on September 23, 1968.
7. Morris Janowitz, "Changing Patterns of Organizational Authority," *Administrative Sciences Quarterly* 3 (March 1959) pp. 480–481.
8. Mike Frome, *American Forests* 76, no. 6 (June 1970) p. 62.
9. Carl H. Reidel, "Environment: New Imperatives for Forest Policy" (Paper delivered to the Division of Economic and Policy Division Meetings, 1970 National Convention, Society of American Foresters, October 13, 1970) p. 2.
10. Charles E. Lindblom, "The Science of Muddling Through," *Public Administration Review* 19 (Spring 1959) pp. 79–88.
11. Personal correspondence.
12. Norman Wengert, "Perennial Problems of Federal Coordination," in *Political Dynamics of Environmental Control*, ed. Lynton Caldwell (Bloomington: Indiana University Press, 1967) pp. 58–59.

13. Thurman H. Trosper, "The Making of a Forest Manager" (Paper delivered to the Joint Meeting of the Division of Forestry Education and Forest Management Society of American Foresters' Annual Meeting, Detroit, Michigan, October 27, 1965) p. 4.

14. James Leland, "Value Theory and Environmental Sciences," Manuscript (Billings: Eastern Montana College, February 1971).

15. Herbert Kaufman, *The Forest Ranger: A Study in Administrative Behavior* (Baltimore: Johns Hopkins Press, 1960) pp. 91–99.

16. Personal correspondence.

17. R. Weidner, in *Federalism, Mature and Emergent,* ed. Arthur W. MacMahon (New York: Doubleday, 1955).

18. Daniel H. Henning, "National Park Wildlife Management Policy: A Field Administration and Political Study at Rocky Mountain National Park," Ph.D. Dissertation, Syracuse University, 1965.

19. Victor A. Thompson, *Modern Organizations: A General Theory* (New York: Knopf, 1963) p. 126.

20. Daniel H. Henning, "National Park Wildlife Management Policy: A Field Administration and Political Study at Rocky Mountain National Park," Ph.D. Dissertation, Syracuse University, 1965, pp. 200–212.

21. Harold Woodward, "Common and Conflicting Responsibilities of Natural Resource Biologists" (Paper delivered to the Second American Institute of Biological Sciences Meeting, University of Wyoming, June 30, 1970).

22. Lawrence Halprin, "The Engineer and the Landscape," *Science and Technology* no. 71 (November 1967) pp. 61–62.

23. Daniel H. Ogden, "The Struggle for a Redwood National Park" (Paper delivered to the Western Political Science Association Conference, Sacramento, California, April 3, 1970).

24. Roscoe C. Martin, *From Forest to Front Page,* Inter-University Case Series No. 34 (University, Ala.: University of Alabama Press, 1956) pp. 9–18.

25. Daniel H. Henning, "National Park Wildlife Management Policy: A Field Administration and Political Study at Rocky Mountain National Park," Ph.D. Dissertation, Syracuse University, 1965, pp. 139–230.

26. John M. Pfiffner and Howard Prestus, Public Administration (New York: Ronald Press, 1967) p. 247.

27. Herbert H. Isaacs, "Computer Systems Technology: Progress, Projections, Problems," *Public Administration Review* 28 (November/December 1968) pp. 488–494.

28. Nicholas J. Oganovic and Harold H. Leich, "Human Resources for Science Administration: Can Quality be Enhanced" (Program for Advanced Study in Public Science Policy and Administration University of New Mexico, Albuquerque, 1969) pp. 10–25.

29. Carl H. Reidel, "Parkinson's Law for Foresters," *Journal of Forestry* 65, no. 64 (April 1967) pp. 240–241.

30. Olaus Murie, "Some Views of the Future of Forestry in the United States" (Society of American Foresters, Washington, D.C., 1963).

31. Wilson F. Clark, "Management Training Problems in Government," *Journal of Soil and Water Conservation* 19, no. 6 (November/December, 1964) p. 228.

32. U.S. Civil Service Commission, *Qualification Standards: Forestry Series* GS–460 (December 1968) p. 1.

33. Personal correspondence, January 18, 1971, with Bernard Rosen, Executive Director, United States Civil Service Commission, Washington, D.C.

34. Interview, April 6, 1971, with Rondeau M. Gurley, Regional Training Officer, U.S. Forest Service, Albuquerque, New Mexico.

35. *Grid Seminars* (Austin, Texas: Scientific Methods, Inc., 1969). Based on B. R. Blake and S. S. Mouton, *The Managerial Grid* (Houston: Gulf Publishing Co., 1964).

36. Leonard Redding, G. Michael Reynolds, Doug Marston, Dennis Meeker, Harry Peltzer, and Ronald Sears. Interviews with federal environmental personnel in conjunction with course on Public Administration (Billings: Eastern Montana College, December 1969).

37. The Wilderness Society, "Public Hearing Alert" (Washington, D.C.: The Wilderness Soc., March 26, 1971) p. 3.

38. *Ibid.*, p. 4.

39. Leonard Redding, G. Michael Reynolds, Doug Marston, Dennis Meeker, Harry Peltzer, and Ronald Sears. Interviews with federal environmental personnel in conjunction with course on Public Administration (Billings: Eastern Montana College, December 1969).

40. Carl H. Reidel, "Environmental Forestry: A Modest Proposal," *Journal of Forestry* 40, no. 2 (February 1970) pp. 100–101.

41. George J. Maslach, "The Reorganization of Educational Resources," in *Undergraduate Education in the Biological Sciences for Students in Agriculture and Natural Resources* (Conference Proceedings) *Daedalus* vol. 96, no. 1 (Fall 1967) p. 1223.

42. Carl H. Reidel, "Environmental Forestry: A Modest Proposal," *Journal of Forestry* 40, no. 2 (February 1970) pp. 100–103.

43. Bernard Rosen, Executive Director, United States Civil Service Commission (Lecture presented to the Perspectives on Intergovernmental Administrative Relations Seminar, University of New Mexico, Albuquerque, December 10, 1970).

Chapter 5

NATURAL RESOURCES POLICY AREAS:
PART ONE

This chapter deals with forest and range, water, and wildlife as they generally relate to environmental policy and administration. A detailed and comprehensive treatment of these policy areas is not our objective here; rather, we shall consider them generally in terms of environmental perspective and quality. A complete listing of available sources appears in the "Bibliography" that follows the text.

FOREST AND RANGE

Forest and range are combined into one policy field because of the general correlations in approach and interspersed location relative to environmental and governmental decisions affecting them. According to Lyle Craine, it is possible to view policy in these areas as a "flexible linkage" that government has constructed to combine: (1) government with a partially independent private economy; (2) federal and state governmental interrelationships; and (3) special, but diverse, groups interested in forest and range, i.e., conservation organizations and lumber and grazing industries. (Craine notes that no realistic "timber shortage" can be predicted for the United States in the foreseeable future).[1] Although private citizens and industry own 70 percent of the commercial forests, much of forest and range policy pertains directly to extensive public ownership by the federal government; two major agencies in this area are the Forest Service (FS) and the Bureau of Land Management (BLM).

Traditionally, the policy of the United States has been to dispose of forest and range lands to private ownership. The free timber of the "cut-out-and-get-out" era of land and timber disposal to railroads and others in the 1800s was counteracted to a degree around the beginning of the twentieth century by the reservation of vast areas of public lands as forests and watersheds. Later, additional forest lands were acquired primarily in the eastern states. The retention and acquisition policy was to an extent a reaction to the dramatic, negative effects of environmental abuses and deterioration arising from unregulated and exploitative timber practices. In contrast, equally negative effects on range lands (many of which were interspersed with forest lands) due to overgrazing were of a less dramatic and obvious nature.

As a result of the reservation policy, the federal government now owns (among its 771 million acres) 20 percent of all commercial forest land, nearly 40 percent of the supply of merchandizable timber, and over 60 percent of softwood sawtimber available in the United States.[2] The Public Land Law Review Commission (PLLRC) notes: "The degree of potential federal control over the supply of timber is greater than over that of any other commodity presently produced from public lands."[3] In all western states, the federal government owns and administers 273 million acres on which grazing is allowed; depending on the season of the year, about half of these lands are grazed by domestic cattle and sheep. Consequently, the PLLRC states that grazing uses more of the public lands than any other economic activity. Although public lands supply only 3 percent of the total forage consumed by livestock in the United States and about 12 percent of forage in the West, the PLLRC indicates that public land grazing plays a significant role in the national livestock economy. Hence, the PLLRC observes that the western-range livestock industry is built around public lands through the availability of seasonal grazing to individual ranch operations.[4]

Thus, a major component of public forest and range policy is extensive public ownership of lands. The second feature of policy relating to forest and range lands correlates with and results from the first. This is that forestry and, to a lesser degree, grazing are public interest concerns of government and require public action. This general policy is now well accepted, and questions appear to center on the types of action that should be permitted. With growing public awareness of recreation since the 1950s, it is now recognized that forest and range lands are owned by the people, and hence must answer their needs and interests. In conjunction with the public interest, there appears to be a commitment on the part of government to economic aspects of forestry and grazing interests. According to many conservationists and environmentalists, this economic commitment is the basis of much governmental policy, resulting in neglect of noneconomic considerations of environmental quality.

Given the commitment of government to economic considerations, forest policy on public lands mainly involves selling stumpage to the highest private bidder with relatively little economic interest beyond this point. A neutral price policy is followed, with no price support (in contrast to agricultural policy). As in Canada, there is no government wood processing and the few government attempts at logging, sawing, and marketing have been unsuccessful. Little study has been done on import–export policies from the standpoint of their influence on forestry. E. E. Crafts notes that private industry exports large quantities of timber to Japan and other nations; over 2.5 billion board feet of softwood logs were exported in 1968.[5] In the private sector of forestry, there is little governmental policy, particularly of an economic nature. Thus, Crafts reports: "The Forest Service, in about 1968, developed a small woodland program but never released it. It is most significant that the greatest potential for timber production is on the farm and miscellaneous private lands which include over 60 percent of the total commercial forest land area of the country but support only 18 percent of the inventory."[6]

On the other hand, some subsidy-type and cooperative policies are in limited operation in the private and state sectors. These consist of: (1) financial inducements (e.g., tax modifications, credit and insurance, financial aid, etc.); (2) technical assistance, especially to small wood-lot owners; (3) research in forestry and wood products (e.g., experimental stations); (4) protection of the public from fire, pests, and diseases; (5) public education (e.g., forestry schools); and (6) payments in lieu of taxes.

In areas of forest and range policy a controversy exists relative to allocation and actual use in terms of environmental quality, particularly under the concept of multiple use. Although the 1960 Multiple Use and Sustained Yield Act for national forests gave it legal sanction, the FS and other agencies had previously operated under this concept with very general statutory guidance. The application of *multiple* uses to a given area is a major component of forest and range policy on public lands, but it is an ambiguous and imprecise concept. In the allocation of uses (logging, grazing, recreation, wildlife, water, minerals, etc.), it is obvious that overemphasis of one use will negatively influence other uses. In some cases, allocation decisions will be made on the basis of power and economic influences rather than according to what may be best for the land in terms of environmental quality. For example, overgrazing or overlogging in a given area may occur with "multiple use" as a convenient slogan for covering a dominant use.

Within the federal framework, a very limited regulation policy can be extended to state and private lands. The federal government must operate through the states in this sphere. Although several states have limited control policies over private lands, much of the activity is of an educational and nonenforceable nature. (In some cases, federal grants and services are available; e.g., the Soil Conservation Service (SCS) provides planning and technical assistance in forestry in conjunction with agriculture programs.) Consequently, environmental quality regulation pertaining to forest practices and grazing on state and private lands relies heavily on each state's legislative and police powers. Given that these lands occupy two-thirds of the nation, except for cities and small communities which have been delegated regulatory powers, relatively little has been done to regulate severe problems of overlogging and overgrazing. On the other hand, public support for environmental stewardship of state and private lands appears to be growing, and this may result in more federal and state regulations.

Nevertheless, under present federal regulatory policies for public lands, various forest and range abuses occur through vested political interests. For example, political pressures to increase timber harvesting have resulted in a biased reclassification system for national forests, from 73 million acres in commercial lands in 1945 to 97 million acres in 1971. The "new" criteria, supposedly based upon ecological and multiple-use policies, did not involve any change in the national forest area of 186 million acres. Rather, the 24-million acre increase in commercial forest lands was taken from protected forest lands that were managed for watershed, wildlife, and recreation, and hence will involve logging marginal slow-growing trees in high-country areas where forest protection is needed.[7] Moreover, a recent White House directive has called for a 60 percent increase in softwood harvests from national forest lands by 1978. Regarding political and procedural pressure, Crafts notes:

> The Forest Service over the past two decades has made two serious mistakes in connection with timber management. First, it has allowed its timber cut to be linked to appropriation justification. And this, of course, puts it under serious pressure to increase the cut in order to get more money. Former Forest Service Chief Lyle Watts told me that he considered this to be the most serious error of his career.

> The second error is that the Service has largely allowed the term "allowable cut" to be substituted for and supersede the term "sutained yield." The first term is not defined by statute and is flexible in meaning. For example, allowable cut used to be the ceiling above which cut would not be allowed to go. Now it is generally considered to be the floor below which cut will not be allowed to fall. On the other hand, sustained yield is defined by statute and the Forest Service should stay with it. The agency may have gotten itself trapped by being drawn away from sustained yield and the statutory protection it gives.[8]

Similarly, the history of range policy is basically that of abuse due to political and economic pressures; for example, overgrazing on both private and public lands. Williamson estimates that 65 percent of the entire range has declined appreciably during the last 60 years and only about 20 percent has improved; forage values have been reduced by more than half, nearly 55 percent of the entire range.[9] On public lands, range conditions and forage production are, on the average, less than half of their potential.[10] Little regulation was extended to grazing on public lands until the Taylor Grazing Act of 1935 which, in turn, was manipulated and abused by livestock interests. Low grazing fees permitted monopolies of public lands and the fees were not raised on an equitable basis until 1969. Grazing permits, which can be obtained only through inheritance or purchase, allow 5 percent of the permit holders to control 52 percent of the grazing, and 11 percent of the permit holders to control 74 percent of the grazing.[11]

Grazing allocations are made on the basis of animal unit months (AUMs) established by grazing advisory boards composed of qualified range users. The final decisions rest with the government, but the grazing advisory boards exert great influence on allocation and range determinations in conjunction with the livestock industry's political pressure groups. Consequently, efforts to reduce AUMs to permit recovery from overgrazing are usually met with subtle, but solid, resistance. Moreover, some public lands end up being managed solely for livestock interests (e.g., sage-removal projects) with little attention to other legitimate uses (e.g., wildlife, recreation, water, etc.). With the advisory boards of the livestock industry exercising control, rather than acting in an advisory capacity in range decisions, it is obvious that recommendations will reflect the direct interests of the members and permit holders. Many grazing advisory board members regard themselves as owners with rights, rather than leasers with privileges. Concerning boards of this nature, the PLLRC notes: "The growing recognition that public lands can serve a variety of uses provides a basis for our conclusion that membership on advisory boards should be chosen to represent a range of interests, and that representation should change as interest in, and uses of, the land change. We believe the appropriate range of representation includes not just the obvious direct interests, such as grazing, recreation, mining, fish and wildlife, and wilderness, but the professor, the laborer, the townsman, the environmentalist, and the poet as well."[12]

A central problem of forest and range policy appears to be a tendency for dominant-use positions under the multiple-use and ecosystems approach of agencies. With sufficient political and economic power, forest and range interests have traditionally dominated, to the detriment of noneconomic environmental quality. The PLLRC recommended, for example, that the Dominant Use Timber Production Units be classified for commercial timber on public lands (it is interesting to note the constant reference by the PLLRC to "timber" rather than "forests").[13] G. L. Woolfolk observes that the term *range* traditionally carries a strong connotation of land used primarily for livestock grazing.[14] Traditional interests and perceptions that result in dominant use, however, may not be compatible with environmental quality or the public interest under public ownership. In effect, real ecosystem approaches to forest and range policy are needed, rather than one-sided manipulation by political and economic forces.

Much of forest and range administration continues to operate under a dominant-use concept. Reidel states:

> And there is little doubt that the pattern of management in the future will continue to be multi-purpose use of forest resources. Multiple use may be the *result* of environmentally integrated forest policy; it cannot be the guide. With its focus on mediating conflict between essentially economic definitions of resources, multiple use either collapses on the issue of assigning values to intangibles, or is forced to accept an inherent bias toward clearly short-run monetary values. This is a flaw in the concept, not in its users, as is too often claimed. . . .[15]
>
> I am not suggesting we merely abandon multiple use, but rather that we integrate it into a broader and more comprehensive systems approach that will make it possible to achieve the balances that were sought by, and abandoned by the Multiple Use Act of 1960. The mandate stated in that historical act must now be interpreted in light of the broader and more comprehensive mandate of the National Environmental Policy Act signed into the law the first day of this decade.[16]

WATER

As an essential prerequisite for life, as well as for economic, urban, and recreational activity, water presents a complex, diverse, and controversial policy issue. Craine notes that water policy is unique due to the peculiarities of water and public policy problems regarding its use. He considers the controversy surrounding questions of water use and development to be more vigorous than that affecting other natural resources.[17] Besides the varied and numerous state and local agencies dealing with water, on the federal level there are some eight departments (e.g., the Department of Interior) with 32 agencies (e.g., the Bureau of Indian Affairs), five agencies under the Executive Office of the President (e.g., the Office of Emergency Planning), and nine independent agencies (e.g., the Atomic Energy Commission) involved.[18] Although a vast amount of water legislation has been passed by Congress, the Water Quality Improvement Act of 1970 in particular applies to federal agencies. This Act provides a statutory basis for bringing environmental quality into the planning and decision making of federal agencies, especially in areas where gaps exist in earlier laws.[19]

Much of the complexity of water policy hinges around its natural characteristics and uses, which include:

1. Pervasive and evasive character: As a flowing substance, water is everywhere—in, under, and over land—which makes it the subject of various governmental and private claims.

2. Drainage basin concept: According to Craine,[20] a drainage basin is the only unit for dealing with water in public management; he notes that there is no governmental jurisdiction that conforms to this water region, and that use in one drainage area may affect another.

3. Degree of immobility: Water is where it is and water problems and uses are typically very localized, with governmental responses occurring at a local or regional level.

4. Variety: Water varies tremendously in quality, quantity over time (seasonal flows), location, and uses.

5. Pollution adjustment: Although naturally susceptible to pollution, water can be treated and, depending on the pollutants, can adjust to varying degrees.

Water renders disservices (e.g., floods and soil erosion) as well as services. The same unit of water, depending on its quality and treatment aspects, can serve a variety of purposes (e.g., household, recreational, wildlife, power, industrial, etc.). This automatically generates competition among users, and places water within the concept of multiple use in terms of comprehensive planning and management. According to Laas and Beicos, the total per capita consumption of water in the United States is 1800 gallons a day. (This is based on all uses, as a given family may use only 15 gallons a day). Thus, they note that overall estimated totals for water use in billions of gallons per day are:

Uses	Now	1980
Public water supplies	12	39
Industry	73	115
Steam power plants	119	162
Agriculture	148	178
TOTAL	352	494

Based on the projected figures for 1980, Laas and Beicos note that the greatest and most rapid increases are expected to occur in industry and the power plants that supply industry, while agriculture will continue to grow as a major user, particularly in western irrigation.[21]

Given the role of government and its numerous agencies with their conflicting policy objectives, water is accepted as a public resource, financed through subsidy and tax money. Water is regarded as a *free* good (commodity of commerce) and price plays only a small part in the market system. In noting the supply management orientation of water, with demands accepted with no relation to price, Hanke and Davis advocate a system of demand management with alteration of demands through responsive pricing. They state: "Although a rather radical departure from conventional practice, a policy of responsive pricing plus effective management of supply will provide the utility manager with the means to assure both a more efficient utilization of the resources employed to produce and distribute water, and a more equitable distribution of the costs incurred in providing water services."[22] Because there is no current relationship between supply and demand and competitive pricing, other factors determine water resource allocation.

Thus, much of water supply allocation depends upon investments and developments that use water. With private economic interests concerned only with some segment of water process, government is required to carry the majority of investment as a public function; about half of the expenditures by government in natural resources are in the area of water developments.[23] Moreover, a recognized traditional role of government is public expenditure on water projects, serving public welfare through local economic growth. Consequently, allocation of expenditures for projects becomes highly political, particularly among congressmen with their concern for constituents.

Much of water policy centers around certain assumptions associated with unlimited development and expansion. These may not be valid under present environmental imperatives. Bruner and Farris hold that certain widely accepted assumptions relating to water serve as common rationale for policy making, regardless of other valid economic, political, social, and environmental criteria. They give as examples: (1) survival, (2) agricultural fundamentalism, and (3) desert assumptions, noting that: (a) an increase in water supply is the necessary if not sufficient answer to most water problems; (b) demand aspects of water problems are relatively important; (c) price is an unsuitable basis for allocation in water administration; (d) water problems require immediate action.[24] They conclude that consideration of these points results in perfunctory support for proposals to increase water supplies without any real examination of alternatives. There is also a sense of urgency attached to consideration of water policy proposals, and a tendency to deny the relative importance of certain noneconomic environmental concerns.

Some individuals associated with water and planning development are beginning to question assumptions concerning water needs for various population, industrial, and urban projections. In some cases, a self-fulfilling prophecy may exist, with water expansion acting as a causal factor for overconcentration of populations, and urban and industrial developments in heavily burdened water areas. This, in turn, creates greater demands for water in an endless cycle. In the Southwest, water can serve as a crucial control factor in population and industrial growth to avoid overuse and concentration. The water control concept has so far, however, had little use in planning.

Moreover, in the West, a major allocation of water resources and governmental expenditures is for irrigation, despite the marginal agricultural gains and low economic efficiency of such use. Much of this misdirection is due to ambiguous and unsound water laws affecting ownership rights, which many experts identify as a major problem in water allocation, and a stimulus for large government projects for new and distant water sources.[25] Thus Hirshleifer, DeHaven, and Milliman note that:

> . . . much of the present misuse of water within the spheres governed by the market can be traced to imperfections in water law and its administration. These ills occur because in most jurisdictions, water rights are not clearly defined, do not have legal certainty, and cannot be transferred with ease as are rights to other types of property, land, mineral rights, etc. As a consequence, the market processes that ordinarily direct resources to uses that maximize their productivity—chiefly voluntary exchange through purchase and sale—are either severely limited or prevented entirely from operating in the case of water.[26]

A major component of water policy allocations and priorities for government projects concerns the benefit—cost ratio. Simply stated, the formula (required under interagency agreements) for justifying a given project on a dollar basis is concerned with a higher return of benefits than costs (i.e., expenditures). It is assumed that social benefits correlate with economic benefits for a given area of the project, and, on this socioeconomic basis, primary and secondary costs and benefits are assigned. Regarding justification criteria, Spurr comments: "Cost—benefit ratios have fallen into disrepute because they have too often been manipulated to justify a project which is wanted for political reasons . . . the principle is sound—provided, first, that the intangible values to mankind are properly introduced into the formula."[27]

Biswas and Durie also make the point that human values should be taken into consideration in water planning. They state:

> Since planning is for people, planners should give more emphasis to the social consequences of water resources development and management. Physical and economic feasibility studies are needed, but equally needed are social and environmental feasibility studies. Finally, the tremendous importance in water resources management of having informed public support for a plan must be realized. With increase in population and the resultant further utilization of our natural resources, this importance will become even greater. It should be noted that the foremost factor in the success of a water resources management program is the public understanding and acceptance of the program.[28]

A case in point is the recently completed Libby Dam and Reservoir at Libby, Montana. Many residents of the small community are highly dissatisfied with the water project and had little to say about its planning and implementation. Further, their way of life has been disrupted with the influx of a large population and consequent social changes. Many local residents note that they have received little economic benefit from the water project, although taxes and cost of living have increased.

In striving for congressional appropriations, various water agencies compete with one another through the political process. In some cases, this involves manipulating a higher benefit–cost ratio than those submitted by other agencies, particularly in long-term investment considerations. Also, one agency may challenge another's ratios, especially when both have made studies of the same area (e.g., the Bureau of Reclamation (BR) and the Corps of Engineers (CE)). The CE claims to be directly responsible to Congress, which naturally contributes to further manipulation of benefit–cost ratio criteria. The end result is that the benefit–cost ratio is regarded with skepticism, rather than as a rational basis for project allocation. With the large federal expenditures involved on a local-welfare basis, there is also considerable logrolling and pork barrel activity by congressmen to obtain water projects for their constituents.

A major criticism of the benefit–cost ratio, in terms of environmental measures, is that it does not take into consideration intangible qualitative aspects of a given project. Although interagency arrangements pertaining to the ratio stipulate that intangibles should be evaluated, the ratio is based pragmatically on quantitative economic data. Consequently, little real emphasis is given to such qualitative values as natural beauty, wildlife, open space, or recreation. Such considerations are usually relegated to minor descriptions in project proposals that emphasize that the enhancement of these intangible mass recreational benefits would be accomplished through the project. Moreover, these items are subjugated to the major orientations of the project. Under cooperative inter-agency arrangements, agencies concerned with recreational and qualitative concerns, such as the Bureau of Sports Fisheries and Wildlife (BSFW), are relegated to surveying and other insignificant activities once a project has been undertaken by a major water resources agency. Bruner and Farris found:

> Given the mystique surrounding water and the concern for water supplies, there is often an unjustified sense of urgency associated with proposals concerning water. If this sense of urgency prompts hasty action, the merit of rational choice may be sacrificed to obtain immediate benefits. You do not change the location of a dam, reincarnate the land area inundated by a reservoir, alter the location of distribution facilities, and rebuild wildlife habitats without substantial if not exorbitant costs. The difficulty of predicting conse-quences of water projects, the irreversibility of decisions, changing value systems, finite reservoir sites, and an improving technology [should obviate] hastily made decisions. Yet conventional wisdom promulgates a sense of urgency that can cause such decisions to be made. . . .[29]

> The value of water used to preserve wildlife sanctuaries and fish spawning grounds, the esthetic appeal of a verdant agriculture, and the recreational benefits accruing from mainte-nance of open stretches of rivers are difficult to measure. Yet these aspects of water use represent a substantial value to society. Conventional wisdom tends to support these preferences only indirectly, if at all. To the extent that these needs are associated with water

and can be satisfied by increasing water supplies, they are apt to be incorporated into policy proposals. To the extent that they can be maintained only at the expense of restricting water supplies, they tend to be disfavored. As an example, the construction of a dam to improve water supply capabilities would probably be favored over the maintenance of an open stretch of river or the preservation of a geological find.[30]

With the passage of the National Environmental Policy Act of 1969, however, new project evaluation standards for environmental quality have been added to the benefit–cost ratio for water agencies. The Act stipulates that federal agencies shall:

(a) Identify and develop methods and procedures, in consultation with the Council on Environmental Quality established by title of this Act, which will insure that presently unquantified environmental amenities and values be given appropriate consideration in decision making along with economic and technical considerations.

(b) Include in every recommendation or report on proposals for legislation and other major Federal actions significantly affecting the quality of the human environment, a detailed statement by the responsible official on—

    (i) the environmental impact of the proposed action;

    (ii) any adverse environmental effects which cannot be avoided should the proposal be implemented;

    (iii) alternatives to the proposed action;

    (iv) the relationship between local short-term uses of man's environment and the maintenance and enhancement of long-term productivity;

    (v) any irreversible and irretrievable commitments of resources which would be involved in the proposed action should it be implemented.[31]

The Act further stipulates that the responsible official preparing the detailed statement shall obtain consultation and comments from any other federal agency with jurisdiction or special expertise on the environmental impact.[32] Recent directives by the Council on Environmental Quality (CEQ) have also required public participation and hearings. The National Environmental Policy Act establishes a potential·for applying more comprehensive criteria than with the benefit–cost ratio; these new criteria appear to be oriented toward utility, with equal consideration for intangibles pertaining to environmental quality. On the other hand, environmental impact statements presented by agencies to the CEQ reveal a tendency to assign to qualitative considerations quantitative values based on dollar amounts and numbers of people. It should be realized that a decision based upon such quantitative data is still no more accurate than the basic assumptions used to construct it. And, in some instances, the public participation requirement may result in an agency's manipulation of support from economic interests committed to a specific proposal.

Although federal water agencies operate under various laws and directives calling for environmental as well as multiple-use objectives, major problems occur with traditional dominant uses relative to specific agencies. Project study, justification, authorizations, and appropriations are highly dependent upon clientele and political support related to a given economic use. Consequently, a given agency works closely with dominant interest groups in obtaining political support. For example, the BR maintains close association with the National Reclamation Association and some agency personnel may serve as quasi-officials in local chapters of that Association during various phases of a project. The end result may be to give undue, and environmentally unsound, emphasis to irrigational aspects of a project to the detriment of other uses. Irrigational use of water is defined as a consumptive use in which 60 percent or more of the water supplied is lost to the atmosphere as vapor and is not subject to reuse.[33]

In building political support and influence, the CE has the reputation of being the most powerful and most independent agency in the federal government in that it answers only to Congress. Dominant uses of flood control and navigation are encompassed where appropriate with other uses such as irrigation, power, water storage, and recreation. In many instances, a common assumption is that man-made protection should be extended against natural flooding, which occurs on the flood plains of rivers. Hence, many of the CE's projects and proposals relate to protecting human life. This bias, coupled with large federal expenditures in local areas, assures the agency little trouble in gaining local and congressional support for effective political power, particularly from interests deriving direct economic benefits from its projects. On the other hand, many of its projects may be environmentally unsound, irreversible, and unnecessary, but little attention is paid to long-range environmental aspects.

WILDLIFE

Numerous agencies are directly (BSFW), partially (NPS), or indirectly (BR) involved with the management of wildlife, which includes wild fowl, aquatic species, and fisheries. Although a variety of agency policies exist, an overall principle is that habitat determines wildlife populations. Consequently, the composition and condition of wildlife populations serve as a barometer of the quality of the environment since these populations are dependent on wise and proper use of the environment by man. Climate, topography, and geology are basic influences on the composition of a given plant community, and the nature and abundance of local plants, in turn, govern the kinds of wildlife that will be supported. In this sense, man-made changes in the environment may radically alter the composition of wildlife populations.[34]

Thus, the Wildlife Management Institute notes:

> Some environmental changes, however, may be extremely damaging to all wildlife. Excessive pollution, repeated uncontrolled forest fires, and farming and forestry practices that destroy soil fertility and the diversity of the plant community can create wildlife deserts. When the balance between wildlife and its habitat is recognized, it is possible to understand why some species that never were hunted extensively became extinct while others that have been hunted intensively are among our most abundant species. The white-tailed deer, for example, is many times more abundant today than it was in 1900 and in most places more numerous than in 1600. Few of the birds and mammals listed as rare and endangered by the

U.S. Bureau of Sport Fisheries and Wildlife ever were hunted. Most are victims of pollution, landfilling, and clearing and other massive man-made environmental changes that have destroyed one or more essential elements in their habitat.

When desirable wildlife begins to disappear from a given area, in spite of legal protection, it is an indication that something is wrong with the environment. And the effects on human beings may extend far beyond the loss of esthetic and recreational values.[35]

Relating wildlife to the environmental movement, Reidel comments:

Intrinsic values are given relative consideration as they are integrated into the total man/nature system. This, I believe, is a major point of departure from traditional conservation. Where the old conservation mourns the loss of an eagle for its intrinsic value alone, or perhaps as a vague symbol of paradise lost, the environmentalist mourns the eagle both for those reasons and in the recognition that its death is a clear warning of systematic disruption. The eagle's death, like the death of the 19th Century coal miner's canary, is a signal that something is wrong in the biological system *and* quite likely in the political, economic, and social realms as well.[36]

With some exceptions (e.g., national parks, fish and wildlife refuges), wildlife is generally considered to be "owned" by the states in which it resides, whether on federal, state, or private lands. On the other hand, it is recognized that activities of a given land-management agency directly affect wildlife through man-made influences on the habitat. Hence, wildlife concerns involve considerable intergovernmental relations and various conflicting policies and clientele groups. The Outdoor Recreation Resources Review Commission estimates that approximately 15 percent of the population over 12 years of age engages in hunting,[37] and that perhaps more than twice this percentage engages in fishing. Consequently, there are considerable political and economic pressures on state wildlife departments to produce abundant supplies of selected species of game and fish. Billions of dollars are spent in the rapidly growing hunting and fishing industries.

The majority of state wildlife agencies derive most of their financial support for operation of wildlife programs from hunting and fishing licenses, and, as a result, are strongly oriented toward the production of game species for the use of the sportsmen who supply their revenues. Little attention, either in operations or research, is directed toward nongame wildlife species. On the legal assumption that wildlife is owned by all the people of a given state, and that a good percentage of the public may have esthetic, environmental, or recreational interests in wildlife (both game and nongame species), it would appear that some state and federal wildlife-associated agencies are not serving the public interest by their emphasis on the development of game species.

In some instances, too much attention is given by state wildlife agencies to overproduction of selected game species (deer, pheasant) and to "put-and-take" fishing (stocking fish that are caught in a short time period). This results from intense political pressure from sportsmen and their organizations. Little attention may be given to wildlife in its broader social and environmental context relative to the general public.[38] Under federal funding of state wildlife agencies through the Pittman–Robertson and Dingell–Johnson Acts, practically all research is oriented toward game species production.[39]

Wildlife policy is based to a degree on wildlife management. As R. E. Trippensee notes:

> The field of wildlife management has many sides and many angles. Fundamentally it is the process of making land and water produce sustained crops of wild animals. The goal is clear and definite, but the roads toward the goal are several and varied. In the first place, many different classes of animals are involved—migratory species, fur bearers, game species, nongame species. Management includes the manipulation of widely varying environments. It is concerned with many occupations, including agriculture, forestry, and range management, and may involve encouragement or restraint of both animal populations and human activities. . . .[40]

> Fortunately, wildlife management often fits admirably into such a plan of multiple use. This is not only true in conjunction with the practice of forestry, but applies also in the science of agriculture. That wildlife management in one form or another may be adapted to nearly all programs of land use is a fact deserving major emphasis.[41]

The Wildlife Management Institute also states that: "Altering or maintaining the environment to favor the needs of certain wildlife species, in fact, is a basic technique of wildlife management."[42]

Given the multiple use and "crop" aspects of wildlife policy and management, a major function of governmental personnel in this area appears to be dealing with the public, sportsmen, and other agencies. Wildlife is a flow resource that obviously involves numerous agency and organizational boundaries, responsibilities, and policies. In some situations, wildlife may be brought into direct competition with other interests (e.g., grazing for limited forage on lands supervised by the FS and the BLM) and may be subject to subsequent human interaction. At the same time, a great deal of political pressure is exerted, particularly on state wildlife agencies, to achieve the highest "crop" of game species. With too much attention being paid to other uses of public lands (e.g., timber harvesting, outdoor recreation, mineral development, grazing, etc.), habitat deterioration may negatively affect wildlife, causing further interagency conflict. Thus, the PLLRC states: "With regard to habitat management, we recommend that all public land uses and management practices that affect vegetative cover and surface water should, to the extent possible, be conducted in a manner designed to leave a quality habitat essentially unchanged in its overall capacity for supporting fish and wildlife."[43]

Four major problems of wildlife policy and management relative to environmental quality are: overpopulation, predator control, protection of rare and endangered wildlife, and the conservation of an adequate habitat. A brief discussion of these problem areas follows.

Overpopulation

Overpopulation of certain wildlife species is a relatively recent phenomenon resulting from protection of wildlife and its adaptability to civilization. Two species in this category are deer and, in some instances, elk. In essence, overpopulation of these species results in destruction and deterioration of the habitat, particularly on the range where the animals concentrate during the winter season. An analogy might be the running of too many livestock on a limited range. The end result of overpopulation is destruction of a quality environment with healthy wildlife. This type of problem continues to occur throughout various parts of the United States. Classic examples are the Kaibab National Forest and Yellowstone National Park. Management efforts to reduce overpopulation include (1) live trapping, and transplanting of overpopulated species to less populated areas; and (2) allowing sportsmen to hunt on public and private lands other than national parks. In the case of national parks, the Leopold Report and the PLLRC both recommend that only federal personnel should directly control overpopulations of wildlife.[44–46]

Predator Control

Predator control is recognized as one of the most controversial areas in wildlife policy, particularly with the recent Sierra Club legal suit calling for termination of all predator control activities by the federal government. The PLLRC has recommended that predator control programs be eliminated or reduced on federal public lands.[47] Under federal monies, supplemented by funds from state and local governments and livestock producers, predator control centers around the BSFW's Division of Wildlife Services, with some state and private control measures. In general, the history of predator control has been one of indiscriminate removal of "bad" animals, as defined in terms of man's interests, with disregard for ecological considerations. The program has been supported by powerful political and economic interests associated with the agriculture and livestock industries, and related government agencies. Often the control measures are unnecessary, and certain species are used as scapegoats. One example is the Golden Eagle, whose populations were decimated despite the lack of scientific evidence of its alleged livestock predation.[48] Serious reduction in numbers of natural predators (e.g., coyote, puma, cougar, bear), although of some benefit to livestock operators, may upset important natural balances for control of other species, such as rodents and deer. Yet, the Leopold Report of 1964 and the Department of Interior recommended the continuation of predator control programs, with emphasis on damage control rather than animal numbers.[49] Under present methods, however, predator control measures still involve little attention to the changing public attitude toward wildlife or environment.

Rare and Endangered Wildlife

Rare and endangered wildlife species are of particular concern because of growing public awareness of environmental quality. The Department of Interior reports that 40 species of wildlife have become extinct in the last 150 years (e.g., eastern elk, prairie wolf) and that 89 more species are on the endangered list (e.g., wolverine, keydeer, grizzly bear).[50] The major requirement for preservation of rare and endangered species is the availability of a sufficient natural habitat excluding man-made influences, that is, a wilderness or sanctuary area. However, grizzly bear hunting is still permitted in some western states, including Montana, and other species (e.g., wolverine) may be taken as predators. Without an adequate habitat and with man's influences, many species (e.g., California condor) are not able even to maintain their declining numbers of breeding stock, let alone attain a comfortable population margin. Ecological and cultural recognition of this decline is more than a concern for a species' survival; it is also a recognition of the quality of life and of man's responsibility to other forms of life, through protection of an undisturbed habitat where animals and plants can live naturally. Under the Endangered Species Act of 1966, the federal government assumed a national responsibility in this area, but little has been done to implement the Act on public lands. Relative to this, the PLLRC recommended that "Protection and propagation of rare and endangered species of wildlife should be given a preference over other uses of public lands," and that "Game and nongame species of resident wildlife should be given equal attention in the administration of public lands."[51]

Adequate Habitat

Establishing an adequate habitat is crucial to wildlife policy, especially with both private and governmental development and utilization of lands. Because the composition and numbers of wildlife species are directly dependent on habitat, manipulations of habitat (including the use of pesticides and herbicides) will bring about various changes that negatively affect native wildlife populations. Although various laws and policies have provided for wildlife preservation, the end result has been a growing destruction of natural habitat, particularly wetlands and wildlands. Although public lands provide a significant portion of wildlife habitat, little actual attention is given to this use as contrasted with conflicting economic uses. In water resource developments, wildlife surveys and arrangements become a farce under "improvement" and "enhancement" provisions. Economic forces of agriculture and industry make little provision for wildlife habitat. On the other hand, changing public attitudes toward wildlife and the stipulations of the National Environmental Policy Act call for definite recognition of the need to provide an adequate habitat as a major concern of wildlife policy.

REFERENCES

1. Lyle E. Craine, Lecture presented at Integrated Resources Management Seminar, Conservation Department, University of Michigan, Ann Arbor, Spring 1958.
2. Public Land Law Review Commission, *One Third of the Nation's Land* (Washington, D.C.: U.S. Gov't Printing Office, 1970) p. 91.
3. *Ibid.,* p. 92.
4. *Ibid.,* p. 105.
5. Edward E. Crafts, U.S. Congress, Senate, *Congressional Record,* 91st Cong. 1st sess., 1969, pp. 28860–28862.
6. *Ibid.*

7. Gordon Robinson, "Why the Status of American Forestry Must Change," in *The Case for a Blue Ribbon Commission on Timber Management in National Forests,* ed. Chuck Stoddard (San Francisco: Sierra Club and the Wilderness Society, 1970) p. 50.

8. Edward E. Crafts, U.S. Congress, Senate, *Congressional Record,* 91st Cong. 1st sess., 1969, pp. 28860–28862.

9. Interview with Robert Williamson, range manager, U.S. Forest Service.

10. Shirley W. Allen, *Conserving Natural Resources* (New York: McGraw-Hill, 1955) p. 219.

11. William L. Reavley, "Big Trouble on the Range: Public Rights Vs.," *National Wildlife* (July 1969) pp. 40–41.

12. Public Land Law Review Commission, *One Third of the Nation's Land* (Washington, D.C.: U.S. Gov't Printing Office, 1970) p. 289.

13. *Ibid.,* p. 92.

14. G. L. Woolfolk, "Range Management in ASRM," *Range Management Journal* 21 (1968) pp. 155–186.

15. Carl H. Reidel, "Environment: New Imperatives for Forest Policy" (Paper delivered to the Division of Economic and Policy Division Meetings, 1970 National Convention, Society of American Foresters, October 13, 1970) p. 14.

16. *Ibid.,* p. 15.

17. Lyle E. Craine, Lecture presented at Integrated Resources Management Seminar, Conservation Department, University of Michigan, Ann Arbor, Spring 1958.

18. Albuquerque Urban Observatory, *Factors Pertinent to Water Quality in the Albuquerque Metropolitan Area* (Albuquerque: Albuquerque Urban Observatory, 1970) pp. 1–5.

19. Public Land Law Review Commission, *One Third of the Nation's Land* (Washington, D.C.: U.S. Gov't Printing Office, 1970) p. 67.

20. Lyle E. Craine, Lecture presented at Integrated Resources Management Seminar, Conservation Department, University of Michigan, Ann Arbor, Spring 1958.

21. William Laas and S. S. Beicos, *The Water in Your Life* (New York: Popular Library, 1967) p. 21.

22. Steve H. Hanke and Robert K. Davis, "Demand Management Through Responsive Pricing," *Journal American Water Works Association* 63, no. 9 (September 1971) pp. 555–556.

23. Lyle E. Craine, Lecture presented at Integrated Resources Management Seminar, Conservation Department, University of Michigan, Ann Arbor, Spring 1958.

24. John M. Bruner and Martin T. Farris, "The Conventional Wisdom in Water Philosophy" (Paper delivered to the Eighth Annual Meeting of the Western Regional Science Association, Newport Beach, California, February 9, 1969).

25. David L. Shapiro, "Water Rights and Wrongs," *The Annals of Regional Science* 3, no. 2 (December 1969) pp. 139–143.

26. J. Hirshleifer, J. C. DeHaven, and J. W. Milliman, *Water Supply: Economics, Technology, and Policy* (Chicago: University of Chicago Press, 1960) p. 362.

27. Stephen Spurr, "Developing a Natural Resources Management Policy," in *No Deposit—No Return* (Menlo Park, Calif.: Addison-Wesley, 1970) p. 105.

28. Asit K. Biswas and Robert W. Durie, "Sociological Aspects of Water Development," *Water Resources Bulletin* 7, no. 6 (December 1971) p. 1143.

29. John M. Bruner and Martin T. Farris, "The Conventional Wisdom in Water Philosophy" (Paper delivered to the Eighth Annual Meeting of the Western Regional Science Association, Newport Beach, California, February 9, 1969) p. 10.

30. *Ibid.,* p. 11.

31. U.S. Congress, The National Environmental Policy Act of 1969, *Public Law no. 91–190,* 91st Cong., 2nd sess. (January 1, 1970).

32. *Ibid.*

33. U.S. Geological Survey, *Water for Recreation—Values and Opportunities,* Outdoor Recreation Resources Review Commission Study Report 10 (Washington, D.C.: U.S. Gov't Printing Office, 1962) p. 11.

34. Wildlife Management Institute, "Wildlife: The Environmental Barometer," Pamphlet (Washington, D.C.: Bureau of Sport Fisheries and Wildlife, 1970).

35. *Ibid.*

36. Carl H. Reidel, "Environment: New Imperatives for Forest Policy" (Paper delivered to the Division of Economic and Policy Division Meetings, 1970 National Convention, Society of American Foresters, October 13, 1970) p. 5.

37. Department of Conservation, The University of Michigan, *Hunting in the United States—Its Present and Future Role,* Outdoor Recreation Resources Review Commission (Washington, D.C.: U.S. Gov't Printing Office, 1962) p. 2.

38. John R. Owens, *A Wildlife Agency and Its Possessive Public,* Interuniversity Case Program: No. 87 (Indianapolis: Bobbs-Merrill, 1965) pp. 1–51.

39. Provided under the Dingell–Johnson and Pittman–Robertson Acts, sometimes known collectively as the Federal Aid Program for Fish and Wildlife Restoration, 16 U.S. Congress no. 667–669b, no. 669c–669i, and no. 777–777k (1964).

40. Reuben Edwin Trippensee, *Wildlife Management: Upland Game and General Principles* (New York: McGraw-Hill, 1948) p. v.

41. Reuben Edwin Trippensee, *Wildlife Management: Fur Bearers, Waterfowl, and Fish,* vol. II (New York: McGraw-Hill, 1953) p. vii.

42. Wildlife Management Institute, "Wildlife: The Environmental Barometer," Pamphlet (Washington, D.C.: Bureau of Sport Fisheries and Wildlife, 1970).

43. Public Land Law Review Commission, *One Third of the Nation's Land* (Washington, D.C.: U.S. Gov't Printing Office, 1970) p. 165.

44. *Ibid.,* p. 164.

45. Advisory Board on Wildlife Management, "Wildlife Management in National Parks" (Manuscript, March 4, 1963) pp. 1–23.

46. Daniel H. Henning, "National Park Wildlife Management Policy: A Field Administration and Political Study at Rocky Mountain National Park," Ph.D. Dissertation, Syracuse University, 1965, pp. 1–464.

47. Public Land Law Review Commission, *One Third of the Nation's Land* (Washington, D.C.: U.S. Gov't Printing Office, 1970) p. 168.

48. Interview with Thomas Smiley, chief naturalist, Sandia Ranger District, U.S. Forest Service.

49. A. S. Leopold, S. A. Cain, C. M. Cotton, I. N. Gabrielson, and T. L. Kimball, "Predator and Rodent Control in the United States," *Transactions of the North American Wildlife Conference* no. 29 (1964) pp. 27–49.

50. National Wildlife Federation, *National Wildlife* 50, no. 6 (August/September, 1969) p. 13.

51. Public Land Law Review Commission, *One Third of the Nation's Land* (Washington, D.C.: U.S. Gov't Printing Office, 1970) p. 160.

Chapter 6

NATURAL RESOURCES POLICY AREAS:
PART TWO

This chapter will deal with soil, minerals, and recreation as they relate to environmental policy and administration. As in Chapter 5, these areas will be considered generally in terms of environmental perspectives. Recreation policy will be included here because of its interrelationships with natural resource policy areas.

SOIL

As an essential for life, soils differ widely in kinds, characteristics, types, textures, combinations, and capabilities. These differences affect their productivity and their susceptibility to environmental influences. Consequently, a major concern in soil policy is the classification of soils for land-use planning and zoning. The major agency concerned with soils, the Soil Conservation Service (SCS), is engaged, together with other federal and state agencies, in a National Cooperative Soil Survey relative to private and governmental lands. Soil in a given area is surveyed and classified according to type and quality characteristics. These features relate to interactions among soil characteristics, land practices, and uses as essential elements in predicting the behavior of various widely distributed soil types.[1] Major private and public land uses in the United States are shown in Table 6-1.

Table 6–1. Total Land Use in the United States

Type	Percentage	Area (in millions of acres)
Forests	32	732
Grazing land	28	640
Crop land	20	444
Limited surface use (deserts, mountains, tundra, etc.)	12	277
Parks, refuges, cities, and other miscellaneous uses	8	173
TOTAL:	100	2,266 million acres

Commenting on the National Cooperative Soil Survey, Charles Kellogg notes:

This work was initiated in 1899 and has continued since in cooperation with the state agricultural experiment stations and several other interested state, federal, and local agencies. Techniques of doing the work have changed a great deal as we have learned more about soils, as new and improved technology has developed, and as people have had new problems. Some of the soils that were barely useful for farming 50 or even 30 years ago are now highly useful because they respond to the whole of new methods. Thus some of the surveys made in the early days, although generally useful, are not useful for operational planning in either cities or rural areas today.

Our purpose in the soil survey is *not* to make recommendations. Rather we make predictions on how soils will behave under certain systems of management, or with methods of manipulation, as in road construction and housing. We try to give the facts but it is up to the individual user or planning board or zoning agency to make the decisions.[3]

Much of the soil survey hinges on classification of *capability units*, indicating what the soil is capable of in terms of use, and relating to the prediction of various limitations, treatments, and risks, and the degree and kinds of problems. Although a survey classification of this nature is oriented toward agricultural productivity, it is increasingly valuable to other private and governmental interests, for urban and county planning, watershed and water project activities, wildlife management, and construction projects. Environmental impact studies under the National Environmental Policy Act of 1969 include soil surveys. The federal government offers advice and furnishes information and assistance to state and local governments, which must take responsibility for prescribing standards and requirements for zoning and planning, particularly in the case of private lands. Little has been done at the state and local level toward effective zoning and planning in the national environmental perspective. According to soil survey classifications, serious soil and land abuses occur under economic and social pressures, with little attention being given to "wise" use. A certain amount of this abuse involves unplanned and unzoned developments, with the daily removal of hundreds of acres of land.

On the other hand, the soil conservation, water conservancy, and drainage districts are legally constituted units of state governments established to administer soil and water conservation work within their boundaries. Soil conservation districts include about 98 percent of the farms and ranches and more than 94 percent of the agricultural land in the United States. In many instances, these state arrangements incorporate various governmental units at the county and metropolitan levels. Although the states prescribe a variety of legal procedures for their operations, each district is self governed and has the authority to enter into working arrangements with other governmental agencies and private concerns to carry out soil and water conservation programs. The SCS and other federal agencies merely provide professional, technical, and economic advice and assistance.[4]

Soil surveys form the foundation for conservation work within the districts by showing the kinds of programs that are necessary, and where they are most urgently needed. With the availability of soil survey information, and with state influences on zoning and planning, however, local districts have been rather ineffective in formulating and implementing soil policies with strong environmental impact. Charles Hardin indicates that districts have not proven effective instruments of land-use regulation as was anticipated, and have usually been organized along "artificial" (usually county) boundaries rather than "natural" boundaries such as watersheds.[6] The National Association of Soil Conservation Districts notes that districts may still be based upon narrow, rural approaches to complex modern demands, and also observes the need to expand participation by a broad cross-section of citizens, particularly in urban areas, in the decision-making process.[7] Although legislation is now being formulated for national land-use policy, with greater federal involvement, districts under local and state authority still provide the potential for many environmentally effective measures in land use and soil policy.

Besides the loss of soil to uncontrolled development, the SCS estimates that 180 million acres of crop land are affected by wind and water erosion with a loss of $1 billion annually or 1.5 percent of the current surface land value to farmers.[8] In this sense, a pollutant might be defined as a resource out of place, with soil sediment from erosion having a twofold effect on the environment: (1) by depleting the land resources from which it is derived, and (2) by impairing the quality of the water it enters. Soil sediment is the largest single water pollutant, exceeding the sewage load by some 500 to 700 times; about half of all sediment originates on agricultural land.[9] Consequently, much of soil policy is concerned with holding soil in place through proper land management and use. In the past, however, soil policy was seen almost exclusively in terms of agricultural need, that is, protecting the productive capacity of agricultural land. Particularly because of ecological considerations and changing attitudes regarding socioeconomic land use, a major trend in government is toward a broader, more comprehensive environmental approach, with more attention being given to nonagricultural areas and urban land problems.

Related to this trend, a relatively new and increasing policy concern is in the area of soil pollution resulting from improper use of fertilizers, herbicides, and pesticides. Ecologically, such use is an almost inevitable consequence of a modern, highly productive agriculture developed with little regard for diversity or crop rotation. Pure monocultures of corn, wheat, rice, or cotton, which extend over thousands of continuous acres, represent the highest sort of ecosystem specialization, and, consequently, often require continuous artificial chemical techniques for survival of their productivity. On the other hand, little is known about fertilizers, herbicides, and pesticides in terms of their ecological effects as they accumulate and pass through the soil. Thus, environmental quality considerations pose conflicts of interest among governmental agencies and others involved with soil policy; the result is the growing realization that the agri-ecosystem and its soil does not exist in an ecological vacuum.

MINERALS

The National Wildlife Federation indicates that a new national policy is urgently needed to control acquisition and use of nonrenewable mineral resources. The Federation recommends that all future mineral exploitation should be done under a leasing arrangement, whereby surface values of the land may be preserved for various uses (e.g., grazing, timber, recreation, and wildlife), noting that about 66 percent of mined land is unreclaimed by any means, with two million acres of wildlife habitat destroyed by surface mining.[10] In analyzing national mineral policy, which is essentially unchanged over the years, Shirley Allen notes:

> Whatever the United States may have in the name of mineral policy is made up of unrelated laws dealing with:
>
> (1) mineral land disposal;
>
> (2) tariffs on imports to protect domestic producers from foreign competition in the sale of minerals which are ample in supply or those whose production needs to be stimulated;
>
> (3) authorization of surveys to locate, test, and rarely to develop new deposits of those minerals which are scarce and needed;
>
> (4) purchasing output at artificially high prices to relieve mining distress;
>
> (5) maintaining government monopoly on certain minerals or on federally owned property but providing procedures for their development by private enterprise and thereby obtaining public revenue;
>
> (6) allocating strategic minerals in wartime;
>
> (7) encouraging mild self-regulation by mineral industries, usually aimed at production control to maintain prices;
>
> (8) stockpiling strategic minerals in time of war or preparation for war;
>
> (9) negotiating agreements for importation of strategic minerals from foreign sources.[11]

Allen points out that only items (3), (5), and (6) place any emphasis on conservation of mineral resources, and comments, "Theoretically, item (1) which has to do with mineral land disposal should operate to conserve these resources, but weak enforcement of patent claims and superficial appraisal of mineral values under these laws have led to widespread fraud and sometimes to wasteful exploitation and inequitable distribution of public resources."[12] Recently, national policy legislation on mining (S. 719) was adopted by the Senate; it was designed to encourage an economically sound domestic mining and mineral industry, help to ensure satisfaction of industrial and security needs for mineral resources and reserves, and provide mining and mineral research for wise and efficient use. The Wilderness Society, however, opposed this legislation on the grounds that it would direct the secretary of Interior to give priority to mining matters, and would continue to exploit public lands. The Wilderness Society also indicated that primary emphasis in any national mining policy should be given to encouraging research into salvaging and recycling wastes.[13] In this regard, the National Wildlife Federation notes: "Our greatest challenge may be the recovery of minerals from our waste. In a typical year, for example, the unburned residues of the country's municipal incinerators contain more than six billion pounds of iron, and 400 million pounds of aluminum, copper, zinc and other nonferrous metals. These valuable wastes are currently being plowed into ground at dumps and landfills."[14]

The recycling and recovery concept (which was highly successful during World War II) recognizes that minerals are essentially nonrenewable, being of a stock or fund nature. That is, their physical quantity is not increased or replenished with time (although some fossil fuels such as petroleum and natural gas will increase over geological time periods) as is the case with such renewable natural resources as forests, soil, and wildlife. Hence, each unit used diminishes the total stock available unless it can be recycled and recovered, as is the case for nonfossil fuels (metals such as copper and nickel). However, it can be argued, following the physical law of conservation of mass, that we do not really consume materials in the ultimate sense. We simply change them from "usables" to "residuals." In the mining and mineral industries, innovations of an economic, technological, and social nature are constantly sought. Thus, economic and social aspects may place a high demand on certain metals, but the trend of technological change may affect all phases of production and use, for example, by lowering costs, substituting other minerals or materials, or making feasible the extraction of lower quality materials. Technology also affects social needs and wants relative to minerals. Consequently, technology may be the most important and the most variable determinant of mineral policy.

Economizing with respect to mineral resources would appear to involve a reasonable rate of exploitation that would yield the greatest social returns over time, with due concern for environmental considerations. Yet, under economic, technological, and social variables, including questionable security stockpiling (over one-third of our mineral supplies are imported, according to the Public Land Law Review Commission),[15] the United States, with one-fifteenth of the world's population, now consumes about half of the world's raw materials each year.[16] On the assumption that technology can stretch minerals only so far, and that minerals, as a limited stock resource, will continue to be consumed under existing allocations, it is obvious that rates of exploitation will continue to be unreasonable in terms of effect on future generations. Consequently, a policy trend might well be toward stronger government involvement in the control of exploitation as well as toward recycling.

There appears to be another factor to consider about exhausting mineral resources, including those associated with energy demands. Intensive scientific research and technological development, responding in part to the alarms that have been sounded, but mostly to the signals sent out by the pricing system, result in upgrading of old resources, discovery of new ones (e.g., solar energy), development of substitutes and alternatives, and application of more efficient ways of utilizing available resources and adjusting to changes in availability. A strong governmental policy for research and development, particularly in the area of energy resources, could do much to avert what many refer to as the *energy crisis*. Unfortunately, long-range preventive programs involving research and development meet resistance under pragmatic political and economic considerations.

Further, commitment by industry to status quo methods may further discourage policy of this dimension. An example is coal strip-mining companies that are currently investing heavily in equipment and facilities to perpetuate this method.

Public lands are a definite concern in mineral policy as a major source of fuel and nonfuel minerals. The PLLRC notes:

> Over 64 million acres of Federal land were under lease for oil and gas in 1968, of which over 90 percent was in the 11 western contiguous states and Alaska.

> Accurate data concerning production of the metallic and other minerals subject to claim location under the General Mining Law are not available since there are no Federal records segregating production among private, state and Federal lands. However, in 1965, the western public land states, in which over 90 percent of the public lands lie, produced over 90 percent of the nation's domestic copper, 95 percent of the mercury and silver, 100 percent of the nickel, molybdenum and potash, and about 50 percent of the lead. In fact, most of the known domestic resources of metallic minerals other than iron are situated in the West.[17]

Based on the above, the PLLRC recommended that:

> Public land mineral policy should encourage exploration, development, and production of minerals on the public lands.

> Mineral exploration and development should have a preference over some or all other uses on much of our public lands.... Also, development of a productive mineral deposit is ordinarily the highest economic use of land.

> The Federal Government generally should rely on the private sector for mineral exploration, development, and production in maintaining a continuing invitation to explore for and develop minerals on the public lands.[18]

Yet this open invitation by public land agencies may show a disregard for other public uses and environmental values. A case in point is the large coal strip-mining operations on Bureau of Land Management (BLM) lands in Montana and Wyoming. Strip-mining companies are currently applying for, leasing, and developing thousands of acres of public lands on a single-use basis with the cooperation, and sometimes the encouragement, of the BLM (although some leases were postponed because of their massive, speculative nature). Further, Congress has yet to pass a national reclamation act (now pending) that would require reasonable reclamation of public lands. Because of the low rainfall, poor soil (which is a biological, as well as a chemical, entity), and the short growing season, serious doubts exist as to the potential success of reclamation, let alone restoration, particularly on a long-term cost basis; for example, adequate reclamation would in some cases cost thousands of dollars per acre. Thus, such short-term and exclusive-use operations as coal strip-mining on western public lands may cause irreversible environmental devastation. The paradox here is that the BLM is supposedly oriented toward multiple use of public lands on a long-term basis.

Much of public lands mineral policy is based on the General Mining Law of 1872, which has been severely criticized over the years by conservationists, government, and environmentalists. In essence, the Law provides that locators may establish rights to public land mineral deposits merely by discovery, without prior administrative approval. The locator may acquire legal title to the land within his claim(s) by a federal "patent" at a small fee or, even without it, may produce minerals without paying royalties to the government. Qualifications as to what constitutes a claim are ambiguous, and under the guise of the Mining Law, public lands may be obtained for other purposes.[19] Besides abuses in public land ownership, however, serious problems are presented for land management planning and other uses when mining claims can be located on public lands at any time, on a random basis, with little concern for overall environmental considerations, and no governmental intervention.

In the case of national forests and the General Mining Law of 1872, the National Wildlife Federation notes: "Conservationists have tried for years to force the Forest Service to require more environmental safeguards for mining in the national forests. The Service consistently claimed it lacked necessary authority because of the 1872 mining law. Agreeing [that] the archaic 1872 law is an invitation to unnecessary destruction, conservationists insist the Service has many regulatory powers it has failed to use."[20] Recently, the FS announced new mining regulations for some 140 million acres of national forest lands based on its unused authority. But the National Wildlife Federation analysts declared them "incomplete and ineffective" to minimize the despoilation of national forests by mineral exploration and mining, and recommended stronger public regulatory powers. Commenting on the situation, Kimball notes: "The National Forest lands involved are not private preserves of either miners or the Forest Service. They are public lands and the people have a right to be heard in deciding what environmental protections are essential for particular mining activities."[21]

On the other hand, the PLLRC, despite objections and a minority report by some of the commissioners, recommended the continuation of the Mining Act of 1872 with amendments based on industry preferences. While noting the environmental impacts of mining, the PLLRC commented that minerals are where you find them and that public lands should be generally open to exploration, development, and production wherever minerals are located.[22] Although mining is an accepted use of public lands, the present mineral policy (particularly under the Mining Act of 1872) permits too many unnecessary and avoidable abuses of the environment through unwise selection and exploitation of locations with little concern for such tangible and intangible effects as pollution. Short-term economic benefits may accrue to given individuals and organizations, but society will pay long-term costs. More regulations based on realistic criteria are needed to protect the environmental public interest, especially in leasing arrangements, to preserve surface values of land. If we are to avoid environmental deterioration, mineral policy is needed, based on environmental quality, and providing for the actual authority of agencies over regulation, allocation, and planning.

Relative to various natural resource policy areas, the National Wildlife Federation's Environmental Quality Index makes the following evaluations.

1. Forests: Fair (holding their own, with little attention to other values, and with a decline in standing timber);

2. Water: Bad (trend toward loss in water quality with virtually every body of water polluted to some degree);

3. Wildlife: Fair (with 89 species endangered and with a continuing loss of habitat);

4. Soil: Fair (with a high erosion toll and with a steady loss of soil land to development);

5. Minerals: Good (with an urgent need for a national policy to avoid waste and to reclaim and reuse).[23]

RECREATION

Although the previously discussed natural resources policy areas are concerned with functional aspects of natural resources, recreation is emerging as a leading interrelated use of these resources. With the phenomenal growth of recreation since World War II, various legislation has provided increasing responsibilities for all levels of government on practically all governmental lands. The major agency at the federal level is the Bureau of Outdoor Recreation (BOR), with responsibility for coordinating and advising federal agencies, planning and administering a national recreation program, and providing assistance to state and local recreation programs. The BOR predicts that outdoor recreation will increase at least fourfold by the year 2000 with increases in income and leisure; the Bureau also notes that 75 percent of all recreation occurs close to urban areas where 75 percent of the population is located (although these areas may not best represent environmental ideals in terms of open space and quality).[24] The outdoor recreation industry usually ranks high in economic importance, particularly in some of the western states.

In 1962, the Outdoor Recreation Resources Review Commission established foundations for a comprehensive national outdoor recreation policy. The guidelines recommended a framework based on a division of responsibility among local, state, and federal governments, to support and furnish various recreational opportunities; individual initiative and private enterprise were to continue being the most important forces. Regarding the federal role in recreation, the Commission made the following points:

> The Federal Government should be responsible for the preservation of scenic areas, natural wonders, primitive areas, and historical sites of national significance; for cooperation with the states through technical and financial assistance; in the promotion of interstate arrangements, including Federal participation where necessary; for the assumption of vigorous cooperative leadership in a nationwide effort; and for management of Federal lands for the broadest recreational benefit consistent with other essential uses.[25]

It is obvious that outdoor recreation policy, particularly at the federal level, is encompassed under the stipulations of the National Environmental Policy Act of 1969. Two major provisions of this Act that apply to recreation are: (1) Section 101, which recognizes that each person should enjoy a healthful environment; and (2) Section 102, which requires that federal agencies should interpret and administer programs that pertain to the environment, in accordance with the policies of this Act.[26] A major reorientation of national outdoor recreation policy may thus be toward environmental quality considerations. Too much attention has been paid in the past to meeting, or attempting to meet, any and all "recreational" needs on a mass basis, with little attention to quality or environmental impact.

A given land or water area has a *carrying capacity* or *environmental saturation point* for people as well as for other forms of life. To exceed the carrying capacity will produce negative effects on the particular land areas, and often a severe reduction in recreational quality and potential for other uses. Thus, a growing micro policy pattern among federal land management agencies is restriction and regulation of the man/land ratio in terms of the carrying capacity of a given area. Earlier policies, particularly of the NPS, have tended toward accommodation, adjustment, and development to meet demands of increasing numbers of people, at the sacrifice of environmental quality. (The budget to each national park is based to an extent on numbers of visitors.) Under that pattern, many federal land agencies had schemes to regulate density of recreational use, depending upon the kind and quantity of land, but efforts are just beginning for recreational management under environmental quality considerations.

Although on a national scale state and local lands receive the bulk of recreational visits (because of their locations near population centers), public lands administered by federal agencies receive growing numbers of visitors. With the exception of a small percentage of lands established specifically for recreation (national parks, national seashores, etc.), or for a major purpose (National Wildlife Refuges), the great majority of public lands are managed under multiple-use guidelines. Given that recreation may be compatible under multiple use, the PLLRC notes: "Some of the sharpest public policy issues in recent years have arisen as a result of real or alleged conflicts between various recreational values and other uses of public lands, or between one and another type of recreational use."[27]

Under the multiple-use concept, value conflicts with economic interest groups may favor a dominant use that reduces recreational and other uses. Moreover, only a small portion of government personnel have professional training in recreation, and so tend to favor their areas of specialization, for example, timber management. Increasing public recreational pressures appear to increase the conflict in multiple use, particularly when recreational values are threatened or lost through incompatible uses.

Besides this conflict between recreational and other uses, there is growing conflict among types of recreation on public lands. Certain of recreational uses may diminish others. The growing impact (including noise pollution), of motorized equipment (e.g., motorbikes and snowmobiles), has created serious conflict with people who wish to enjoy quiet, natural beauty in hiking and other activities; high-density use of areas may seriously reduce the quality of the recreational experience as well as the scenic or environmental quality. In many instances, federal land management agencies may be oriented toward motorized recreational uses on the basis of quantitative arguments (with some budget justification), with little attention to recreational conflict or environmental quality. On the other hand, relatively little federal regulation, planning enforcement, or zoning has been directed at reducing conflicts among types of recreation, despite the government's broad powers. With increasing recreational pressures, however, more governmental involvement is certain to occur in this area to maximize quality and minimize conflict.

The PLLRC identifies a major conflict area in recreational policy occurring when, on land reserved to maintain environmental quality, any use, including certain recreational uses (e.g., by motorized vehicles), that would disturb that environment must be prohibited.[28] Federal wilderness occupies approximately two percent of the United States. It is located in national parks, national forests, national wildlife refuges, and other public lands. Under the Wilderness Act of 1964, wilderness and potential wilderness areas are being considered for classification as part of a legal and permanent national wilderness system. Wilderness, however, means many things to many people. The Wilderness Act defines it as a natural community, untrammeled by man, who is regarded as a visitor. When man adapts such an area to meet his civilized needs, it can no longer be considered a wilderness; the natural area and biotic community have been modified. Thus, with use and development (lumbering, mining, mass recreation), an ecological and cultural resource is removed forever. Much of wilderness remains today only because it has been uneconomical to develop it, or because recreational pressures to do so have not yet been strong enough. Value decisions for wilderness call for recognition of qualitative values for future generations and other forms of life as important intangible aspects of environmental stewardship.[29]

In observing the federal policy vacuum in recreation, Phillip Foss notes:

> ... None of these, or any other Federal agency, started out to provide public outdoor recreation, but they have had recreation and recreationists thrust upon them. Recreation has been an incidental, and almost an accidental, by-product of the "primary" purposes of Federal agencies. Consequently there is no unified national policy on recreation, and few of the agencies have any real recreation policy. Agency practices have been established usually without adequate research and long-range planning and oftentimes as defensive measures against the recreationists. Lack of anything resembling a national recreational policy is therefore at the root of most of the recreation problems of the Federal government.[30]

Although governmental efforts have been made toward formulating recreational policy with expenditures and programs, Foss's comments appear quite relevant. Moreover, in terms of environmental quality criteria put forward by the legislative or public bodies, it is obvious that an even greater policy vacuum exists.

As in many other areas of environmental policy, one of the problems in formulating a unified policy involves complex pluralistic public and private interests of a competing, conflicting, and overlapping nature.[31] Despite coordinating efforts of the BOR, particularly at the federal level, most organizations continue to deal with recreation in terms of their own vested interests and missions. The result may be fragmented policies and ineffective programs in terms of environmental and recreational quality. For example, a pressing need in recreation is the public (governmental) acquisition of open space or natural areas before the lands are purchased and developed by private sources. Although some authorization and funds are available for this purpose, Huey D. Johnson, western regional director of the Nature Conservancy, notes that governmental programs are relatively ineffective and slow in acquiring essential lands before their removal to the private sector. Consequently, he finds the Nature Conservancy and other organizations actually doing the job that government should be doing, and, in some cases, being involved in serious conflicts with some governmental organizations.[32]

Nevertheless, the acquisition of open space or creation of new major national parks by government is a pressing public need which has been generally neglected. Although full funding for this purpose was finally planned for the 1971 fiscal year under the Land and Water Conservation Fund ($327 million), past neglect and manipulation have resulted in serious loss of land to other uses, and also in a price increase. There are now about 11 acres of general land for every American (one-third of the acreage available for each citizen at the beginning of the century) and this will have dwindled to about seven acres by the year 2000.[33] It is well known that open space recreation satisfies man's deep psychological and emotional needs, but government planning and acquisition of land has been hampered by the difficulty of acting in behalf of highly personal and intangible public benefits in contrast to concrete, economic considerations. Yet Dubos notes that failure to have contact with open space and natural situations may result in losses in quality of numan life and creativity. He states:

> The primordial habitat in which the human race evolved still shapes man's most basic responses in adapting to conditions of modern life. Our reaction to crowding and to strangers, our sense of social order, even our forms of conflict, are conditioned by deep imprints from the biological past. A human environment must allow ways for man to express his aboriginal nature, to satisfy those needs that are rooted in the Stone Age, however great the outward changes brought by urbanization and technology.... The problem of the environment involves the salvation and enhancement of those positive values which man uses to develop his humanness.... Seeing the milky way, experiencing the fragrance of spring and observing other forms of life continue to play an immense role in the development of humanness. Survival is not enough.[34]

REFERENCES

1. Charles E. Kellogg, *Soil Interpretation in the Soil Survey* (Washington, D.C.: Soil Conservation Service, April 1961) p. 6.
2. "Comment," *National Wildlife* 7, no. 5 (August/September 1969) p. 13.

3. Charles E. Kellogg, deputy administrator for Soil Survey, Soil Conservation Service, Washington, D.C., July 14, 1969. Personal correspondence.

4. Soil Conservation Service, "Soil Conservation Districts," Pamphlet (Washington, D.C.: U.S. Department of Agriculture, 1965) pp. 1–7.

5. Roy D. Hockensmith, "The National Cooperative Soil Survey in the United States," Pamphlet (Washington, D.C.: Soil Conservation Service, SCS-TP-138, August 1960) p. 10.

6. Charles M. Hardin, *Soil Conservation and the Struggle for Power in Rural America* (New York: The Free Press, 1952) pp. 70–84.

7. Special Committee on District Outlook, "The Future of the Districts: Strengthening Local Self-Government in Conservation and Resource Development" (Washington, D.C.: The National Association of Soil and Water Conservation Districts, n.d.) p. 10.

8. "Comment," *National Wildlife* 7, no. 5 (August/September 1969) p. 12.

9. James E. Tatum, "The Environmental Concerns in Soil Conservation." Research paper delivered to the Environmental Policy and Administration Seminar, Division of Public Administration, University of New Mexico, Albuquerque, Spring 1971.

10. "Comment," *National Wildlife* 7, no. 5 (August/September 1969) p. 15.

11. Shirley W. Allen, *Conserving Natural Resources* (New York: McGraw-Hill, 1955) p. 265.

12. *Ibid.*, pp. 265–266.

13. Rocky Mountain Center of Environment, *Open Space Report* (April 1970).

14. "Comment," *National Wildlife* 7, no. 5 (August/September 1969) p. 15.

15. Public Land Law Review Commission, *One-third of the Nation's Land* (Washington, D.C.: U.S. Gov't Printing Office, 1970) p. 121.

16. Paul R. Ehrlich, *The Population Bomb* (New York: Ballantine, 1969) p. 133.

17. Public Land Law Review Commission, *One-third of the Nation's Land* (Washington, D.C.: U.S. Gov't Printing Office, 1970) p. 121.

18. *Ibid.*, p. 122.

19. *Ibid.*, p. 124.

20. *Conservation News* (May 15, 1971), p. 2.

21. *Ibid.*, p. 3.

22. Public Land Law Review Commission, *One-third of the Nation's Land* (Washington, D.C.: U.S. Gov't Printing Office, 1970) pp. 124–127.

23. "Comment," *National Wildlife* 7, no. 5 (August/September 1969) pp. 6–10.

24. Bureau of Outdoor Recreation. "The Recreation Imperative," Pamphlet (Washington, D.C.: U.S. Department of the Interior, 1969).

25. Public Land Law Review Commission, *One-third of the Nation's Land* (Washington, D.C.: U.S. Gov't Printing Office, 1970) p. 197.

26. U.S. Congress, *The National Environmental Policy Act of 1969,* Public Law no. 91–190, 91st Cong., 2d sess. (January 1, 1970).

27. Public Land Law Review Commission, *One-third of the Nation's Land* (Washington, D.C.: U.S. Gov't Printing Office, 1970) p. 205.

28. *Ibid.*, pp. 204–206.

29. Daniel H. Henning, "The Ecology of the Political/Administrative Process for Wilderness Classification," *Natural Resources Journal* 2, no. 1 (January 1971) pp. 69–75.

30. Phillip O. Foss, *Federal Agencies and Outdoor Recreation,* Outdoor Recreation Resources Review Commission, Study Report No. 13 (Washington, D.C.: U.S. Gov't Printing Office, 1962) p. 1.

31. Morton Grodzins, "The Many American Governments and Outdoor Recreation," in *Trends in American Living and Outdoor Recreation* (Washington, D.C.: U.S. Gov't Printing Office, 1962) pp. 62–68.

32. Huey D. Johnson, "Natural Areas." Paper delivered to the Natural Areas Symposium of the Northwest Scientific Association, March 27, 1970, Salem, Oregon.

33. "Man's Control of the Environment" (Washington, D.C.: *Congressional Quarterly,* 1970) p. 36.

34. Rene Dubos, "Guest Privilege," *Life* (July 24, 1970).

Chapter 7

POLLUTION CONTROL POLICY AREAS

Various policies are being formulated hastily in response to public and political demands for pollution control. Pollution might be defined as the unfavorable alteration of the environment wholly or largely as a result of man's actions. Although pollution can take many forms (e.g., pesticides, solid wastes, noise), it becomes a governmental problem only in relation to man and society. A recent Gallup poll revealed that more than 85 percent of the population of the United States is concerned about environmental pollution and that three out of four people questioned said they would be willing to pay additional taxes to improve the environment.[1] In defining pollution, the Council on Environmental Quality (CEQ) states: "Although pollution may be the most prominent and immediately pressing environmental concern, it is only one facet of the many-sided environmental problem. It is a highly visible, sometimes dangerous sign of environmental deterioration. Pollution occurs when materials occur where they are not wanted. Overburdened natural processes cannot quickly adjust to the heavy load of materials which man, or sometimes nature, adds to them. Pollution threatens natural systems, human health, and esthetic sensibilities; it often represents valuable resources out of place."[2]

Davies maintains that a definition of pollution is dependent upon the public's decisions concerning the tolerable pollution level and proper use of the environment. Although scientists may be able to define requirements for some uses or to describe harmful effects of particular substances, Davies indicates that they transcend the bounds of science when they try to prescribe the levels and uses of given substances in the environment. Thus, he states, "Only by linking scientific knowledge with a concept of the public interest can one arrive at a working definition of pollution."[3] Consequently, much of pollution control hinges upon value determinations and political decisions under a broad concept of the public interest. With the recognition that science cannot provide final answers or values in determining pollution policy, private and governmental forces emerge and compete through the political process.

Given the conceptual nature of pollution relative to the public interest, another dimension of pollution control policy is environmental quality. James Nettleson indicates that respondents in a correspondence survey of private and governmental sources failed to pinpoint a single definition of environmental quality or even to agree generally. Although the responses did indicate a positive awareness, with a variety of measures being applied to a number of problems, an underlying theme appeared to be the necessity for a degree of *balance* between man and nature. Response categories were: (1) private industry—in terms of the impact of its plants, products, and services; (2) federal agencies—in terms of natural resources and other areas for which they were primarily responsible; (3) congressmen—in terms of their cautious and vaguely worded support for bettering the physical environment, and (4) private environmental groups—in terms of their efforts (to date, blocked or modified) regarding the programs of private industry and government relative to environmental considerations. Nettleson also observed that the majority of responses indicated implicit desire for more federal government direction through environmental laws, policies, standards, and regulations.

Pertaining to the above, Sen. Henry Jackson (Democrat, Washington) notes:

> I cannot provide you with a definition of environmental quality, because I do not believe that one presently exists. Environmental management has only recently become a recognized function of government. The scope of what should be included in environmental management is now being defined by legislation, court decisions, and executive reorganization around the concept.

> The next step, and one which we have barely undertaken, will be to develop a set of criteria of environmental quality and a methodology for measuring them. These criteria would provide the specific definition of environmental quality which you seek.[5]

The National Environmental Policy Act of 1969 espouses broad and idealistic environmental quality goals, for example, to "encourage productive and enjoyable harmony between man and his environment; to promote efforts which will prevent or eliminate damage to the environment and biosphere and stimulate the health and welfare of man."[6] This allows a great deal of discretion in interpreting "environmental quality."

In the process of defining and determining environmental quality for a pollution control policy, formulation of quantitative standards involves interrelations of federal, state, and local governments. A great deal of emphasis is placed upon the legal authority of the states in presenting and regulating standards. Yet, a national survey by *The New York Times* revealed members of air and water pollution control boards in 35 states were also employees of major polluting industries; this was followed by a request to the governors from the Environmental Protection Agency, urging that state boards remain free from the influence of "foxes guarding chicken coops."[7] Under the complex political processes affecting all levels of government concerned with environmental quality, optimum, or even adequate, standards are generally slow to emerge and be enforced. As a result, pollution abatement has proceeded very slowly. A major force of resistance involves high economic costs and their political interrelationships in pollution control. Preventive and reductive measures that allow for quality considerations in pollution control obviously require allocations of funds that could be utilized more directly in enhancing a given organization's interests and profits.

Many governmental and private efforts for pollution control have been directed toward treatment of symptoms, rather than toward eliminating sources of pollution on a long-range basis. Many legal and economic institutions support continuing pollution because it is profitable for them to do so, regardless of social and ecological costs. Peter Schrag notes, "We are in the early stages of a revolt against growth and traditional efficiency, but we have not yet decided who the enemy is and who should pay the price."[8] Economic imperatives are combined with technological innovations, population growth and concentration, and business ideologies, all unfavorable to self assessment, to produce a major source of pollution. Within a period of time, interests involved in creating pollution are so far-reaching politically and economically that they cannot respond adequately to piecemeal direct control measures.

In this sense, a sound, long-range pollution control policy, besides being directed at symptoms, on a short-term basis, should be applied to the sources of pollution. Now that limited governmental activity exists in the following spheres, institutional change calls for control of: (1) technology—with assessment at various governmental levels; (2) population—with definite governmental action to control population growth and concentration; (3) the economic system—with institutional arrangements to control and limit causes of pollution by assessing and factoring in its social costs; and (4) public involvement—in private decisions that affect public environmental interests. Regarding economic aspects and governmental policies, Larry Ruff argues:

> In a market economy, prices convey information about needs and priorities.
>
> . . . the politician's natural reaction is to apply direct control: require this device or forbid that action. When this is tried on any large scale, it always founders on the same problems which plague centrally directed economics.
>
> A better approach is to attack the basic cause of the problem by providing the missing prices. Ordinary markets cannot determine these prices and force payments, so new institutions are needed. There must be an agency which sets the prices, measures the outputs of the various pollutants from each source, and collects payments. Once such an agency is established, the same forces of self interest which provide beefsteak and beer will provide clean air and water.[9]

A major factor in pollution control policy is the priority actually assigned to it by the public and government. Given growing awareness of environmental deterioration, Sprout notes that environmental imperatives are competing with other substantial demands for scarce resources, such as the large and inflexible military budget, and clusters of social needs, including poverty measures, urban renewal, etc.[10] Consequently, the presidential request to Congress for environmental relief funds represented two percent of the federal budget in 1971,[11] and this included water development projects. Yet, in various public addresses, President Nixon stated that the environment would be given a top priority in governmental affairs. It is obvious that a funding request of two percent does not match this priority emphasis, especially since the president impounded the 1971 federal environmental appropriations. Given various political and governmental commitments to pollution control activities, proportionate appropriations have not been forthcoming in most cases. Serious questions are also raised about the exercise and degree of governmental regulatory and enforcement measures by agencies authorized and responsible for pollution control. Although various efforts are being made in this area, severe public and political pressures are sometimes necessary before a given agency will use its actual powers.[12] Moreover, much of the governmental process in this area involves a closed, secret system, geared not to make waves. John Esposito notes: "The real reason for secrecy is that disclosure of such information would raise questions about why government agencies have not been doing their jobs—and would facilitate legal action by injured persons against the polluters."[13]

Priorities regarding pollution control are quite dependent on the values and attitudes of the general public. Given public awareness, the Council of State Governments blames an information gap as the major public problem in this area.[14] Sprout also considers that there is a distinction between environmental conditions, particularly the less obvious ones, as they are perceived by experts and by the general public.[15] Dubos notes: "The worst effects of environmental pollution are probably yet to come since it is only during recent decades that certain chemical pollutants have reached high levels almost everywhere and that children have been exposed to these pollutants almost constantly since birth." Yet, Dubos believes that the greatest danger to mankind is loss of quality and "humanness" even though mankind will survive through immense adaptability.[16] Adaptability to various forms of pollution, which may appear less obvious with time, can become an important variable in public attitudes toward pollution control.

DISPOSAL OF SOLID AND OTHER WASTES

According to the Bureau of Solid Waste Management, the total solid wastes produced in the United States in 1969 amounted to 4.3 billion tons, distributed in the following categories.

Source	Millions of Tons
Residential, commercial, and institutional wastes	250
Collected (190)	
Uncollected (60)	
Industrial wastes	110
Mineral wastes	1,700
Agricultural wastes	2,280
TOTAL	4,340

Refuse collected in urban areas averaged five pounds per person per day in 1970, and if the trend continues, is expected to reach eight pounds by 1980. Although wastes from residential, business, and institutional sources are a small part of the total, they are considered to be the most offensive and the most dangerous to health when accumulated near population centers.[17]

A major problem in improving urban waste-disposal methods is political in nature. Urban waste and related environmental effects are regional, but communities approach them on a local basis. Funds and interest do not allow for adequate disposal or for pooling resources on a common problem. Another major aspect of this problem is that city council members are interested only in short-term, low-cost solutions, as an aid to re-election. However, short-term solutions are seldom efficient, and often create long-term problems. Former Secretary of Health, Education and Welfare, and founder of Common Cause, John W. Gardner, indicates:

> There must be an inducement so strong for state and local governments to do comprehensive planning on an appropriate geographic scale and to conform with national goals and objectives that it is politically and economically unpalatable for them to do otherwise. . . . Participation on the part of local government in any regional environmental program should be as great as possible, but it must be recognized that environmental protection problems will have to be solved on the metropolitan or regional scale. We must engage in experimentation and research in order to increase our capacity to make decisions at the metropolitan or regional level.[18]

For example, Los Angeles County, with 70 separate communities, has an areawide approach to waste disposal; the countywide waste disposal system has one of the lowest costs in the United States.

Dumps and sanitary landfills are the usual methods of disposal of urban solid wastes, but this method presents various environmental problems (94 percent of dumps are classified substandard by the Bureau of Solid Waste Management.) Water pollution results from effects on the purity of the ground water while air pollution results from burning at dumps as well as in municipal incinerators. Moreover, nonbiodegradable materials (i.e., their breakdown by microorganisms is either slow or incomplete) do not compact easily and hence lessen the fill utility. About three-fourths of the urban waste disposal is collected, and an estimated 77 percent of the collected waste is placed in 14,000 open dumps.[19] Given research efforts on collection and disposal, (e.g., the Mole, which will compact refuse and dispose of it below ground level), further environmental consideration points toward recycling and reuse of urban and other solid wastes. For example, only eight of every 100 beverage bottles, of the 30 billion bottles produced in 1966, were returnable.[20]

While techniques for separating and recovering waste materials are to a great extent both primitive and expensive, the key factor in effective recycling and reuse is still economics. Economic considerations and the abundance of resources have delayed development and application of recycling technology and markets in the United States. The Resources Recovery Act of 1970, however, extends the Solid Waste Disposal Act of

1965, and redirects the shift in federal emphasis from disposal to recycling. This 1970 Act established a National Commission on Materials Policy concerned with extraction, development, and use of solid waste materials susceptible to recycling, reuse, or self destruction. Although much solid waste has some salvage value, a major concern is social and environmental costs not taken into consideration in the economics of solid waste disposal. Hence, the price of a given product does not incorporate the cost of its disposal or its long-term environmental potential.

The largest single source of solid wastes is agriculture, contributing about half the total, or more than two billion tons.[21] A major problem in this area involves growing feedlot operations, in which cattle produce enormous and concentrated quantities of manure. Surface and underground water is polluted by manure assimilated into the soil, and substantial problems arise from insects, dust, and odors. Roughly 80 percent of American cattle are produced on feedlots, and, with most manure treated as sewage, this more than doubles the sewage output of the United States. Although contemporary agriculture depends primarily on chemical fertilizer, Ehrlich and Ehrlich recommend legal means to stop the treatment of manure as a waste product, to stop the nutrient runoff from soil.[22] At present, little governmental regulation or control exists in feedlot operations. Another area of weak governmental controls involves logging debris, which accumulates at 25 million tons a year, and is a source of forest fire, disease, and insects. Burning, the only feasible method of disposal, contributes to air pollution.[23]

The federal role in solid waste disposal was not of major consequence until 1965, with the passage of the Solid Waste Disposal Act. With local governments largely responsible for solid waste disposal, the federal government, particularly through the Bureau of Mines and Bureau of Solid Waste Management, assumes a supportive role. Under recent legislation, emphasis is on recycling, rather than disposal, and involves: (1) research and development—demonstrations of new techniques; (2) training—university programs; (3) technical assistance; and (4) cooperative activities—regional and intermunicipal, especially through grants-in-aid. With growing environmental problems in solid waste disposal, it is obvious that the federal government will play an increasing role, particularly because of the need for regional coordination to compensate for the lack of finances, facilities, and equipment available to local government. The CEQ notes: "Public appreciation of the magnitude of the economic and social costs of solid waste is building and a concept of solid waste management is evolving. It assumes that man can devise a social–technological system that will wisely control the quantity and characteristics of wastes, efficiently collect those that must be removed, creatively recycle those that can be reused, and properly dispose of those that have no further use."[24]

In this regard, it is obvious that the federal government has an important educational responsibility in solid waste disposal. The recommendations made by Jacobs and Biswas to the Canadian government are equally pertinent here. Their idea of a twofold role included: "(1) the collection of information and the establishment of a data bank which would include such items as an inventory of types of disposal sites, inputs, and life expectancy; trends in current materials consumption and disposal, and projections of future trends are invaluable information when formulating broad national policies; and (2) the federal government should be expected to make a substantial contribution to the public's awareness of the environment problem with respect to solid wastes generation."[25] They also indicate that the federal government should provide leadership in consumer behavior relative to the marketing of materials salvaged through recycling. Specifically, they suggest: "development of a nationwide public awareness program to entrench notions of the need for individual concern for environmental protection and possible public contribution to recycling schemes; and investigation of product specification regulations which establish minimum recycled material content for federal purchases."[26]

Littering, although of considerably less importance in solid waste disposal policy, is nevertheless a very significant problem in terms of environmental quality and esthetics. Severe accumulations of litter can also disrupt the natural environment. Billions of dollars are spent annually by various levels of government in an attempt to clean up the vast array of materials carelessly deposited by the general public. Also, the advent of nonreturnable bottles has contributed considerably to general littering; governmental regulations requiring returnable deposit bottles would greatly reduce this source. For example, in France, few bottles are littered due to their high deposit value and, in Oregon, the littering problem has been greatly reduced through the state law forbidding the use of disposable bottles. Given the various means used by government to control littering, relatively little has been accomplished; private and public lands continue to suffer the severe impacts of littering, particularly with growing recreational pressures. On the federal level, the overall policy appears to reflect acceptance of this environmental abuse; micro-policy procedures and efforts are directed at reducing or controlling litter on a token basis. Effective control of littering appears to require: (1) a change in public attitude (which seems to be positively influenced by the environmental movement); (2) intensive and extensive research into the causes of littering (many European nations have few problems in this area); and (3) definite policies for effective control through rigorous enforcement and regulation (few littering offenses actually result in a penalty).

Nuclear effluents, although small in quantity compared to other solid wastes, are considered to be a source of severe danger to ecosystems and human health. The Atomic Energy Commission (AEC) has the responsibility for regulating the use of nuclear facilities, and cooperates with the Federal Radiation Council and the Bureau of Radiological Health. One area of growing concern involves nuclear power plants that produce small amounts of radioactivity in their effluents. In 1969, nuclear power plants produced 1.4 percent of the total electric power, but the AEC estimates that nuclear plants will furnish about 25 percent of the total in 1980, and between 60 and 70 percent by the year 2000 (estimated 950 plants).[27] Senator Gaylord Nelson (Democrat, Wisconsin) also notes that thermal effects from nuclear plants result in expelled heated water that raises water temperature with adverse environmental effects. He states: "On a nationwide basis, more than 100 nuclear power plants will be installed within the next five years. By 1980, the electric power industry—with both nuclear and fossil fuel plants—will be using one-fifth of the total fresh water runoff in the United States for cooling."[28]

Under the National Environmental Policy Act of 1969, the AEC is required to submit budget proposals that include an assessment of all new projects, and to prepare impact statements (Monitor 102) in terms of environmental effects. Preparation of such statements under Monitor 102 requires AEC contractors to assess all new projects in their budget proposals to determine if they will degrade the environment. These projects may include solid waste disposal, settling ponds for contaminated fluids and plant effluents, and other potentially contaminating actions. The contractor must prepare a detailed analysis of environmental effects and present alternative actions, and must justify the proposed activity on the basis of program requirements. Regular review processes center around the requirements of the Act, yet various criticisms are voiced concerning: (1) lack of public participation and public hearings; (2) the commitment of the AEC (it legislates, initiates, and investigates projects) to nuclear power plants; (3) lack of research into the complex ecological interactions pertaining to radiation waste standards and influences; and (4) the propensity for going ahead with project construction without real consideration of the factors outlined.

An indirect problem of radioactive, superheated effluents is the inherent risk of nuclear disaster occurring in a given power plant, particularly with projected increases in numbers of plants. Insurance companies will not insure reactors because the risks are too high. Excessive accidental heating, despite safety precautions, could melt the core of a nuclear reactor and spill large quantities of radioactive materials into the environment; two incidents of this type have revealed the possibilities for such accidents.[29] An obvious result would be the creation of human and ecological disaster areas with unpredictable consequences. Yet, little public participation is permitted in the determination of plant locations or in risk evaluation and acceptance. Given the demands for power increases, the federal government, through the AEC, has generally backed the expansion of nuclear power plants, with their risk potential, regardless of controversial ecological concerns. Various scientists, including David Lilienthal, former chairman of the AEC, and Edward Teller, the inventor of the hydrogen bomb, have opposed the government's nuclear power plant policy.

AIR QUALITY

Although not a new problem, the CEQ believes that air pollution control should have a very high priority, and considers it to be, for the most part, a phenomenon of urban living (concentrated populations, industrial growth, high motor vehicle usage) that occurs when

Table 7–1. Major Sources and Types of Air Pollution over a One-Year Period in the United States (in millions of tons per year)

Source	Carbon monoxide (47%)	Partic- ulates (13%)	Sulphur oxides (15%)	Hydro- carbons (15%)	Nitrogen oxides (10%)	Total (in millions of tons per year)
Transportation (42%)	63.8	1.2	0.8	16.6	8.1	90.5
Fuel combustion in stationary sources (21%)	1.9	8.9	24.4	.7	10.0	45.9
Industrial processes (14%)	9.7	7.5	7.3	4.6	0.2	29.3
Solid waste disposal (5%)	7.8	1.1	0.1	1.6	0.6	11.2
Miscellaneous: primarily forest fires, agricultural burning, coal waste fires (18%)	16.9	9.6	0.6	8.5	1.7	37.3
Total	100.1	28.3	33.2	32.0	20.6	214.2

From Council on Environmental Quality, *Environmental Quality: The First Annual Report* (Washington, D.C.: U.S. Gov't Printing Office, 1970) pp. 63–64.

the capacity of air to dilute pollutants is overburdened.[30] The National Air Pollution Control Administration released data on the major sources and types of pollution in the United States (table 7-1).

The CEQ also identifies environmental problems associated with air pollution, including combinations of chemical constituents thereof, which include the following.

1. Human health. A relatively recent increase in deaths and serious illnesses from preexisting respiratory or cardiac conditions has been linked to air pollution; inversions and other varieties of weather conditions produce unpredictable effects with occasional tragic results, for example, Donora, Pennsylvania, with about 7000 ill and 20 dead, or the deaths, including that of T. S. Eliot in London, from a major smog inversion.

2. Vegetation and animal life. Slower and more chronic injury is inflicted on agricultural, forest, and ornamental vegetation by increasing quantities and varieties of air pollution throughout the United States; for example, livestock and wildlife, grazing on fluoride-tainted vegetation, develop a crippling condition known as fluorosis.

3. Materials. Sulphur oxide contributes to the early aging and damaging of a variety of materials; ozone and particulate matter result in costly damage and soiling of paints, dyes, rubber, and other materials.

4. Visibility. Air pollution dims visibility, obscures scenic views, and interferes with the safe operation of transportation.

5. Climate. Air pollution alters natural climate unpredictably.[31]

The negative effects of air pollution are compounded by combinations of pollutants, and by the lack of ecological and other research to determine the extent of the effects.

The CEQ notes that progress in improving air quality has not kept pace with increased population and urbanization, but that the costs of control measures would be low in comparison (costing about 1 percent of the annual output of most industries involved or about $5 per year per car on a 10-year basis).[32] Former Secretary of Interior Stewart Udall stated that if governmental funding priorities had been directed to research on a pollution-free automobile engine, rather than to the space program and moon landing, it would now be possible to control automobile emissions that account for 60 percent of urban air pollution.[33] The CEQ indicates:

> The costs and institutional barriers to higher air quality are not as massive as in water pollution control. Abatement technology can be installed rapidly when available. Clearly the technological gaps in air pollution control must be overcome, but once breakthroughs are made, rapid progress will be possible.

> The Council on Environmental Quality believes that a very high priority should be given to air pollution control. The opportunities for making significant improvements in the environment, at relatively low costs, are impressive. Indeed, the benefits which can be derived from greater control of air pollution far outweigh the costs of the control measures.[34]

The primary responsibility for air pollution control, however, rests with state and local governments. In 1955, when the first federal air pollution control legislation was passed, no state programs were in operation. This legislation authorized the Department of Health, Education, and Welfare to engage in research, data collection, and technical assistance to state and local governments. Subsequent legislation strengthened the role of the federal government in air pollution control, particularly in setting regional standards, but the emphasis remained on state and local governments. Although air quality control regions are being established along the same conceptual lines as watersheds, major problems (especially through industrial pressures) occur regarding the formulation of sound and effective standards for Federal approval. Consequently, new legislation is necessary to assure more federal involvement and the design of national standards set primarily by the federal government. One positive step has been the inclusion of production-line spot checks of emission control devices on motor vehicles, to avoid earlier discrepancies that allowed new automobiles to fall below standards.

On the other hand, air pollution continues to increase steadily. In explaining some of the resistance to controlling air pollution, R. G. Vaughn notes:

> The difficulty arises because the conditions of industrial development which create pollution also tend to create a concept of progress that often prevents society from dealing effectively with pollution. The economic survival of not simply individual businesses, but the whole of the industrial complex, is reliant upon the continued evaluation of pollution problems against the assumptions of the nature of progress contained in industrial relations.

> Cooperation of threatened economic interests should not be expected, and, even with the

realization of the air pollution menace, has not been offered. It is true that industry, in reaction to the threat of governmental regulation, is making some investment in air pollution equipment. However, the record of industrial concern and cooperation has not been outstanding. The background of industrial development and business attitude explains in part why industry was successful in its interest group activities. This background also explains why industry sought decentralization of control and indicates the probable impact of that decentralization.[35]

John Esposito also indicates that corporate polluters are fighting local efforts at air pollution throughout the United States, while spending their advertising budgets portraying themselves as concerned citizens.[36]

At the same time, government has come under attack for ineffective measures to control air pollution. In referring to the National Air Pollution Control Administration, Ralph Nader said: "The deep loss of popular belief that government is capable of protecting and advancing the public interest against this airborne epidemic and its corporate sources reflects a broader absence of confidence, particularly among the young, that government can be honest and courageous to administer law for the people."[37] Thomas Devany indicates that efforts to interest the agency in the Four Corners area (Utah, Colorado, New Mexico, and Arizona) in the pollution activities of the Farmington power plant in New Mexico were ineffective and "bureaucratized." Yet, he had data available to indicate that the power plant emitted more particulate matter (coal burning) than all stationary sources in New York City and Los Angeles combined; the smoke covered up to 10,000 miles, with direct effects on surrounding public lands and national parks. It was the only man-made pollution stream visible in a 1966 earth photograph taken from Gemini 12 at an altitude of 170 miles. Through the state government, Devany was appointed to the special air pollution committee of New Mexico to study the matter, but he resigned after unsuccessful efforts to work with the other members who represented industrial interests.[38]

VANISHING AIR

In *Vanishing Air,* a special Nader group report on air pollution, Esposito indicated that the first priority of pollution control agencies should be to determine the best means for controlling all forms of atmospheric pollution, and then to enforce them across the board. Yet the study revealed that too much collusion was present between government and industry to achieve these goals. It also revealed the lack of an aggressive, firm position on air quality standards among many administrators and political representatives, with a resulting compromise favoring the status quo. Moreover, it indicated that an express policy did not exist to provide free and candid public information. Although much of the weakness in effective air pollution control stems from interrelationships between politics and administration, another major factor might be the orientation of the governmental mind toward quantitative arguments and facts that "prove beyond doubt" or "give

109

absolute proof," when it already may be too late for positive action. At the same time, an imperative for air pollution control is enlightened value judgments and foresight based on limited circumstantial evidence. Otherwise, with the complex and largely unknown effects of increasing air pollution, government may be permitting dangerous experiments on its citizens.

An emerging area in air pollution control may relate to avoidable noxious odors. Sensory devices to measure such odors are now in operation in Albuquerque, New Mexico, and other metropolitan areas. Given that this may not be a serious problem, esthetic, and sometimes economic, influences are involved, as are environmental quality considerations. Various technological devices and innovations can reduce or remove unpleasant odors for the improvement of urban living. As Shakespeare wrote in *Macbeth,* "The air nimbly and sweetly recommends itself unto our general senses." It is obvious that many urban citizens could partake of this recommendation through adequate control measures, under present public nuisance legislation.

PESTICIDE USE

The Academy of Sciences Waste Management Committee notes: "The damage done to food crops in the United States by insects and pests is estimated at 17 billion dollars a year. The pesticides man uses to control this damage, on the other hand, have been a contributing cause of lethal blood diseases suffered by as many as 50 thousand persons a year. To combat the damage done to crops, some 400 million pounds of insecticides, fumigants, and rodent killers are applied to the nation's land every year."[41] Man must be concerned about the delayed, as well as immediate short-term, effects of absorbing small amounts of pesticides that invisibly contaminate the environment, and affect both human and other forms of life. In *Silent Spring,* Carson states: "The current vogue for poisons has failed utterly to take into account these most fundamental considerations. As crude a weapon as the cave man's club, the chemical barrage has been hurled against the fabric of life—a fabric on the one hand delicate and destructable, on the other miraculously tough and resilient and capable of striking back in unexpected ways. These extraordinary capabilities of life have been ignored by the practitioners of chemical control who have brought to their task no 'high-minded orientation,' no humility before the vast forces with which they tamper."[41]

The general public is rapidly becoming concerned about the contamination of the environment by pesticide pollutants, which in many cases may be irrecoverable and irreversible. Yet, progress in banning the use of dangerous chemicals is slow; governmental agencies are hesitant to take necessary actions. Moreover, industry has been reluctant to invest in alternative solutions.[42] Each year nearly one billion pounds of pesticides of all kinds are sprayed, dusted, fogged, or dumped in the United States (about five pounds per person). The pesticide residues drift through the air, disperse in water to destroy aquatic organisms, and seep through the soil with consequent contamination of the entire environment.[43] With the tendency of pesticides to concentrate and recycle through food chains and ecosystems, dangerous levels of DDT and other deadly chemical pesticides have been found in food, human mother's milk, and a variety of substances and organisms. A recent survey by the U.S. Bureau of Sport Fisheries and Wildlife, for example, found DDT in 584 of 590 samples of fish taken from 44 lakes and rivers across the United States. The study revealed that DDT residues in the fish were nine times higher than the current Food and Drug Administration guide level for DDT in fish.[44]

Senator Nelson notes that the Department of Agriculture (including state control programs) has generally resisted control of DDT and has supported the propesticide arguments of chemical companies without undertaking intensive research in the area.[45] However, with the public impact of *Silent Spring,* the Department of Agriculture, under the Insecticide, Fungicide, and Rodenticide Act of 1947 (amended 1954), has undertaken various measures to control and suspend the use of DDT and other persistent pesticides. But the area remains controversial and some governmental actions are being contested by industry. A certain amount of this hinges around the complex interrelations of pesticides and their effects and the lack of research data. Although various negative effects of pesticides have been proven in birds, mammals, fish, and other organisms (e.g., mortality, eggshell inhibition, damage to the nervous system, cancers, birth defects, and genetic mutation), few supportive data are available regarding the long-term effects on man. Consequently, extrapolative judgments must be based on animal findings, despite the complex variables relating to pesticide effects on man. On the other hand, given the potential danger to man, protection of wildlife from adverse effects of pesticides can be considered a legitimate concern of environmental quality legislation.

However, a report from the secretary of the Department of Health, Education, and Welfare, advises:

> While there is no evidence to indicate that pesticides presently in use actually cause carcinogenic or teratogenic effects in man, nevertheless, the fact that some pesticides cause these effects in experimental mammals indicates cause for concern and careful evaluations.
> . . . the field of pesticide toxicology exemplifies the absurdity of a situation in which 200 million Americans are undergoing lifelong exposure, yet our knowledge of what is happening to them is at best fragmentary and for the most part indirect and inferential. While there is little ground for forebodings of disaster, there is even less for complacency.[46]

The 1954 amendments to the Food, Drug, and Cosmetic Act require the Food and Drug Administration of HEW to establish residue tolerances for all pesticides used on human and animal foods. Given the nature of human tolerance and the lack of information regarding pesticides' effects on man, however, this effort has suffered from ambiguity and lack of effective controls and enforcement. Forty-eight states have legislation similar to the 1947 federal law with regard to marketing pesticides, while 39 states regulate their use through licensing.[47] But with the ambiguous aspects of pesticides, discrepancies occur in state control. Further complications are: (i) the liberal use of pesticides by farmers due to their low cost and heavy individual promotion; (2) the disposal problems (on an environmentally acceptable basis) of by-products of pesticide manufacture, particularly with the imperfectly understood nature of various toxic products used in pesticide production.

Pesticides are utilized by various federal agencies in their numerous control programs. A subcommittee on pesticides of the CEQ was established to review 45 pesticide programs that embraced 1033 projects from 30 federal agencies. Significant changes, including substitutions of pesticides and improved control procedures, resulted from the review.[48] The secretary of Interior has banned the use of 16 types of pesticide on 70 percent of public lands managed by agencies of the department, including use in programs operated by the agencies; another group of pesticides has been designated for restricted use.[49] On the other hand, utilization of pesticides by many federal agencies and programs, particularly in the Department of Agriculture, continues without adequate exploration or ecological study of alternatives. Frank Graham, Jr. notes that the interests and convenience of industry have generally dictated national policy on pesticides, and that a great deal of harm has been done by the failure of various government agencies to agree to a general pesticide policy.[50]

Since regulations on pesticide programs for federal lands have been strengthened, only five percent of pesticides used in the United States are applied by federal agencies. The remainder of the 1.25 billion pounds per year, with the exception of 400 million pounds sent abroad, is used at the discretion of state and local agencies or private citizens. And this discretion reflects a regulatory void in governmental efforts to achieve effective pest control and the wise use of pesticides.[51] An unpublished federal study on pesticides concluded that environmental pollution by pesticides could be materially reduced (up to one-half in certain cases), with no loss to pest control, by making use of methods already available; this would, however, require public and private recognition that 100 percent control of pests may not occur, and that complete reliance upon chemical pesticides is a mistake.[52] A major published federal study in the pesticides area was done by the Myak Commission in 1969.[53]

Although the Department of Agriculture has a national monitoring system on pesticides, there appears to be resistance to the Department's pesticide control regulation for governmental and private agricultural programs because of its vested interests and clientele. Under cooperative arrangements with the Pesticides Office of the Environmental Protection Agency (EPA), the CEQ, the Department of Health, Education, and Welfare, the Department of Agriculture and its Pesticides Regulation Division have recently come under criticism by the General Accounting Office (GAO) and Congress for failure to adequately regulate and enforce pesticide control policy, particularly in market operations. Although 750 pesticide products were found to violate the law, and 562 of these were deemed major violations that warranted either seizure or prosecution, the Department of Agriculture initiated only 106 enforcement actions to remove from the market products violating standards. It rarely took action to obtain data on faulty or dangerous products. Moreover, the Department of Agriculture had taken no action in 13 years to report these violations to the Department of Justice, and had approved numerous pesticides for registration over the safety objections of the Department of Health, Education, and Welfare.[54]

Related areas of pesticide control policy concern the use of herbicides and predator and rodent control through poisons. Ehrlich and Ehrlich observe the enormous upsurge in the use of herbicides as a substitute for farm machinery and labor to remove weeds for purposes of cultivating crops and clearing roadsides, and for military defolliants in Vietnam. They note that the rate of increase in herbicide use far outstrips synthetic pesticide use. Although direct toxity to animals is low, Ehrlich and Ehrlich indicate that herbicides have a large impact on animal populations through their modification and eradication of plants used for food and cover, particularly for specialized needs of herbivores.[55] Nevertheless, various governmental agencies have numerous programs involving herbicides; the BLM, for example, is presently carrying out extensive programs of sagebrush removal with herbicides to increase desirable grasses for livestock interests; as a result, populations of antelope (a specific feeder on sagebrush) are being reduced on public lands. The PLLRC recommends that use of herbicides and pesticides on public lands should be considered in the light of their significant short- and long-term environmental effects, and that the ecological impact of these factors should be evaluated in terms of overall environmental quality.[56]

Control of rodents and other "pests" through use of poisons remains an important function of government, particularly through the BSFW and state agencies. Yet, many of the poisons or chemicals used provide only short-term solutions, and are not environmentally acceptable. Further, some rodents may become immune to them after a period of time. For example, warfarin, a specific top-world rodenticide for rats, is now losing its effectiveness because rats are developing a genetic resistance to it.[57] Indiscriminate use of poisons such as 1080 (1080 is currently restricted in a formal legal sense, but is used on a private basis) and others has various secondary effects; for example, one animal is poisoned by eating the carcass of another animal that has been poisoned. Graham notes that control becomes an end in itself without economic or human health justifications, and that it results in the unnecessary poisoning and death of many innocent animals and birds. Moreover, indiscriminate poisoning may be a serious threat to rare and endangered species such as the black-footed ferret, timber wolf, and Golden Eagle.[58] Despite the obvious environmental quality considerations, governmental and private users of poisons for pest control face few *real* constraints. Regardless of recent policy directives from Washington, D.C., calling for limited, wise, and specific use, and for study of such poisons, little control is exerted at the decentralized level because of vested interests.[59]

NOISE ABATEMENT

Noise is sound without value and of an unwanted, obnoxious, and disturbing nature. It is receiving governmental recognition as a new area for pollution control. Noise is very important to environmental quality in an esthetic sense, and medical research reveals that noise also presents serious health hazards such as deafness, illness, and even death. Hearing loss is the most significant physical health problem caused by excessive noise exposure and it is considered to be a major hazard in cerain work environments (16 million Americans are in this category of work situation). However, it is also possible that exposure to the aggregate noise that characterizes life in a modern, technological society can cause varying degrees of hearing loss. It is generally accepted that steady exposure to about 90 decibels can cause permanent hearing loss, yet traffic noise and other urban noise such as a jet takeoff, riveting machines, subways, and certain types of "music" (with decibel levels of 130 to 150) exceed this level of noise pressure. Thus, besides the annoying and disturbing characteristics of noise, temporary or permanent injury to the eardrum and other parts of the hearing system is a definite danger from noise pollution for many urban Americans.[60]

Increasing evidence points toward other physical and mental illnesses resulting from noise pollution. Excessive noise can constrict blood vessels and can, in turn, lead to high blood pressure and cardiac illnesses. It may also be a factor in many stress-related diseases such as peptic ulcer and hypertension.[61] In a U.S. Senate Committee hearing, Sontag, a medical witness, indicated that high-level noise may disturb and cause permanent harm to unborn children whose mothers are exposed to excessive sound.[62] Noise can affect the entire autonomic nervous system and produce emotional distress, neurosis, and mental illness.[63] It can also affect the normal process of sleep and relaxation essential to good health and peace of mind, producing irritable, unproductive, unsociable behavior.[64] Excessive noise may also interfere with the use and enjoyment of property and, consequently, may reduce property values. Moreover, noise-shock waves can actually cause physical and structural damage to buildings and homes.[65]

Intangible aspects of environmental quality can be seriously impaired by excessive unwanted noise. In recreation, the relatively recent advent of motorized equipment (motorcycles, snowmobiles, scramblers) interferes and conflicts with other forms of recreation on public lands. Many forms of recreation require quiet, undisturbed contact with nature (e.g., hiking, nature study, fishing, and hunting), and have low noise tolerances within a given area. Moreover, many users of public lands have made strenuous efforts to seek out quiet open space, away from urban and other noise that intrudes upon their enjoyment. Noise from motorized equipment disturbs them, and may also have adverse effects on wildlife. In a study of snowmobiles and public lands, Thomas McQuillan indicates that governmental land managers are becoming increasingly concerned about the effects of snowmobile noise in disturbing the limited winter range of deer, elk, and other wildlife; many animals were found to be weakened or killed by indirect and direct effects, especially harassment, of snowmobile noise. Yet McQuillan notes that relatively few efforts have been made by government officials to control the noise of snowmobiles on the range of their use.[66] On the assumption that every recreational use is valid, little planning, zoning, or regulation appear to be expended relative to control of motorized noise problems to ensure recreational quality.

Although almost everything makes some type of sound, the main source of urban noise is transportation facilities that depend on the number and speed of vehicles. It is interesting to note that the ancient Romans had similar problems; chariot traffic was banned from the city at night. Yet, there are no federal laws or regulations to control surface transportation noise.[67] Given that the general causes of noise pollution are increased congestion in urban areas and use of mechanical equipment in an advancing technology, noise control has traditionally been the responsibility of state and local governments. Yet these governments have had great difficulty establishing and enforcing effective controls for reducing avoidable noise. In this sense, state and local problems, associated with lack of knowledge and technical expertise, are compounded by the obvious problems associated with setting noise standards for products manufactured for national markets.[68]

Noise as a pollutant has only recently been recognized by all levels of government. Although noise may be easier to control than other forms of pollution affecting air and water, there has been little governmental involvement in setting control measures. Despite its dangerous and annoying aspects, noise pollution has continued to grow, particularly in urban areas. In fiscal 1970, the federal government spent only $32 million on noise control programs with $29 million being used to combat aircraft noise.[69] Some federal authorization, however, has been granted to certain areas for noise abatement. The Federal Aviation Administration was authorized in 1968 to control the amount of noise generated by civil aircraft. The Department of Transportation is authorized to set highway noise levels, but efforts are mainly confined to research at this stage. The Department of Health, Education, and Welfare and the Labor Department are charged with regulating the occupational noise exposure of workers engaged in interstate commerce.[70] Yet, authorization may or may not mean control, and little effective control exists so far.

Major political and economic resistance to noise control measures naturally comes from industry, which would have to assume much of the additional cost in modifying production methods for noise abatement. Present and anticipated technological controls offer great potential for definite noise reduction. Motor vehicles could be muffled easily at comparatively little cost. Legislation is sought to provide federal standards and to regulate major sources of noise in addition to those within present departmental authorization areas, for example, transportation vehicles, construction equipment, home appliances, and machinery. The standards would be formulated by the EPA. Because state and local legislation and enforcement have been generally ineffective in this area, the new legislation also calls for more regulation through interstate commerce by the federal government, especially the EPA.[71] However, because of public pressure, state and local action is gradually emerging specifically to control noise pollution, for example, the recent New York State legislation and the new noise control city ordinance of Billings, Montana.

One of the most serious noise pollution problems appears to center on aircraft noise, particularly around airports. A low-flying jet may blast people in the areas surrounding airports with about 115 decibels. A recent British study indicated that people living around London's Heathrow Airport had a much higher rate of mental hospital admissions than those in nearby quieter areas. About half of the 140 major airports have been involved in noise-related suits, complaints, or political disputes within the last ten years. It is estimated that by 1975 more than 15 million people will live near major airports and be subjected to intense noise. Under a Supreme Court ruling of 1962, which permits people to sue airport operators for damage liability due to noise, there are potential costs for compensation for hearing loss as well as property and other damages due to aircraft noise. Over $6 million in claims was filed against the U.S. Air Force for sonic boom damage during 1969. Under the Federal Aviation Administration, however, little effective regulation or control has been extended to aircraft noise and pollution.[72] It can be argued that the new generation of aircraft is quieter. Roughly, 727s are one-half as noisy as 707s and the giant 747s are half as noisy as 727s, that is, a quarter as noisy as early 707s.

The recent defeat of the SST (supersonic transport) appears to illustrate the growing recognition and concern by the public toward aircraft noise and noise pollution control. Social surveys on noise reveal an increasing percentage of people who are disturbed and annoyed by noise pollution in metropolitan areas.[73] Although noise control technology is available to control many sources of noise, the Environmental Health Service notes that such technological advances are not being applied for various reasons.[74] The growing public awareness and concern should lead to governmental and industrial action involving increased costs (which appear not to be politically acceptable without substantial public demand); nevertheless, uniform national noise standards and controls for noise sources that affect society and the environment appear to be forthcoming. The question, however, appears to be one of when, and to what degree of effectiveness.

A certain amount of noise and other pollution could be effectively controlled before it occurs through proper technological assessment and preventive measures. In considering that technological advance has typically produced social problems, and that social control over technology is by no means a new one, Harold Green notes that these social problems are typically met and dealt with on an *ad hoc* basis. When the extension of old legal principles to new social and technological problems proves too slow and inadequate, legislative bodies superimpose statutory law over judicial law by establishing standards of conduct and liability, or by providing for outright governmental regulation. Green believes that this responsive approach to social control over technology is crisis-oriented and can no longer be tolerated under present conditions and under the explosive growth of science and technology during the last 30 years. He argues that effective social controls on adverse, or dangerous, technological developments must be undertaken at an earlier stage than has been the case in the past.[75] It is obvious that today's pollution problems, if put under earlier social controls, would now be of a less severe nature and magnitude. Green states:

> Congressman Daddario's [Democrat, Connecticut] proposal for a Technology Assessment Board is intended primarily to force the process of balancing benefits against risks into an open forum, in which all relevant information is freely available and in which the determinations will be made by disinterested officials. Presumably such an arrangement would create a situation in which feedback from the public will become possible in a meaningful sense.

> At the same time, it should be recognized that the type of technology assessment institution which is proposed will perform its function primarily on the basis of sophisticated prediction of the consequences of technological development. In many instances, the prediction will be based on only the fragmentary evidence available in the early stages of development. This process can undoubtedly determine the effects which are already desirable or clearly undesirable and also those which are uncertain. It is in the area of uncertain effects that the greatest problem exists.[76]

WATER QUALITY

In essence, water pollution results from the many activities of man and nature. Pollution occurs when wastes from these activities flow into the water in such quantities that the natural ability of water to cleanse itself (i.e., its assimilative capacity) is lessened or destroyed. The natural purification process uses oxygen to break down organic pollutants (with some exceptions, e.g., mercury) into harmless and inoffensive forms. But when too much waste, especially from urban and industrial sources, is placed in the water, the natural processes cannot perform adequately. The consequence is polluted water that may not be acceptable for a variety of uses and may appear visibly polluted. In this sense, water quality implies a comparison against an acceptable standard, which, in turn, varies with the criteria for numerous uses. Yet, Melvin Benarde states, ". . . the public must be prepared to accept the fact that there are degrees of pollution; and that the mere statement that a body of water is polluted does not necessarily imply that it is *in extremis.*"[77]

Although water pollution in the United States has generally been accepted as the price of progress, the CEQ considers three reasons for the relatively recent public concern and governmental activity extending beyond health orientations: (1) the growth and expansion of industries and cities with the multiplication of pollution in most waterways; (2) demands for outdoor recreation centering around water or water locations; and

(3) man's unexplainable attraction and affinity toward water, for the enjoyment, tranquility, inspiration, and appreciation he derives from it. Yet the CEQ observes that recreational and esthetic appreciation is difficult or impossible to achieve under the current conditions of many bodies of water.[78] Nevertheless, it is obvious that much of the public motivation toward water pollution control policy hinges around intangibles associated with environmental quality. At the same time, it should be recognized that, with sufficient economic and technological inputs, even the most polluted stream can be transformed into high quality water.

The major sources of water pollution are industrial, municipal, and agricultural. Over half of industrial waste volume discharged into the water comes from the paper, organic chemicals, petroleum, and steel industries. CEQ notes that most industrial water waste can be greatly reduced by treatment and by production process designs that keep waste at a minimum. The treatment processes are currently available at an estimated cost of one percent of the gross sales of most industries.[79] Much industrial and other waste in water is measured in terms of biological oxygen demand (BOD) or chemical oxygen demand (COD) with the former more commonly used as an indication of ecological health. Bacteria use oxygen in breaking down water waste and hence reduce the amount of oxygen in water. With little or no oxygen in the water, different mixtures of bacteria occur under an anaerobic (without air) decomposing process that results in extreme water pollution.[80] A growing problem is thermal pollution of water, mainly by the electric power industry, which requires vast amounts of water for cooling (1980 estimates indicate power plants will require one-fifth of total fresh water runoff; also, see previous discussion on nuclear plants and thermal pollution). The increase of temperature in the returned waters results in severe problems and changes aquatic life and bacterial decomposition processes.[81]

Municipal waste treatment plants derive 45 percent of their total processed wastes from industry, and 55 percent from homes and commercial establishments. The CEQ notes that less than one-third of the population of the United States is served by a system of sewers and an adequate treatment plant. Overflowing wastes from septic tanks, with pollution of surface and ground water, appear to be a very common problem in America today. Moreover, waste loads from municipal systems are expected almost to quadruple within the next 50 years.[82] In the agricultural area, wastes from feedlots are major sources of pollution, while animal wastes in general are estimated to equal the wastes of two billion people (although much of this waste never reaches the water). Chemical fertilizers and pesticides used in agriculture contribute to water pollution in many areas.[83] Some other sources of general water pollution are: (1) sediment and erosion, (2) oil, (3) mine drainage, and (4) watercraft wastes.[84]

Given the variety, accumulation, and complexity of water pollution sources and problems, the relatively recent strong public concern for water quality and improvement of polluted waters has caused water pollution to become an important political issue as well as an essential element of the environmental movement. Although much of early governmental action was centered around water pollution control as it relates to health, with little attention to recreational, esthetic, and other quality values, policy and legislation have gradually emerged that are broader and more comprehensive, encompassing environmental quality values.[85] Under federal legislation on water pollution over the years (e.g., temporary legislation in 1948, the Federal Water Pollution Control Act of 1956, amendments to the Act, the Clean Water Restoration Act of 1966, the Water Quality Acts of 1965 and 1970, etc.), a complex array of pollution control and water quality standards has emerged, as has federal involvement through administration (e.g., the EPA), assistance, grants, and enforcement. Further, the Refuse Act (Section 13 of the Rivers and Harbors Act of 1899: 33 U.S.C. 407) has recently been reactivated relative to federal enforcement and court actions on water pollution problems; this Act prohibits the discharge of any refuse matter, with exception of liquid wastes flowing from streets and sewers, into navigable waters without a permit from the Corps of Engineers.[86]

Traditionally, most water pollution control has been and still (despite federal legislation and involvement) is considered to be the responsibility of the states. Particularly in association with public health matters, all states have had water pollution control laws on their books for years. Under the requirements of recent federal legislation on water quality, however, states have been required, through public hearings, to establish water quality standards for interstate and coastal waters within their borders. These standards, in turn, were submitted to the federal government for approval. All 50 states submitted water quality standards rather than have federal standards imposed. State standards become federal standards after approval by the secretary of Interior, and may be used in federal enforcement programs and actions. The two most controversial areas in this arrangement are federal demands for secondary treatment of all wastes (or the equivalent for industrial wastes) and the adoption of nondegradation clauses.[87]

For example, on the nondegradation clauses that stipulate that a state may not degrade water quality from the time the water enters its boundaries until it passes into an adjoining state, in New Mexico, a state engineer, S. E. Reynolds, recently made a request to reject the water salinity standards promulgated by the Federal Water Quality Administration on the grounds that the standards were too high and that they did not reflect the salinity pollution from other states upstream.[88] In an analysis of enforcement efforts directed to water pollution abatement by the states and through their water quality standards, the GAO indicated that many states were unclear about or omitted interim dates for implementation of measurement and enforcing of water pollution control standards for industry and municipalities. Thus, the GAO states: "Our review showed that, although the implementation plans were to serve as a basis for initiating enforcement actions, their use in this regard was limited. All too frequently the States did not take enforcement actions against polluters not complying with the implementation plans, but, rather, merely extended the dates for compliance. According to EPA officials, 34 states had extended, by as much as six years, the dates included in their implementation plans."[89]

Further, in an intensive study of six states, the GAO revealed that 259 municipalities and industrial plants, as of February 28, 1972, had not constructed waste treatment plants in compliance with the plans (1965) of the given states. The review indicated that projects were delayed from an average of 14 months in one state to 31 months in another.[90] According to GAO interviews with the state, local, and industrial officials involved, the delays were attributed to one or more of the following factors.

1. A lack of federal and state financial assistance
2. Reluctance of some municipalities to participate in regional waste treatment systems
3. Failure of voters to approve local bond issues for the construction of facilities
4. Inability to find economical methods to treat wastes
5. Recalcitrance on the part of some polluters to comply with the state's implementation plans[91]

Under the state-oriented plan for water pollution control, federal and state legislation, policy, and implementation for adequate, or better, water quality standards is very limited. This is to a great extent a result of leaving the states to make their own decisions on pollution control goals, and implementation thereof, in determining the uses to which particular waterways will be put. For example, each state decides what the temperature of a given stream or river should be relative to a particular use, often without attention to the overall body of water or its ecology; that is, the emphasis is on economic uses. Some states facing each other across a river may have different standards for the same river, rather than having general standards for a given river that might flow through several states. Consequently, it would appear that unified regional and national standards are needed; geographic and political boundaries are not effective barriers to the flow and spread of polluted waters.

Water quality standards for pollution control include three elements: (1) determination of uses for each stretch of interstate and coastal water in the United States; (2) central limits on the amounts of various pollutants allowed into the waters; and (3) an implementation plan with a documented, step-by-step outline of remedial measures needed to prevent or control pollution in a given stretch of water, including enhancement measures. Some of the major limitations and problems of water quality standards with pollution controls follow.

1. Authority and responsibility are not clearly defined.
2. Insufficient incentive is provided to public and private institutions to take into account the consequences of their actions that affect water quality.

3. Planning is often separated from operating responsibilities, with a consequent lack of follow-up.

4. In many instances, there is no agency with appropriate geographic and jurisdictional authority, responsibility, and resources.

5. Existing policy and institutional arrangements suffer limitations that are somewhat attributable to the emphasis on action by state and local governments.

6. Serious problems throughout the governmental system are associated with the enforcement of water quality standards and pollution controls with obvious political and economic overtones.

7. There is a lack of integration of water quality standards into comprehensive environmental programs, for example through coordination with land use planning and management.[92]

Taking governmental involvement for water quality and pollution control at various levels in the Albuquerque, New Mexico, area as an example, the Albuquerque Urban Observatory indicated: "At least 29 Federal, eight New Mexico, one Bernalillo County, one joint City–County, four Albuquerque, and six regional agencies, as well as three military bases, have responsibilities relevant to water quality in the Albuquerque area. At least 13 Federal agencies and four State agencies provide funding or technical assistance for solving water quality problems at the local level."[93] Assuming that similar arrangements of varying degrees exist for other areas, it is recognized that water pollution control involves complex interagency relations. Coordination thus appears essential among agencies at the federal, regional, state, county, and local levels. For the federal level, the EPA (combining the duties of the Water Quality Administration and Bureau of Solid Waste Management, among others) is considered to be the main coordinating agency. States usually have some type of agency or commission to serve in a coordinating capacity for various state water agencies (e.g., the New Mexico Water Quality Control Commission), but it is obvious that there is much overlapping of policies and jurisdiction among agencies at all levels.

Yet, the general operational rule of most coordination in governmental administration is that of token cooperation, particularly under specific mission orientations. Each agency tends to place emphasis on its own policies, budgets, values, and interests, and cooperation reflects this emphasis. Consequently, water pollution control policy, including its water quality aspects, becomes a complex compendium of specific policies of various agencies, further complicated by industrial and other private spheres of involvement. In attempting to control *avoidable* pollution, however, various micro-policies and values are interjected into the political and administrative process which may not result in an effective system or effective implementation of governmental action on water quality, despite cooperative efforts and public environmental pressures.

121

It is an ecological principle that consumption of any resource leads inevitably to the discharge of waste, and that high concentrations of waste have a detrimental effect upon the environment. In controlling avoidable pollution, economic and political questions necessarily arise relative to the degree of quality and control. However, consideration by government and society should include not only the political and economic costs of dealing with water pollution, but the costs (including social costs) of *not* dealing with it.

REFERENCES

1. Harvey Lieber, "Public Administration and Environmental Quality," *Public Administration Review* 30, no. 3 (May/June, 1970) p. 277.
2. Council on Environmental Quality, *Environmental Quality: The First Annual Report* (Washington, D.C.: U.S. Gov't Printing Office, 1970) p. 8.
3. J. Clarence Davies, III, *The Politics of Pollution* (New York: Pegasus, 1970) p. 19.
4. James Nettleson, "Definition of and Efforts Toward Environmental Quality." Paper delivered to the Seminar in Environmental Policy and Administration, University of New Mexico, Albuquerque, May 1971.
5. Sen. Henry Jackson, letter of April 27, 1971.
6. Council on Environmental Quality, *Environmental Quality: The First Annual Report* (Washington, D.C.: U.S. Gov't Printing Office, 1970) p. 243.
7. Colorado Plateau Environmental Advisory Council, *Newsletter* (February 1971) p. 3.
8. Peter Schrag, "Who Owns the Environment," *Saturday Review* 53, no. 27 (July 4, 1970) p. 10.
9. Larry E. Ruff, "Price Pollution Out of Existence," *Los Angeles Times,* December 7, 1969.
10. Harold Sprout, "The Environmental Crisis in the Context of American Politics," in *The Crisis of Survival,* ed. Eugene Odum et al. (Glenview, Ill.: Scott, Foresman, 1970) p. 202.
11. Rocky Mountain Center on Environment, *Open Space Report* (March 1971).
12. Joseph J. Brecher and Manuel E. Nestle, *Environmental Law Handbook* (Berkeley, Calif.: Continuing Education for the Bar, 1970) pp. 175–288.
13. John C. Esposito, *Vanishing Air* (New York: Grossman, 1970).
14. Council of State Governments, *Environmental Quality and State Government* (Lexington, Ky.: The Council of State Governments, 1970) p. 3.
15. Harold Sprout, "The Environmental Crisis in the Context of American Politics," in *The Crisis of Survival,* ed. Eugene Odum et al. (Glenview, Ill.: Scott, Foresman, 1970) p. 200.
16. Rene Dubos, "Guest Privilege," *Life* (July 24, 1970).
17. Council on Environmental Quality, *Environmental Quality: The First Annual Report* (Washington, D.C.: U.S. Gov't Printing Office, 1970) p. 107.
18. Congressional Quarterly, *Man's Control of the Environment* (Washington, D.C.: *Congressional Quarterly,* 1970) p. 35.
19. Council on Environmental Quality, *Environmental Quality: The First Annual Report* (Washington, D.C.: U.S. Gov't Printing Office, 1970) p. 109–110.
20. Congressional Quarterly, *Man's Control of the Environment* (Washington, D.C.: *Congressional Quarterly,* 1970) p. 32.
21. Council on Environmental Quality, *Environmental Quality: The First Annual Report* (Washington, D.C.: U.S. Gov't Printing Office, 1970) p. 107.
22. Paul R. Ehrlich and Anne H. Ehrlich, *Population, Resources, Environment* (San Francisco: Freeman, 1970) p. 189.
23. Congressional Quarterly, *Man's Control of the Environment* (Washington, D.C.: *Congressional Quarterly,* 1970) p. 33.

24. Council on Environmental Quality, *Environmental Quality: The First Annual Report* (Washington, D.C.: U.S. Gov't Printing Office, 1970) p. 106.
25. Hersch Jacobs and Asit K. Biswas, *Solid Wastes Management: Problems and Perspectives* (Ottawa: Research Coordination Directorate: Environment Canada, March 1972) pp. 288–289.
26. *Ibid.*, pp. 289–290.
27. Council on Environmental Quality, *Environmental Quality: The First Annual Report* (Washington, D.C.: U.S. Gov't Printing Office, 1970) p. 163.
28. Sen. Gaylord A. Nelson, "Our Polluted Planet," in *The Crisis of Survival,* ed. Eugene Odum et al. (Glenview, Ill.: Scott, Foresman, 1970) p. 190.
29. Council on Environmental Quality, *Environmental Quality: The First Annual Report* (Washington, D.C.: U.S. Gov't Printing Office, 1970) p. 166.
30. *Ibid.*, p. 62.
31. *Ibid.*, pp. 66–71.
32. *Ibid.*, p. 72.
33. Informal seminar with Stewart Udall, November 20, 1969, Eastern Montana College, Billings, Montana.
34. Council on Environmental Quality, *Environmental Quality: The First Annual Report* (Washington, D.C.: U.S. Gov't Printing Office, 1970) pp. 90–91.
35. Robert G. Vaughn, "State Air Pollution Control Boards: The Interest Group Model and the Lawyer's Role," *Oklahoma Law Review* 24, no. 25 (1971) p. vii.
36. John C. Esposito, *Vanishing Air* (New York: Grossman, 1970) pp. 299–310.
37. Ralph Nader, "Introduction," in John C. Esposito, *Vanishing Air* (New York; Grossman, 1970) p. vii.
38. Thomas Devany, Lecture delivered to the Environmental Policy and Administration Seminar, University of New Mexico, Albuquerque, April 28, 1971.
39. John C. Esposito, *Vanishing Air* (New York: Grossman, 1970) pp. 258–331.
40. The Episcopal Foundation of New York, "Pollution," *Program Release,* May 1970.
41. Rachel Carson, *Silent Spring* (Greenwich, Conn.: Fawcett, 1970) p. 261.
42. Joseph J. Brecher and Manuel E. Nestle, *Environmental Law Handbook* (Berkeley, Calif.: Continuing Education for the Bar, 1970) p. 29.
43. Sen. Gaylord A. Nelson, "Our Polluted Planet," in *The Crisis of Survival,* ed. Eugene T. Odum et al. (Glenview, Ill.: Scott, Foresman, 1970) p. 187.
44. *Ibid.*, p. 188.
45. *Ibid.*, p. 189.
46. Council on Environmental Quality, *Environmental Quality: The First Annual Report* (Washington, D.C.: U.S. Gov't Printing Office, 1970) p. 135.
47. Council of State Governments, *Environmental Quality and State Government* (Lexington, Ky.: The Council of State Governments, 1970) p. 40.
48. Council on Environmental Quality, *Environmental Quality: The First Annual Report* (Washington, D.C.: U.S. Gov't Printing Office, 1970) p. 138.
49. Council of State Governments, *Environmental Quality and State Government* (Lexington, Ky.: The Council of State Governments, 1970) p. 40.
50. Frank Graham, Jr., *Since Silent Spring* (Boston: Houghton Mifflin, 1970) pp. 185–186.
51. *Ibid.*, pp. 185–186.
52. *Ibid.*, p. 187.
53. Myak Commission Study, *Report of the Secretary's Commission on Pesticides and Their Relationship to Environmental Health* (Washington, D.C.: U.S. Department of Health, Education, and Welfare, December 1969).
54. Congressional Quarterly, *Man's Control of the Environment* (Washington, D.C.: *Congressional Quarterly,* 1970) p. 49.
55. Paul R. Ehrlich and Anne H. Ehrlich, *Population, Resources, Environment* (San Francisco: Freeman, 1970) pp. 182–183.

56. Public Land Law Review Commission, *One-third of the Nation's Land* (Washington, D.C.: U.S. Gov't Printing Office, 1970) p. 70.
57. David Brand, "Warfarin—Its Potency Against Some Rodents," *The Wall Street Journal,* September 27, 1972.
58. Frank Graham, Jr., *Since Silent Spring* (Boston: Houghton Mifflin, 1970) pp. 193–202.
59. *Ibid.,* pp. 202–203.
60. Council on Environmental Quality, *Environmental Quality: The First Annual Report* (Washington, D.C.: U.S. Gov't Printing Office, 1970) pp. 124–125.
61. Paul R. Ehrlich and Anne H. Ehrlich, *Population, Resources, Environment* (San Francisco, Freeman, 1970) p. 140.
62. Congressional Quarterly, *Man's Control of the Environment* (Washington, D.C.: *Congressional Quarterly,* 1970) p. 54.
63. Joseph J. Brecher and Manuel E. Nestle, *Environmental Law Handbook* (Berkeley, Calif.: Continuing Education for the Bar, 1970) p. 285.
64. Congressional Quarterly, *Man's Control of the Environment* (Washington, D.C.: *Congressional Quarterly,* 1970) p. 54.
65. Joseph J. Brecher and Manuel E. Nestle, *Environmental Law Handbook* (Berkeley, Calif.: Continuing Education for the Bar, 1970) p. 285.
66. Thomas McQuillan, "The Administration of Snowmobiles and Their Effect on the Environment." Research paper delivered to the Public Administration Seminar, University of New Mexico, Albuquerque, May, 1971.
67. Congressional Quarterly, *Man's Control of the Environment* (Washington, D.C.: *Congressional Quarterly,* 1970) p. 54.
68. The Domestic Council, Executive Office of the President, *The President's 1971 Environmental Program: Emerging Problems* (Washington, D.C.: U.S. Gov't Printing Office, 1971) p. 7.
69. Congressional Quarterly, *Man's Control of the Environment* (Washington, D.C.: *Congressional Quarterly,* 1970) p. 54.
70. The Domestic Council, Executive Office of the President, *The President's 1971 Environmental Program: Emerging Problems* (Washington, D.C.: U.S. Gov't Printing Office, 1971) p. 8.
71. *Ibid.,* pp. 8–9.
72. Congressional Quarterly: *Man's Control of the Environment* (Washington, D.C.: *Congressional Quarterly,* 1970) pp. 55–56.
73. Environmental Health Service, *Environmental Health Problems* (Rockville, Md.: Department of Health, Education, and Welfare, 1970) p. 15.
74. *Ibid.,* pp. 15–16.
75. Harold P. Green, "Technology Assessment and the Law; Introduction and Perspective," *The George Washington Law Review* (Spring 1968) pp. 1033–1034.
76. *Ibid.,* p. 1041.
77. Melvin A. Benarde, *Our Precious Habitat* (New York: Norton, 1970) p. 131.
78. Council on Environmental Quality, *Environmental Quality: The First Annual Report* (Washington, D.C.: U.S. Gov't Printing Office, 1970) pp. 29–30.
79. *Ibid.,* p. 31.
80. *Ibid.,* pp. 30–31.
81. *Ibid.,* pp. 30–34.
82. *Ibid.,* p. 35.
83. *Ibid.,* pp. 36–37.
84. *Ibid.,* pp. 37–39.
85. Lynton Keith Caldwell, *Environment: A Challenge for Modern Society* (Garden City, N.Y.: Natural History Press, 1970) pp. 45–47.
86. Comptroller General of the United States, *Water Pollution Abatement Program: Assessment of Federal and State Enforcement Efforts* (Washington, D.C.: U.S. General Accounting Office, March 23, 1972) pp. 6–7.

87. Terry R. Dixon, "The Environmental Problem of Water Pollution." Research paper delivered to the Environmental Policy and Administration Seminar, Public Administration Division, University of New Mexico, Albuquerque, May 1971.

88. *Albuquerque Journal*, June 10, 1970, p. A–5.

89. Comptroller General of the United States, *Water Pollution Abatement Program: Assessment of Federal and State Enforcement Efforts* (Washington, D.C.: U.S. General Accounting Office, March 23, 1972) pp. 13–16.

90. *Ibid.*, pp. 16–17.

91. *Ibid.*, p. 16.

92. Terry R. Dixon, "The Environmental Problem of Water Pollution." Research paper delivered to the Environmental Policy and Administration Seminar, University of New Mexico, Albuquerque, May, 1971.

93. Albuquerque Urban Observatory, *Factors Pertinent to Water Quality in the Albuquerque Metropolitan Area* (Albuquerque, N. Mex.: Albuquerque Urban Observatory, 1970) p. vi.

Chapter 8

URBAN AND REGIONAL ENVIRONMENTAL POLICY

Environmental considerations, as well as growing political, social, and economic pressures, require that urban policy be approached by government on a regional basis. In redefining urban fields, Friedman and Miller note that urban life has broken through the symbolic boundaries of the classic city and that the metropolitan age is here. They consider that the *urban field* for more and more people is an area extending between 30 and 100 miles from the old central zones, and that these urban fields are increasingly adjoining and overlapping.[1] Although Shakespeare asked, "what is the city but the people?" it is obvious that the city or urban field can no longer be approached as an extension of man. Policy innovations based on environmental quality considerations call for recognition of the underlying basis of the regional ecology, and of human population concentrations and their influences on the land and on other forms of life.

Government is very much involved in what is happening in urban areas relative to the environment. The Advisory Commission on Intergovernmental Relations in *Urban America and the Federal System* comments through a proponent argument: "We need to remember that governments—state and local included—already condition urban and economic growth. We seek here a more rational playing out of this government role. . . . I concede a genuine national policy on urban growth must have a geographical foundation. I also admit that it will be difficult to work out—since ultimately it involves all three levels of government, as well as the Congress at the national level."[2]

The present complex array of federal, state, and local governments contains countless intergovernmental arrangements with no unifying policy for urban environmental considerations. Local economic (i.e., private sector) and political forces appear to dominate the scene. With the complex interdependencies of environmental problems and quality, not to mention their social costs, it becomes increasingly difficult to recognize the independent micro-policies of given political entities or uncontrolled economic units in urban and regional areas.

On the other hand, the trend toward recognition of regional arrangements for urban policy is observed by Walter Scheiber who indicates: "Over the past two decades, a new species of government and quasi-government has emerged in urban areas across America. Created out of a growing awareness that our traditional patterns of local government cannot treat adequately problems which transcend municipal and county boundaries, problems which require areawide planning for their solution, these regional entities comprise the most striking development on the local government scene since the advent of the council-manager plan."[3] Yet, he notes that many of these multipurpose regional governmental organizations have little power to compel adherence to their policies. Many are of a voluntary nature and are financially dependent on local governments with grant supplements from a variety of federal and state governments.[4] It is further obvious that a given governmental unit will automatically safeguard and advance its own interests and territory in any overall regional policy.

For many urban organizations, the *nonplace urban realm* (i.e., without real governmental identity), a term used by Melvin Webber, has become the major frame of reference.[5] Thus, John Friedman notes: "The urban experience of these groups is conditioned by a complex network of guidance institutions, none of which has complete control over events in its own area of jurisdiction nor the knowledge or ability to make such control effective. To accomplish anything, different interests must be concerted through intricate procedures of persuasion. In the urban field, and even more in the nonplace urban realm, there is no single hierarchy of authority, but rather many possible configurations of guidance institutions whose composition becomes apparent only by considering each situation separately and by itself."[6] Consequently, considering each situation as an isolated event, political manipulations and power clusters become dominant in urban policy decision making. Under this orientation, long-range environmental considerations often play an insignificant role in the short-range economics of brokerage politics in a given organization.

There are also severe limitations on the perceptions of policy-making groups and individuals relative to regional and urban environmental perspectives. In many ways, the postindustrial man is cut off from these perceptions except in abstract and symbolic terms which, in turn, creates a policy vacuum with respect to value conflicts and environmental abuses. And self-limiting public policy, with its countless fragmented decisions, permits, or even encourages, many environmental and pollution problems of modern society. A system of short-range, independent, and politically expedient decisions oriented to local interests and values does not add up to a long-range urban and regional policy responsive to the dimensions of environmental quality and pollution control problems. And every region of the United States today, in varying degrees, reflects environmental abuses and pollution resulting from expedient policy; the physical and esthetic deterioration of the environment is most apparent in urban areas. Sound regional environmental values, perceptions, and orientations must be realistically encompassed in the system of policy making for urban areas.

In essence, an urban area is an integrated ecosystem of man and his environment. Concentrations and distributions of populations associated with man's technoscientific and industrial resources are subject to the principle of *environmental unity*. Simply stated, this concept is that all the elements and processes of environment are interrelated and interdependent, and that a change in one will lead to changes in the others.[7] And urban or metropolitan societies are constantly overwhelmed by accelerated change through population increase and technological developments, as well as by their social and biological needs and wants. The consequence is a constantly changing and erratic ecosystem relative to this environmental unity. On the decision-making level, much of this change, with its forces and influences, remains uncontrolled in terms of the ecosystem. An instant, crisis-spawned policy is formulated and administered in response to the symptoms, pressures, and economics of change; hence, the total ecosystem, including its regional dimensions, is disregarded.

A major factor in such changes is the constant growth and concentration of human populations in urban areas. The Census Bureau classifies as urban populations all those who live in towns or cities of 2500 or more. The metropolitan area, consisting of a central city of over 50,000 with its satellite suburbs or subdivisions, now represents home to two out of every three Americans. (The various categories, cities, towns, suburbs, and central cities, will be considered "urban.") James Swan notes:

> Since 1900 people and land in cities have more than quadrupled and if present trends continue it is likely that they will double again by the year 2000. Seventy percent of the more than 200 million people in the United States now live in cities, which constitute little more than one percent of the total land surface. To accommodate the prospective growth of the next 35 years we can anticipate twice as much urban development as has occurred since this country was founded. In our technologically advanced, affluent society this will mean twice as much waste, twice as much almost everything, just to maintain the present standard of living. In light of this prediction two questions must be asked: Can we? And should we?[8]

It is only in very recent times that questions of this nature with "cans" or "shoulds," are being asked in terms of urban and regional policy. For example, a recent charter amendment proposal to the City of Boulder, Colorado, called for setting a ceiling of 100,000 on the population (the current population is 72,000). Although the amendment was not passed, concern is increasing over the city's rapid population growth and development.[9] In most urban areas, progress, growth, and economic development have generally been the dominant values underlying policy. Powerful governmental and corporate interests have operated too long in an opportunistic and expansionistic manner, ignoring environmental impacts of their policy decisions. Moreover, the increasing percentages of Americans in urban areas have supplied the physical force behind much of this orientation. The 1970 Census indicates that some 73 percent of the American population lives in urban or suburban areas. If present trends continue, by the year 2000, from 70 to 80 percent of all Americans will be located in five large urban areas.[10]

Given the physical force of growing populations in urban areas, an array of federal, state, and local agencies has appeared to deal with present and anticipated impacts. This has resulted in myopic, fragmented, and ineffective urban policy in terms of the environment and other important problems. Ranging from the Department of Housing and Urban Development down to any local, urban agency, little in the way of actual, operational, and realistic urban environmental policy exists on a regional basis. In this sense, Dennis McElrath observes that "the political culture (including agencies) has not kept pace with the dramatic changes which are occurring in society, nor with their environmental correlates."[11] He attributes important societal changes to a growing interdependence of society and environment which goes beyond political boundaries, activities, and policies. McElrath further considers two major obstacles to effective environmental policy in any area to be: (1) lack of an integrated concept of public responsibility for environmental quality, and, (2) a political structure that impedes the formation of comprehensive policy issues in meaningful terms.[12]

On the other hand, there is a definite recognition of environmental needs, and efforts are being made to translate them into an effective urban policy. At the April 1971 White House Conference on Youth, an environmental task force reported: "Although environmental degradation has become recognized in recent years as a major social crisis, the public focus on this issue has usually been directed toward problems that are important to middle class Americans. The issues of urban transportation, slum housing, inadequate health care, recreation and education and unemployment are vital to urban poor people; but have not been properly understood in an environmental context or dealt with from an ecological perspective."[13] Environmental impact statements and plans are now required of many urban projects that involve federal agencies and funding, with additional requirements for interagency review and input from the federal, state, and local agencies involved. This forces some environmental orientation.

The environmental impact statements also require public participation and hearings in many cases, as do other programs concerned with urban environmental affairs. Although this public participation may take many forms in terms of actual and potential influences on urban policy, disadvantages of public responsiveness also exist. Politically powerful groups and individuals may dictate priorities (the "noisy wheel gets the grease"), with little attention being paid to important values of the environmental public interest. Further, interpretations and manipulations by public officials can result in public participation merely being "used" by the established political administrative system; that is, public participation is incorporated into the system's own power base. In *The New Grass Roots Governments: Decentralization and Citizen Participation in Urban Areas*, the Advisory Commission on Intergovernmental Relations notes: "To sum up, several cities and a few counties are making progress in decentralizing services and involving citizens in decision making concerning their delivery. Yet most of the activity to date can be classified as territorial or administrative decentralization, with citizens playing an advisory and, to a lesser extent, a policy-making role. . . . With respect to political decentralization or community control, the survey results suggest that it will take quite a while for reality to catch up with rhetoric."[14]

Also, with the high mobility of Americans today, many citizens of urban areas may lack the environmental familiarity, identification, and concern that go with long experience in an area. This has a definite influence on urban policy administration which, in essence, deals with a citizenry composed of many temporary, or transient, residents. Impersonalization, apathy, and alienation characterize many citizen–government relationships, resulting in the lack of a sense of permanence, stability, or long-range commitment to the urban or regional environment. Further, habitual acceptance by both spheres of environmental abuses and pollution can weaken the quality of urban environmental policy on either a short- or long-range basis. As one citizen of Los Angeles recently remarked about the smog, "You learn to live with it."

Yet, residents of urban areas are the most apparent contributors to, and victims of, environmental deterioration and pollution, and the majority of Americans will be spending most of their lives in urban areas. As citizens, they certainly have the right and the responsibility to achieve environmental quality and freedom from avoidable pollution. Thus, in *The Urban Crisis*, the President's Council on Recreation and Natural Beauty notes:

> By the year 2000, according to an Urban Land Institute projection, 90 percent of Americans are expected to live in cities. By the year 2000, 60 percent of the American people are expected to be living on only seven percent of the land, concentrated in the three largest metropolitan areas. One megalopolis reaching from west of Chicago to Maine and down the Atlantic coast to south of Norfolk, a second stretching down California from 150 miles north of San Francisco to the Mexican border, and a third extending the length of the Florida peninsula.

> This staggering prospect carries with it the possibility that the metropolitan areas can destroy themselves as decent places to live, owing to an inability to plan and govern on a regional basis.

> It seems clear that in these urban agglomerations the problems of air pollution, water pollution, disposal of solid wastes, and the destruction of open land will grow in such proportions as to demand radical innovations in planning (policy) and governmental techniques and organizations.[15]

In observing historical patterns of urban policy in private and governmental spheres, the Advisory Commission on Intergovernmental relations notes: "Most of these decisions—including those made in the public sector and even those ostensibly concerned with orderly urban growth—are discrete, frequently disconnected, and often disappointing. And no wonder, given the multiplicity of governmental programs and jurisdictions operating in this area, the weakness of areawide mechanisms, and the absence of any real policy at the national, state, or areawide level to help provide the framework for coordinative program action and for the targeting of long-range urban goals."[16] If present urban growth trends continue with consequent severe increases in environmental and other major problems, it is obvious that extremely powerful pressures will cause a national urban regional policy to be forged. And some experts indicate that this would mean new life styles for future Americans in contrast to present urbanization.[17] It is also obvious that a national policy of this nature would have to exert some control on areas

130

currently uncontrolled, including decisions involving private development, local government autonomy, and population distribution, in terms of environmental and other major problems and constraints. But large changes and innovations in national urban and regional policy are inevitable in the urbanization process itself.

THE INNER CITY

In its 1971 annual report, the Council on Environmental Quality (CEQ) indicated that special attention should be given to the inner city where many of the most severe environmental problems are juxtaposed with social and economic strains. The "inner city" describes the decaying, older urban areas, which generally intertwine with the center portion of the city, as well as surrounding sections that share the same environmental characteristics. Life in the inner city embraces a range of environmental problems both evident and disguised, and noted for their severity and concentration. The inner city is noted for its inferior and deteriorated environment. Some environmental problems, such as air pollution and the absence of open space, occur to a greater degree here than in other areas. And the inner city's noise, sanitation problems, and congestion affect all urban sectors. Typical inner city problems include overcrowding, rats, flaking leaded paint, deteriorating housing, litter, and garbage.[18]

Due to the complexity of the problems and the absence of simple solutions, the CEQ indicates that environmental problems in the urban setting cannot be sharply differentiated from nonenvironmental problems. Moreover, the CEQ observes that many of the traditional environmental objectives are not the central concerns of most inner city poor whose focus is mainly on economic and social interests. Thus, the CEQ notes:

> For many inner city residents, the overwhelming concern is poverty and its accompanying ills—inadequate housing, high crime rates, poor health, unsanitary conditions, inadequate education and recreation, and drug addiction—all of which are exacerbated by racial discrimination. These factors may not be environmental when looked at individually, but their net effect is to lower the quality of life.

> Nevertheless, there is growing evidence that among the urban poor—those with the most to gain from environmental improvement—are some who have decided to embrace environmentalism in their own distinct way. Their use of the term environment is broader than the traditional definition. Their concept embraces not only more parks, but better housing; not only cleaner air and water, but rat extermination.[19]

The White House Conference on Youth in April 1971 passed the resolution, "that national priority be given to the actions necessary to improve the quality of the environment of the people of America's inner cities."[20] Yet, one might question whether in some respects this goal is not directed to symptoms, rather than underlying causes, in terms of its environmental perspective. Thus, Iltis notes: "If the concrete and steel cities . . . turn man into a social, erratic, and sick animal; if urbanization degrades human society through increased emotional stress, crime, delinquency, slums, and other neuroses and psychoses, it is because the genetic flexibility of the human animal . . . is not great enough."[21]

Before anything else, the inner city or urban area is an ecosystem that includes all life and substances within a particular space, and ecosystems are complex and interdependent networks. Although a given city may be considered a partial ecosystem, lacking photosynthesis through green plants, it is dependent on other regional ecosystems for energy and materials provided through mechanical means. This, in turn, creates major alterations and growing disturbances in ecosystems, for example, pollution, environmental deterioration, etc.[22] Consequently, Stewart Marquis notes: "As unique human dominant ecosystems, cities might be looked at as evolutionary experiments in the ability of one species to create and control its own ecological systems. At this point in time we cannot say whether or not the experiments will succeed or whether or not cities will prove to be stable experiments. What we can say is that most of them are not stable."[23]

Marquis attributes much of destructive power of the city ecosystem to private and governmental management, which is largely deluded by the possibilities and applications of mechanical force technology, and lacks understanding and discrimination necessary for ecosystem control or for combining natural and human control.[24] He suggests the social planning and engineering of complete ecosystems, including man and his activities as critical parts, and states: "But we are suggesting still more strongly the need to deal with the complex interdependencies between lesser systems—the social life, artifactual, the natural—as they function in the larger ecosystem. The means to achieve this may involve large measures of social engineering, since we are suggesting that these problems must be dealt with by men, through their social systems. But the matters to be dealt with go far beyond the social."[25]

By a symptomatic approach to isolated human problems of the inner city, which neglects consideration of ecosystems or environment, underlying causes and effective solutions may be disregarded. For the inner city, the vast array of socially or environmentally involved organizations (government and private) has little real orientation along environmental lines. Countless divergent organizational approaches, with specific and isolated missions, do not add up to integrated social environmental programs for the quality of life. Human and social problems need to be approached on a unified basis within the context of actual environmental controls. In essence this involves ecological perspectives, foundations, and orientations to pressing problems of the inner city.

The CEQ recommends that efforts to overcome the variety and complexity of environmental problems of the inner city should be tailored to the needs and problems of each locality. The CEQ observes that most of the resources used for coping with broad environmental problems are raised within the locality itself, with federal assistance being only a portion of the total resources available. Thus, the CEQ recommends that local resources be used in a planned and effective way to meet locally determined priorities, with federal aid helping the locality to meet its own recognized needs. Some federal programs deal with physical circumstances of the inner city environment (e.g., air and water pollution control) that affect all citizens, while a few programs (e.g., federal assistance for rat control) are concerned primarily with inner city problems.[26]

The CEQ indicates that effective and comprehensive approaches are lacking to focus on local priorities and problems of the inner city: "Inner city residents and federal, state, and local officials all have found that the fragmental approach—dealing separately with causes and effects—is generally inadequate to deal with the interdependent nature of the inner city environment. Programs have also faltered when they failed to involve the residents themselves. And the way the financial assistance was provided often impeded the effort."[27] Also, questions might be raised concerning attention to environmental or ecosystem considerations in the various programs, particularly as contrasted with political economic expediencies. Moreover, the politics of federal grantsmanship can become dominant in many local programs, to the detriment of important social and environmental concerns. At the same time, a lack of funding, particularly because of the weak tax base of the inner city, precludes solid, and comprehensive, long-range programs.

There is an obvious need for more and better community participation by inner city residents in the decision-making processes. Often, this process is a procedural farce of centralization—decentralization—centralization without any consideration of the residents' wishes, life styles, or social structures. Yet, their help and guidance are very much needed for improving the quality of life and environment in the inner city; the community's goals should be included, rather than having goals imposed, which can be only ineffectively implemented. On the other hand, the public participation process itself can be complicated through pressure-group representation and political conflict, disregarding the genuine public and environmental interest of the inner city resident. Governmental responsiveness and comprehensive new institutions such as NEEDS (Neighborhood Environmental Evaluation and Decision System) are appropriate. Located in the Department of Health, Education, and Welfare's Bureau of Community Environmental Management, NEEDS is designed to help local communities identify their interrelated problems of environmental and social stresses on a cause and effect basis, and to set comprehensive, action-oriented priorities for solving them. Nevertheless, the CEQ considers that the focus of such public participation, "should not obscure the fact that many of the forces that shape the intimate environment of the inner city resident are often beyond his knowledge and control."[28]

Some of the major environmental problems of the inner city include the following.

Air Pollution. Central business districts and nearby industrial areas absorb and bear the heaviest air pollution loads, and the largest concentrations of urban poor live near such areas. An Environmental Protection Agency (EPA) study indicated that the average

133

concentrations of particulates in the air in nonurban areas are between 10 and 50 percent of the average concentrations occurring in urban areas, with similar variations being found between suburbia and the inner city within metropolitan regions.[29]

Water Pollution. Water pipes in inner city housing are often old and inadequately maintained; they frequently contain a pipe or joint cementing compound of lead. As a result, water containing as much as 920 μg of lead per liter (as contrasted to a 20 μg per liter level elsewhere) can be found in inner city areas. Residents have very limited access to water recreation. Economic restrictions on travel limit their sources of water recreation to river courses, harbors, or other bodies of water at hand. And these often contain dangerously high levels of bacteria and pollutants.[30]

Solid Waste. Junk, litter, and garbage are abundant and familiar in poverty areas and have a psychological effect on those who live there, discouraging individual and community efforts toward sanitation and a cleaner neighborhood. Although reasons for failure to control solid waste, including governmental efforts, are complex and interrelated, it is a constant source of frustration. Besides being odorous and unattractive, strewn garbage invites disease-carrying rats. An estimated 60 to 80 percent of rat bites occur in inner city areas.[31]

Neighborhood Deterioration. Abandonment of buildings by landlords, widespread dilapidation from lack of maintenance, overcrowding of individual dwellings, and deleterious effects of lead paint are common problems of many inner city neighborhoods. Lead is present in the paint, plaster, and caulking of older dwellings, and particles of this material are sometimes eaten by small children. Prolonged or recurrent ingestion of lead produces dangerous levels of lead in the bloodstream. It is estimated that 400,000 children are afflicted. Lethargy, convulsions, mental retardation, and death can result from lead poisoning.[32]

Open Space and Recreation. Less than three percent of the 491 million acres of public recreation area in the United States is within 40 miles (or an hour's drive) of the center of a metropolitan area with a population over 500,000, although 90 million people live in these areas. Moreover, despite current acquisition programs, inner city areas are now suffering from decreases in available open space or parklands. There has been a loss of more than 22,000 acres of urban parkland in the past six years, much of it close to the inner city. Transportation corridors and industries along waterways have cut off access to many areas suitable for recreation. Increasing traffic has often congested streets used as playgrounds by the urban poor.[33]

Transportation. The ownership of an automobile often means the difference between access to recreation and confinement. On the other hand, constant new highway construction throughout the inner city can cost a resident his home, increase immediate air pollution, and add to noise. Better public participation and displacement costs relative to highway planning are needed.[34]

Noise. The inner city has intensive, combined noise problems ranging in source from transportation and construction to the accumulated noise of crowds of people engaged in their everyday activities. With little escape from this concentrated noise pollution, there are serious negative effects on the general and mental health of inner city people, as well as on their quality of life.

Given these and other problems, serious questions are raised concerning the quality of life in the inner city. It is obvious that the environment influences and molds the individual, both physically and mentally. Pleasure, health, and other human considerations are negatively influenced by a deteriorating and polluted environment. Ehrlich and Ehrlich note that the dehumanizing effects of life in the slums, ghettos, and other crowded, noisy, and smoggy environments, aggravate the problems of people with symptoms of mental disturbance and emotional stress.[35] A life of quality for the inner city resident appears to involve an environment of quality. It is obvious that government can do much to provide such quality, particularly with adequate public participation and proper, comprehensive environmental perspectives for the inner city.

SUBURBIA

In describing the growth of suburbia, a land developer and mortgage banker who was a witness before a congressional committee, stated:

> A farm is sold and begins raising houses instead of potatoes—then another farm. Forests are cut, valleys are filled, streams are buried in storm sewers.

> Traffic grows, roads are widened, service stations . . . hamburger stands pockmark the highways, traffic strangles. An expressway is cut through and brings cloverleafs which bring shopping centers. Relentlessly, the bits and pieces of a city are splattered across the landscape.

> By this irrational process, noncommunities are born—formless, without order, beauty or reason—with no visible respect for people or the land. Thousands of small, separate decisions—made with little or no relationship to one another nor to their composite impact—produce a major decision about the future of our cities and our civilization, a decision we have come to label "sprawl."[36]

In essence, there appears to be little governmental policy to control or deal with this sprawl. Each year, urban sprawl consumes an estimated 420,000 acres of land in this uncontrolled outward push.[37] Max Ways refers to sprawl and land consumption as the "tyranny of small decisions," with each small decision being made on the basis of individual gain and profit for one or a few people. Yet, he considers that each sprawl decision that contributes to the general decay is almost invariably one that is most profitable to the real estate developer.[38] And there appears to be little reduction in the suburban sprawl trend. From 1950 to 1969, the population of suburbia climbed 91 percent while the population of central cities increased only 12 percent. By 1969, suburbanites numbered more than 71 million against a central city of 59 million

135

residents. Also, since World War II, industry appears to be foregoing the central city for rambling suburban plants, because of space requirements for assembly line production. In consequence, three of every four new manufacturing jobs are being created in the suburbs.[39]

Socioeconomic preference, the automobile, escape from city problems, the "American Dream," real estate entrepreneurship, and promotion are only some of the factors behind the suburban tide. Although involved in problems and services relating to the sprawl, the government has a minimal controlling or planning role; suburbia and its sprawl are generally considered to be the autonomous domain of private enterprise. Still, the impacts of suburban growth in the context of environmental awareness point toward increasing governmental involvement. Open space is also absorbed by the numerous facilities, such as shopping centers and highway interchanges, serving suburbia. Airports and industrial developments also subtract space. The end result is less and less available public or private space. Yet this open space is essential to the quality of urban life and environment. The CEQ notes: "Man requires a feeling of permanence to attain a sense of place, importance, and identity. For many persons in the city, the presence of nature is the harmonizing thread in an environment otherwise of man's own making."[40]

Construction and zoning practices in suburbia frequently abuse the land with high public costs. Some subdivisions, for example, are stripped of all tree and plant cover before construction, and this results in heavy soil runoff and sedimentation in various waterways. Consequently, expensive downstream dredging and upstream flood control are required, and the quality of lakes, streams, and rivers suffers from this runoff.[41] Suburban developments along *flood plains* (where flooding is a natural process of rivers) create public pressures for flood control projects. Besides the destruction of a fertile habitat with its plant and animal life, construction on flood plains accelerates rapid runoff, increases flooding, and adds to water shortages. In terms of intangible environmental quality, CEQ notes:

> Esthetically, this current pattern of growth triggers at least three adverse consequences. First, much commercial development along roads and highways through suburbs is of cheap and unimaginative construction. Gaudy neon signs, billboards, powerlines, and clutter characterize this development. Second, many residential subdivisions are visually boring— block after block of treeless lawns, uniform setbacks and repetitious housing designs and street layouts. Finally, wooded streambeds, slopes, and ridges, which could help break the monotony of uniform housing developments, are often destroyed.[42]

Developments of suburbia show little sensitivity to natural features and environmental quality. Ridges, slopes, and trees are enveloped in the sprawl, regardless of their beauty or utility as watersheds and wildlife habitats. Inadequate governmental controls are exercised relative to development of flood plains, steep slopes, or land above aquifer (i.e., geological formations containing water) recharge areas, with soil instability and erosion resulting. Data and expert advice are available on subsoil composition, aquifers, cover, wetlands, and other ecological features, but are generally not sought by most planning and zoning boards.[43] In many ways, the developments operate "apart" from nature and the land, with resulting negative effects on a physical, as well as an esthetic basis. Too often economics, expediency, and environmental insensitivity are dominant forces in sprawl, in both private and governmental spheres.

In *Design with Nature,* Ian McHarg considers that uncontrolled models of development bear no relation to definitions of natural processes, values, or intrinsic suitability.[44] If anything, these features become targets of more expensive suburban developments. Thus, a natural and scenic rimrock above Billings, Montana, is now under subdivision development, with many of the unbuilt lots selling for several thousand dollars. Billings failed to purchase the property for parkland when it was offered; now the development on the top of the rim will destroy the esthetic qualities of a natural feature, and pollution of ground and surface water is predicted for dwellings below, in addition to erosion and disturbance of the fragile plant cover. Similar examples of negative development of natural features and processes can be cited throughout the spectrum of urban sprawl in the United States. In fact, examples of the reverse aspect of this uncontrolled process would probably be the exception.

County government units, where the greater portion of the sprawl descends, are ill equipped to control or plan orderly growth, let alone to conserve natural features. Given the potential for strong governmental administration in the counties relative to sprawl, most county-based units remain ineffective, politically dominated, unresponsive, and weak. This is due, to an extent, to inadequate financing of county government through poor tax arrangements and the lack of other revenue sources. In many cases, financial problems are responsible for insufficient and inadequate personnel, and resources to cope with suburbia and related county problems. Well trained personnel are usually not attracted by low salaries, although supplemental federal funds are now being made available for personnel and resources in many instances.

Further, many county commissioners, as major policy and decision makers, are of low caliber, because of relatively low salaries attached to their elected office. Older politicians, who might handle the office inadequately on a part-time basis, are sometimes attracted to the county commissioner's job because of various intergovernmental arrangements such as city–county planning boards and regional governmental councils. Counties thus become "weak sisters," and are ineffective in formulating and implementing various policy decisions regarding suburbia and its growth. As the one governmental unit that includes much of suburbia within its boundaries and jurisdiction, the county generally remains autonomous (although subject to manipulations and economic influences), and suburbia and its subdivisions remain aloof. Thus, suburbia becomes a "no place" political unit lacking in governmental controls for environmental and other problems. There are also county problems, such as open space and scenic consumption, deriving from the "second homes" of many suburban residents. These, in turn, create a "second" suburbia in other regions. It is obvious that effective urban policy on suburbia should encompass strengthening of county governments and their intergovernmental arrangements.

Max Ways considers that much environmental damage resulting from uncontrolled urban sprawl is irreversible, particularly that involving destruction of topsoil. Concrete and asphalt permanently cover topsoil as a result of development of dwellings, driveways, parking lots, etc. Besides removing topsoil from natural processes and agricultural use, such artificial covers permit little rain to enter the soil, and cause a high runoff of water with detrimental effects on water tables.[45] Further, natural features, such as flood plains and ridges, and certain plant and animal populations associated with given natural habitats, will never recover fully from the influences of suburban developments. Trees and forests, under proper planting and land encouragement as renewable natural resources, will attain good size within a lifetime. But, in the meantime, their beauty and value as sources of habitat, watershed, temperature control, and air pollution reduction, are destroyed or are only partially effective. The point is that a policy (or nonpolicy) of uncontrolled development allowing urban sprawl causes irreversible damage of the environment for present and future generations.

On the other hand, some trends toward control appear to be emerging, with concern for environmental esthetics. An effort is being made to enhance the full potential of specific areas. McHarg, in formulating ecological development plans for valleys of the Baltimore region, noted that the land was examined for intrinsic opportunities for or constraints on urban development. Further, he noted that the concept of "photographic determinism" was used, which suggested that optimum development should respond to natural processes; observance of this concept, taking advantage of natural opportunities and constraints, would result in an anticipated excess value of $7 million, in addition to environmental benefits, as contrasted to the negative projection for the uncontrolled growth model. Relative to the concept of accumulation of powers, McHarg proposed the following sequence for both private and public actions.

> The area is beautiful and vulnerable.
> Development is inevitable and must be accommodated.
> Uncontrolled growth is inevitably destructive.
> Development must conform to regional goals.
> Observance of conservation principles can avert destruction and ensure enhancement.
> The area can absorb all prospective growth without depreciation.
> Planned growth is more desirable than uncontrolled growth, and more profitable.
> Public and private powers can be joined in partnership in a process to realize this plan.[46]

Besides the suggested trend toward blending of economics and ecology and private and public powers in control of suburban development, there appears to be some trend toward resistance of development of scenic natural areas. Given limited governmental programs for acquisition of public park lands, legal, economic, and political activity by organized and *ad hoc* pressure groups is increasingly a factor. In many instances public participation is now required under the law. The Nature Conservancy, for example, has national and regional programs for acquiring natural areas for public use before they are subject to development, and organizes the defense of natural areas on a local basis. In the Rimrock natural area development at Billings, Montana, thousands of signatures were collected on a petition to "Save the Rimrocks," and establish it as public parkland. This effort was undertaken by a local organization composed mainly of college students. Although the county commissioners were unresponsive to the petition, and the City of Billings declined to purchase the land to forestall development, the effort did indicate strong public resistance to unrestrained suburban development of a natural area. Also, legal actions by George C. Matthews of Saint Petersburg, Florida, have resulted in frustration or termination of plans proposed by many real estate developers for the coastal mangrove swamps.[47] A result of the actions may be public and private recognition that urban sprawl developers cannot do everything they want to do.

Within the development of suburbia itself, new trends are emerging in terms of environmental considerations for quality of life. Government and developers are becoming more oriented toward wise planning and site selection, thus avoiding abuses to the natural environment while meeting both housing and environmental goals.[48] Moreover, McHarg notes that wise planning of developments will present minimum disturbance through absorption into the natural landscape. However, he considers that this must be accomplished in terms of the entire landscape, regardless of well designed individual subdivisions that include small parks. The overall effect would be the "expunging" of the great landscape without a total environmental orientation in planning and development.[49] It is obvious that the great landscape orientation requires some loss of subdivision autonomy, and a movement toward stronger private and governmental policy, arrangements, and responsibilities.

In considering innovations in suburbia, the CEQ notes: "The combination of open space with cluster zoning or planned unit development lowers the initial community service costs because of smaller networks of roads and utilities, and it makes a more livable environment for the long term. These developments can vary from new satellite communities like Columbia, Md., to small, sensitively designed clusters of townhouses around a common green. The challenge is to change traditional ways of building and development and to break down the economic and institutional barriers that obstruct widespread use of these innovations."[50] Many changes required for environmental quality in suburbia depend upon planning processes that involve the inner city and region.

METROPOLITAN REGIONAL PLANNING

In the past, from an environmental or ecological perspective, little attention has been given to planning processes. Limitations imposed by training, time in office, public awareness, and the current state of the art, generally led to economic, architectural, civil

139

engineering, or efficiency oriented decisions with indirect reference to man–land–environmental relationships. Recent trends in planning appear to be responsive to environmental pressures and constraints, including environmental impact studies and government statements. Perhaps some of these environmental aspects have been neglected for so long that they have finally emerged on a crisis basis. Yet, planning is also a political process responsive to value and power conflicts. Environmental aspects may actually be incorporated in planning relative to political processes and realities and, in some cases, environment may be the actual focus for planning and implementation, or it may be totally disregarded while lip service is paid to platitudes.

Further complications of regional planning for metropolitan environments involve the complexity of intergovernmental relations. Each agency, whether federal, state, county, or local, has interests that affect political planning. Moreover, there is no governmental agency that has *full* responsibility for the *whole* environment, particularly on the regional level. Consequently, planning agencies must interact with a multitude of other agencies that are, or might be, involved in a given plan. Since each agency has its own power base, brokerage politics—with manipulation, bargaining, and dealing—becomes an integral part of the planning process. Environmental considerations are often neglected, although they are necessary for quality.

Many planning processes involve an overconcern for economic development and population growth in light of present environmental considerations. Granted that economic development and population are vital, predictions and projections may act as self-fulfilling prophecies bringing overconcentrations of population and overdevelopment to a given environment, with eventual detrimental effects. For example, water engineers and other planners in the Southwest, where population and developments are particularly likely to center around water, may plan water developments to meet the future needs of a given metropolitan or regional area. But these water plans and developments will, in turn, encourage further population growth and economic development in the same area, thus creating immediate water needs and other problems because of overconcentration. Little thought has been given in the planning processes to optimum compatible populations and economic developments in terms of environmental constraints and quality, let alone to planned population distributions that would follow ecological principles. An overriding assumption made by many planners is that substantial future growth is good and must be encouraged and accommodated, regardless of environmental considerations.

Yet, a trend in planning appears to be to pay more attention to the environment, and perhaps even, through ecological perspectives, to the place of urban man in nature. Within this trend, an important element (as portrayed in McHarg's *Design with Nature*) is accommodation of necessary urban developments within natural values, and the order of metropolitan and regional areas with emphasis on ecological principles and the consequences of planning.[51] Further applications of ecology in economics and regional planning are conceptualized by Walter Isard, who writes:

140

The combination of the two words, *ecologic* and *economic,* while an unusual one, is set forth as a true combination, in the sense of a synthesis of analysis of two systems within the world of actuality. Throughout the book, we stress the need for this synthesis. Having constantly in mind the mounting air, water, and sonic pollution problems of society, its solid waste problem, its need for open spaces, its diverse impingements on the environment, we assert that no longer can regional development and regional planning be treated in their traditionally narrow garb. Emphasis on the strict economics of such developments and planning, with only passing consideration of physical environment and design, let alone social, political, and other cultural factors, can no longer be tolerated. Whether we look at the problems of planning and development within the New England states, or in innumerable other regions of the world, we are confronted with the reality that control of the disturbance to the ecological and physical processes, and design of the environment are key elements of economic development and planning work. Even conscious redesign of the environment may be.[52]

While there is a great potential and a need for considering ecology in planning for environmental quality of metropolitan and regional areas, the planning process itself is a very complex one. Le Blanc and Allensworth note that much of this complexity involves conflict over just what government should do by way of planning the future. They also observe wide community acceptance of planning as a governmental function and responsibility.[53] Although some may prefer to think of planning as nonpolitical or "administrative," Blanc and Allensworth note the growing emphasis on planning as a political institution, and comment: "Politics in this sense means conflict over the values, priorities, and means of implementation that should govern the determination of community policy over planning."[54] Thus various values, including those pertaining to ecology, economics, recreation, esthetics, and transportation, are involved in the political processes of planning.

Planning and implementation, through political conflicts and compromises, exclude and include and reduce and increase emphasis on various values and their alternatives in terms of power allocations. In this sense, "private" values in planning and development may be considered part of environmental planning in terms of influences and results. On ecological perspective, McHarg notes: "The basic proposition employed is that any place is the sum of historical, physical, and biological processes, that these are dynamic, that they constitute social values, that each area has an intrinsic suitability for certain land uses and finally, that certain areas lend themselves to multiple coexisting uses."[55] Yet, McHarg observes that a plan based on these assumptions is not complete until society resolves through politics the entire question of supply and demand for a given area and values.[56] Nevertheless, under this proposition, he notes that most planning criteria are "obscure and covert" with arbitrary and distant judgments, and methods that employ natural processes as values (e.g., geology, hydrology, wildlife, etc.) as well as applying the value system of the community concerning localities, sites, or spaces that it cherishes.[57]

The CEQ notes that planning, unless it is comprehensive and long range, cannot really evaluate ecological factors adequately. Master plans sometimes become a set of comple-

141

mentary, functional goals (transportation, schools, etc.), emphasizing economic growth and efficiency and with no real regional and environmental considerations.[58] The CEQ further observes that public officials have a growing base of sophisticated land-use tools at various governmental levels for planning and directing development to achieve a balance between economic and public interests, but that little effective use is made of them, often because of inadequate institutional arrangements.[59] Thus, the CEQ indicates:

> Conflicts among the rights of an individual landowner, his neighbors, and the community should be resolved by the unit of government best able to take into account broad regional interests. Urban growth has outstripped the ability of small government units to handle environmental decisions that have metropolitan, regional, or even statewide impact. To offset this, many State governments have begun taking back some of the land use powers that they had delegated to municipalities. Although it has been long in coming, Americans are recognizing the need to examine carefully what government can do to assure that land is treated as a resource to be managed and not merely as a commodity to be marketed.[60]

In essence, a plan is: (1) a description of current physical and human resource conditions, (2) an assessment of the direction in which the community or region is developing, (3) an expression of desired goals, and (4) recommendations for governmental programs to reach the goals.[61] However, planners, such as O'Donnell, Smutz, McCallum, and Varma, observe that environmental impact is increasingly being considered in numerous plans. With various forms of federal financial assistance supporting at least one-half to two-thirds of the planning bodies, planning falls under federal legislation and requirements relative to the environment (e.g., the National Environmental Policy Act of 1969, and the EPA). Thus, environmental impact statements, inventories, and reports are required from planning bodies that operate as legally constituted entities through state laws. Yet, authority is generally lacking in the planning process, even with federal involvement; much reliance for environmental consideration is consequently placed on persuasion, through renewal and increase of federal funding.[62]

O'Donnell, Smutz, McCallum, and Varma also observe that most planning bodies owe their beginnings and continued operations to federal financial support and programs, such as the U.S. Housing and Urban Development's urban planning assistance.[63] A recent survey by the National Commission on Urban Problems indicates that about half the county governments in the United States, including four-fifths of those in metropolitan areas, have planning boards, and there has been a substantial increase in both boards and master plans since 1966. Yet, in terms of land itself, municipal planning generally relates to relatively small local areas with large populations. Nevertheless, recent federal and state legislation requires that some federal grants to metropolitan governments and their planning bodies be conditional upon review and comment by an areawide agency with planning functions.[64] At the same time, these areawide agencies (e.g., Council of Governments, etc.) are heavily funded by the federal government.

The previously named planners observe that areawide or regional governmental organizations, as legally constituted entities with planning functions, have little real authority and must depend upon voluntary compliance and funding. Consequently, political considerations, fragmentation and lack of coordination, ambiguity of role and area definitions, and other problems beset them. Under growing environmental and other regional problems, however, intergovernmental planning organizations require greater authority and coordination, particularly through state government. The planners consider that too often a given planning agency's legal jurisdiction, responsibilities, and plans terminate at political boundaries, and suffer from ineffective and inadequate controls within the boundaries. Consequently, various developments are uncontrolled, with decisions being made "someplace" that affect the whole community. In Montana, for example, the only real requirement for a building permit is that there be a proper septic tank approved by the state board of health. Nationwide, little real power is available to planning agencies to refuse or regulate subdivisions; governmental approval is automatically assured, in most cases, including what the subdivision developer wants in the form of zoning.[65]

In this sense, many planning agencies are basically concerned with zoning, excluding important environmental and public considerations in favor of vested interests. Yet, effective zoning, geared to regional and ecological concerns, can be a powerful tool for ensuring quality of life and environment. In discussing zoning in urban land utilization, Dreyfus notes: "Land use zoning has traditionally been a responsibility of local government, and it is not surprising that no federal program is established with zoning as an objective. Increasingly, however, zoning as a tool of land use planning is being discussed as a primary means for environmental control. Indirect federal action has been suggested regarding flood plain zoning and coastal zone management. The zoning activity therefore appears to be a valid activity and a possible indication of a need for new programs."[66] In many other nations, zoning is a definite and accepted policy and activity of various levels of government, particularly in densely populated countries where strong enforcement as well as compensation for economic loss may be involved. For example, in England, open and green space and rural areas, as well as agricultural areas, are zoned and protected to prevent encroachment by urban sprawls and other developments.

Yet in the United States, little zoning action of this nature is undertaken, and the result is removal and deterioration of open space and agricultural lands surrounding urban areas. The CEQ admonishes: "The traditional local zoning system is ill suited to protect broader regional, state, and national values. Local governments have a limited perspective on and little incentive to protect scenic or ecologically vital areas located partially or even entirely within their borders. Economic pressures often spur development to the detriment of the environment because of local government dependence on property taxes."[67]

Basically, zoning is police power to protect the welfare of the general public; it is delegated by the state to local governmental units within its boundaries, but zoning is subject to easy change. Zoning implies limitations on property rights relative to the public interest involved. Yet the Advisory Commission on Intergovernmental Relations observes that much of zoning is based on fiscal considerations and competition. With an orientation toward keeping governmental costs to a minimum, or protecting large lots of homes, this zoning approach is self defeating. It reinforces socioeconomic disparities, since only high-income families can purchase homes in protected areas. Also, among other environmental problems, it forces a continual sprawl of developments into surrounding areas and elimination of open land. Consequently, the Advisory Commission on Intergovernmental Relations recommends that states restrict zoning authority in metropolitan areas to larger municipalities and to county government, and that they require greater diversity in home price ranges to guard the public interest.[68] With larger areawide zoning arrangements and authority, including state and regional programs, there appear to be better possibilities for applying perspectives beyond local fiscal and subdivision interests.

The CEQ notes that present zoning is not very successful in preserving open space or in channeling growth and development, let alone in implementing sound land-use plans. When the pressure of development and speculation is on, zoning changes, through amendments and variances, weaken, reduce, or destroy its effectiveness. Further, there is a "relationship" between land developers and members of zoning boards.[69] In the previously mentioned Rimrock development in Billings, Montana, for example, two land developers of the Rimrock also held official public positions related to zoning. *Eminent domain,* which gives the government the right (with just compensation and for public benefit) to acquire land, also presents great potential for environmental quality. Unfortunately, it has been used mainly to acquire property for urban renewal and highway-construction projects. The CEQ notes that eminent domain has had relatively little use for public benefits pertaining to the environment or for controlling urban sprawl. This is particularly true of local governments that fail to acquire land for proper development or to set aside open space on a preventive basis before high land prices occur. Because of financial and political pressures, local governments usually fail to act, and the result is loss of scenic areas, public access to water, and other features of environmental quality.[70]

It is obvious that greater perspective and sensitivity, and more value emphasis on environmental quality are needed in metropolitan and regional planning. And some of this should come from the planners themselves. McHarg notes: "Each year I confront a new generation of graduate students, secure in their excellence, incipient or confirmed professionals in one or another of the planning or design fields. My most important objectives in this first encounter are to challenge professional myopia, exclusively man-centered views, to initiate consideration of basic values and to focus particularly on the place of nature in man's world—the place of man in nature."[71]

Conversely, Swan considers that the new type of urban professional should combine a planning and social-work perspective on problems and needs with an ability to integrate them along conceptual lines.[72] Nevertheless, the important concept is that broader orientations toward the environment and quality of life are needed in the planning process and from planners. And these orientations require a departure from uncontrolled sprawl, economic development interests, and other forces that have dominated the scene, leading to environmental inequality, deterioration, and destruction.

Recognizing that urban policy and planning with its interrelated regional and environmental problems can no longer go the way of the uncontrolled and destructive, Sen. Henry Jackson (Democrat, Washington) has proposed legislation for a National Land Use Policy that will encompass some urban and environmental controls. Excerpts from this legislation (*S. 992*) include:

> To establish a national land use policy; to authorize the Secretary of the Interior to make grants to encourage and assist the states to prepare and implement land use programs for the protection of areas of critical environmental concern and the control and direction of growth and development of more than local significance; and for other purposes.

> Sec. 101(a) The Congress hereby finds and declares that decisions about the use of land significantly influence the quality of the environment, and that present state and local institutional arrangements for planning and regulating land use of more than local impact are inadequate, with the result

> (1) that important ecological, cultural, historic, and aesthetic values in areas of critical environmental concern which are essential to the well-being of all citizens are being irretrievably damaged or lost.

> (2) that coastal zones and estuaries, flood plains, shorelands, and other lands near or under major bodies or courses of water which possess special natural and scenic characteristics are being damaged by ill-planned development that threatens these values.

> (3) that key facilities such as major airports, highway interchanges, and recreational facilities are inducing disorderly development and urbanization of more than local impact;

> (4) that the implementation of standards for the control of air, water, noise, and other pollution is impeded;[74]

> (5) that the selection and development of sites for essential private development of regional benefit has been delayed or prevented.

> (6) that the usefulness of federal or federally assisted projects and the administration of federal programs is impaired.

> (7) that large-scale development often creates a significant adverse impact upon the environment.

> (b) The Congress further finds and declares that there is a national interest in encouraging the states to exercise their full authority over planning and regulation of non-federal lands by assisting the states, in cooperation with local governments, in developing land use programs including unified authorities, policies, criteria, standards and methods, and processes for dealing with land use decisions of more than local significance.[75]

The proposed legislation along with general public and governmental concern may signify important changes in urban policy relative to the environment. It is obvious that more controls will have to be exerted over private spheres and economic developments that have politically dominated local governmental decisions and planning. Further, many

145

of the controls would have to center in state government as the basic holder of police and public powers, regardless of past delegations of these powers to local government. The pattern of possible future megalopolises that may involve several states (e.g., Boston to Washington, D.C., and other regional areas) certainly suggests the need for strong governmental intervention to prevent this pattern, which involves the artificial accumulation and concentration of severe social problems (crime, depersonalization, etc.) as well as environmental problems. Moreover, the megalopolis pattern points toward unwarranted, artificial, and unreasonable demands on energy sources and other resources. Yet, under present patterns of urban policy, the energy crisis, water pollution, inadequate transportation, and social problems are emerging with environmental impacts that destroy or diminish the quality of life on a local, regional, and national scale. Consequently, the environmental public interest points toward strong changes, innovations, and controls in urban regional policy.

REFERENCES

1. John Friedman and John Miller, "The Urban Field," *Journal of the American Institute of Planners* 31, no. 4 (Nov. 1965) pp. 312–320.
2. Advisory Commission on Intergovernmental Relations, *Urban America and the Federal System* (Washington, D.C.: U.S. Gov't Printing Office, 1969) p. 67.
3. Walter Scheiber, "Regionalism: Its Implications for the Urban Manager," *Public Administration Review* 31, no. 1 (Jan.-Feb. 1971) p. 43.
4. *Ibid.*, pp. 45–46.
5. Melvin M. Webber, "The Urban Place and the Nonplace Urban Realm," in *Explorations into Urban Structure*, ed. Melvin M. Webber (Philadelphia: The University of Pennsylvania Press, 1964).
6. John Friedman, "The Future of Comprehensive Urban Planning: A Critique," *Public Administration Review* 31, no. 3 (May-June 1971) p. 319.
7. Melvin G. Marcus and Thomas R. Detwyler, "Urbanization and Environment in Perspective," in *Urbanization and Environment*, eds. Thomas R. Detwyler and Melvin G. Marcus (Belmont, Calif.: Wadsworth, 1972) p. 10.
8. James Swan, "Urban Environment," in *Recycle this Book!*, eds. J. David Allan and Arthur J. Hanson (Belmont, Calif.: Wadsworth, 1972) p. 59.
9. *Time*, August 21, 1972, p. 15.
10. Phillip W. Foster, *Programmed Learning Aid for Introduction to Environmental Sciences* (Homewood, Ill.: Richard D. Irwin, 1972) p. 95.
11. Dennis C. McElrath, "Public Response to Environmental Problems," in *Political Dynamics of Environmental Control*, ed. Lynton K. Caldwell (Bloomington, Ind.: Institute of Public Administration, 1967) p. 3.
12. *Ibid.*, pp. 1–8.
13. Council on Environmental Quality, *Environmental Quality: The Second Annual Report* (Washington, D.C.: U.S. Gov't Printing Office, 1971) p. 191.
14. Advisory Commission on Intergovernmental Relations, *The New Grass Roots Government, Decentralization and Citizen Participation in Urban Areas* (Washington, D.C.: Advisory Commission on Intergovernmental Relations, 1972) p. 21.
15. The President's Council on Recreation and Natural Beauty, "The Urban Crisis," in *The Politics of Neglect: The Environmental Crisis*, eds. Roy L. Meek and John A. Straayer (Boston: Houghton Mifflin, 1971) p. 82.

16. Advisory Commission on Intergovernmental Relations, *Urban America and the Federal System* (Washington, D.C.: U.S. Gov't Printing Office, 1969) p. 66.
17. *Ibid.,* pp. 66–67.
18. Council on Environmental Quality, *Environmental Quality: The Second Annual Report* (Washington, D.C.: U.S. Gov't Printing Office, 1971) p. 189.
19. *Ibid.,* p. 190.
20. *Ibid.,* p. 191.
21. Environmental Health Service, *Environmental Health Problems* (Washington, D.C.: U.S. Gov't Printing Office, n.d.) p. 20.
22. Stewart Marquis, "Ecosystems, Societies, and Cities," in *The Politics of Neglect: The Environmental Crisis,* eds. Roy L. Meek and John A. Straayer (Boston: Houghton Mifflin, 1971) pp. 122–128.
23. *Ibid.,* p. 128.
24. *Ibid.,* pp. 130–131.
25. *Ibid.,* p. 130.
26. Council on Environmental Quality, *Environmental Quality: The Second Annual Report* (Washington, D.C.: U.S. Gov't Printing Office, 1971) p. 191.
27. *Ibid.,* p. 204.
28. *Ibid.,* p. 207.
29. *Ibid.,* pp. 191–192.
30. *Ibid.,* p. 196.
31. *Ibid.,* pp. 196–197.
32. *Ibid.,* pp. 197–200.
33. *Ibid.,* pp. 200–201.
34. *Ibid.,* pp. 202–203.
35. Paul R. Ehrlich and Anne H. Ehrlich, *Population, Resources, and Environment* (San Francisco: Freeman, 1970) pp. 141–143.
36. The President's Council on Recreation and Natural Beauty, *From Sea to Shining Sea, A Report on the American Environment—Our Natural Heritage* (Washington, D.C.: U.S. Gov't Printing Office, 1968) p. 104.
37. Council on Environmental Quality, *Environmental Quality: The First Annual Report* (Washington, D.C.: U.S. Gov't Printing Office, 1970) p. 171.
38. Max Ways, "Urban Sprawl: A Smathering of People," in *People, Their Needs, Environment, Ecology,* ed. Bruce Wallace (Englewood Cliffs, N.J.: Prentice-Hall, 1972) p. 177.
39. Council on Environmental Quality, *Environmental Quality: The First Annual Report* (Washington, D.C.: U.S. Gov't Printing Office, 1970) pp. 170–171.
40. *Ibid.,* p. 170.
41. *Ibid.,* p. 172.
42. *Ibid.,* p. 172.
43. *Ibid.,* pp. 171–172.
44. Ian L. McHarg, *Design With Nature* (Garden City, New York: Doubleday/Natural History Press, 1971) pp. 80–85.
45. Max Ways, "Urban Sprawl: A Smathering of People," in *People, Their Needs, Environment, Ecology,* ed. Bruce Wallace (Englewood Cliffs, N.J.: Prentice-Hall, 1972) pp. 178–179.
46. Ian L. McHarg, *Design with Nature* (Garden City, New York: Doubleday/Natural History Press, 1971) pp. 81–82.
47. *Time Magazine,* August 14, 1972, p. 40.
48. Council on Environmental Quality, *Environmental Quality: The First Annual Report* (Washington, D.C.: U.S. Gov't Printing Office, 1970) p. 172.
49. Ian L. McHarg, *Design with Nature* (Garden City, New York: Doubleday/Natural History Press, 1971) pp. 81–87.
50. Council on Environmental Quality, *Environmental Quality: The First Annual Report* (Washington, D.C.: U.S. Gov't Printing Office, 1970) p. 173.

51. Ian L. McHarg, *Design with Nature* (Garden City, New York: Doubleday/Natural History Press, 1971) pp. 1–197.
52. Walter Isard, "Some Notes on the Linkage of the Ecologic and Economic Systems." (Manuscript, Department of Landscape Architecture, Harvard University, March 27, 1969, and paper presented at the Budapest Conference, Regional Science Association, August, 1968) p. 1.
53. Hugh L. LeBlanc and D. Trudeau Allensworth, *The Politics of State and Urban Communities* (New York: Harper & Row, 1971) p. 392.
54. *Ibid.*, p. 393.
55. Ian L. McHarg, *Design with Nature* (Garden City, New York: Doubleday/Natural History Press, 1971) p. 104.
56. *Ibid.*, p. 105.
57. *Ibid.*, pp. 104–105.
58. Council on Environmental Quality, *Environmental Quality: The First Annual Report* (Washington, D.C.: U.S. Gov't Printing Office, 1970) p. 188.
59. *Ibid.*, pp. 184–185.
60. *Ibid.*, p. 185.
61. Advisory Commission on Intergovernmental Relations, *Urban America and the Federal System* (Washington, D.C.: U.S. Gov't Printing Office, 1969) p. 61.
62. Group interview with planners: John O'Donnell, urban planner, and Clyde E. Smutz, financial and management officer of the Community Planning and Management Division, U.S. Department of Housing and Urban Development, Region VIII, Denver, Colorado; and Mike McCallum, planning director, and Ved Varma, assistant planning director, of the Billings–Yellowstone City–County Planning Board at Billings, Montana on August 28, 1972.
63. *Ibid.*
64. Advisory Commission on Intergovernmental Relations, *Urban America and the Federal System* (Washington, D.C.: U.S. Gov't Printing Office, 1969) p. 61.
65. Group interview with planners: John O'Donnell, urban planner, and Clyde E. Smutz, financial and management officer of the Community Planning and Management Division, U.S. Department of Housing and Urban Development, Region VIII, Denver, Colorado; and Mike McCallum, planning director, and Ved Varma, assistant planning director, of the Billings–Yellowstone City–County Planning Board at Billings, Montana on August 28, 1972.
66. U.S., Congress, Senate, Committee on Interior and Insular Affairs *A Definition of the Scope of Environmental Management,* by Daniel A. Dreyfus (Washington, D.C.: U.S. Gov't Printing Office, 1970) p. 15.
67. Council on Environmental Quality, *Environmental Quality: Second Annual Report* (Washington, D.C.: U.S. Gov't Printing Office, 1971) p. 61.
68. Advisory Commission on Intergovernmental Relations, *Urban America and the Federal System* (Washington, D.C.: U.S. Gov't Printing Office, 1969) pp. 68–69.
69. Council on Environmental Quality, *Environmental Quality: First Annual Report* (Washington, D.C.: U.S. Gov't Printing Office, 1970) p. 185.
70. *Ibid.*, p. 187.
71. Ian L. McHarg, *Design with Nature* (Garden City, New York: Doubleday/Natural History Press, 1971) p. 43.
72. James Swan, "Urban Environment," in *Recycle this Book!,* eds. J. David Allan and Arthur J. Hanson (Belmont, Calif.: Wadsworth, 1972) pp. 61–62.
73. U.S., Congress, Senate, Committee on Interior and Insular Affairs, *National Land Use Policy* (Washington, D.C.: U.S. Gov't Printing Office, 1972) p. 191.
74. *Ibid.*, p. 192.
75. *Ibid.*, p. 193.

Chapter 9

INTERDISCIPLINARY ENVIRONMENTAL ADMINISTRATION

GENERAL AND SYSTEMS PLANNING

The National Environmental Policy Act of 1969 requires that all agencies of the federal government shall "utilize a systematic, interdisciplinary approach which will insure the integrated use of the natural and social sciences and the environmental design arts in planning and in decision-making which may have an impact on man's environment."[1] While there is legal recognition of the need for an interdisciplinary approach to environmental administration, little *real* attention has been given to its theory and application, particularly for the social sciences. Daniel Dreyfus indicates that only recently has the comprehensive nature of environmental management been recognized in governmental activities, which have taken the form of problem-oriented, single-purpose programs. He also notes that no recognized discipline exists that is concerned with environmental science or management in a comprehensive sense. Although many diverse disciplines (e.g., biology, engineering, ecology, and architecture) consider environmental study and control to be within their purview, Dreyfus observes that they concentrate on only a part of the environmental system, and lack a comprehensive perspective.[2]

On the other hand, it is generally recognized that various disciplines from the social, natural, and applied arts and sciences can play an important role in environmental analysis as separate entities and on an interdisciplinary basis. For example, Martin Goldberger notes that a physicist can contribute: "a style of research, an openmindedness, and a confidence in man's ability to solve problems. These attributes are the result of training and successful research in physics. A physicist is not frightened by complexity; he knows how to isolate parts of a problem and he knows how to utilize computers instead of worshiping them."[3] Relative to this, Goldberger sees new roles for physicists in the environment in: (1) direct research and development (instrumentation), (2) interdisciplinary environmental education, and (3) participation in interdisciplinary teamwork and projects (e.g., theoretical analysis, models, phenomenological descriptions, etc.).[4]

Given the applicability of various disciplines, Eugene Odum states that a true interdisciplinary approach toward the environment requires a theoretical framework and basic principles for agreement among the several individuals and disciplines. Otherwise, he notes: "Whenever 'unstructured' groups try to make decisions so much time is required in communication and expression of conflicting viewpoints that the actual decisions end up being made in terms of short-term economics as usual! Without some kind of principle as a guide for organizing the input of specialists, action tends to be only that which compromises or alleviates the immediate crisis."[5] Thus, a major consideration for interdisciplinary environmental administration involves formulation of a common frame of ecological reference. On this basis, long-range, objective principles can then be evolved and implemented through interdisciplinary cooperation and coordination. In part, these principles could deal with adding dimensions of environmental quality, enhancing intangibles, and preventing future destruction of the environment.

Hopeman and Wilemon consider several general advantages of the interdisciplinary approach.

1. *Cross-fertilization of ideas.* Personal interaction among members of various disciplines encourages the synthesis and development of ideas and concepts; the resulting "synergistic effect" encourages "new knowledge," particularly in the face of perplexing conceptual problems.

2. *Synthesis of microsopic and macrosopic viewpoints.* Much of problem solving depends on understanding the cogent dimensions of a problem; this, in turn, depends upon an understanding and synthesis of the micro and macro aspects of a given problem and its potential resolution, e.g., a blend of the psychologist's concern for the individual and the sociologist's concern for the group or community.

3. *Personal development.* Interdisciplinary approaches are not natural processes, and so involve a learning process and a different working posture; this contributes to the participant's professional development and perspective.

4. *Complexity of research problems.* Many of the problems encountered in an interdisciplinary approach are too complex for the individual researcher or single discipline, particularly when broad policy issues are involved. The limitations of scope inherent in a single discipline are diminished somewhat through the combination of various, appropriate disciplines.

In summing up, the authors consider the cooperative interdisciplinary approach as a vehicle for solving complex problems, which require a variety of specialized inputs, and as a mechanism for breaking down organizational barriers.[6]

On the other hand, there are various problems confronting the individual disciplines participating in an interdisciplinary approach. Commitments and reward systems are built into "tradition-bound" professions, and interdisciplinary efforts are often resisted. Further complications arise in the form of dogmas and vested interests imposed on a given specialization within the context of an agency's policy indoctrination, e.g., the role of a wildlife manager with the Bureau of Sport Fisheries and Wildlife (BSFW) as contrasted with that of a wildlife manager with a given state game and fish department. Within a discipline or agency, efforts are also made to carve out actual and symbolic territories, with aggressive and defensive behavior toward boundaries; unnecessary conflicts and futile overlapping are among the human and professional interferences with an interdisciplinary environmental approach. In this sense, a politically dominant discipline or agency (by virtue of funds, personnel, clientele, or hierarchial position) may carve out a territory to the serious detriment of other disciplines and of a comprehensive environmental approach.[7]

Important factors in interdisciplinary efforts are the management, administration, and leadership of the individuals and disciplines involved. Eugene Drucker considers that frequent contact among interdisciplinary participants is critical, and observes, "An interdisciplinary team is very much like an oil–water mixture. Left undisturbed, the mixture will stratify."[8] Campbell points out that the present state of interdisciplinary studies is "ethnocentric;" disciplines tend to cluster around similar disciplines with little involvement outside their clusters. Consequently, he observes, "gaps" exist between these clusters and he recommends that training be undertaken to achieve an orientation toward "interdisciplinary specialties."[9] Administrative problems of interdisciplinary efforts also involve timing, leadership, and personalities, as well as the effective development and implementation of conclusions, and alternative solutions. Political considerations and involvements must be realistically considered. It is obvious that a great difference exists between real and effective utilization of the interdisciplinary approach for planning and problem solving and its use as a procedure to justify or manipulate under the influence of vested interests.

An interdisciplinary approach involves the concept of systems planning. Churchman considers that all systems approaches to planning have limitations. He identifies some of the major systems types as: (1) teleological, with emphasis on the client and performance measurement; (2) structural, concerning environmental components and boundaries, with emphasis on analysis of interrelations (e.g., benefit–cost analysis); (3) dynamic, involving adaptive systems and cybernetics, with emphasis on deteriorating, stabilizing, or progressing; and (4) self-reflective or psychoanalytical, with emphasis on advisory committees and organizational analysis. While a given systems approach may enlarge the overall perspective and encourage critical questions, Churchman believes that too much reliance upon such approaches is unsound, and that they will not provide solutions. He indicates that some limitations involve failures of: (1) enlarging the system to encompass the entire decision-making process (not legal or political boundaries, but decision making should be the orientation); (2) lack of due regard for values (including values of ambiguity and uncertainty); (3) inadequate assignment of quantitative weights or measures, particularly in qualitative and intangible areas; (4) categorization of and lack of consideration for the individual decision maker; and (5) separation of management and research.[10]

While the problems and limitations of systems approaches are recognized, much of modern planning supposedly operates under this orientation. Planning is little more than an intelligent look into the future; the soundness of this outlook from an environmental point of view is dependent upon the comprehensiveness and perspective of a given system and approach. When important variables and values are excluded, planning may have negative effects for environmental administration. Planning implies change and determination of goals in terms of degree of environmental impact; further, planning has economic and physical bases with associated implications for specific actions.

A major consideration in the planning process involves assumptions and priorities that determine the types of input and output. Too often, real assumptions and priorities (as contrasted to artificial or public relations ones) are concerned with expedient, short-term, vested interests, and "assumed" needs that relate to a given agency and its clientele. Under such an orientation, environmental parameters, and long-term ecological considerations encounter serious conflicts and are treated as platitudes in the planning process. To be effective environmental planning requires an interdisciplinary focus on ecology as a basic assumption and priority, and an "open-system" approach to value considerations.

In this sense, much of governmental planning is done on a closed-system basis. Besides the total exclusion of or token regard for public participation, the orientation is toward political, economic, and technological priorities. Consequently, an actual comprehensive, interdisciplinary approach based on environmental considerations and values would cause serious changes and conflicts in governmental planning. Much of this would hinge upon the input of valid noneconomic environmental values into the planning system, from which they have been largely excluded in the past. Besides the political and economic resistance to such interdisciplinary considerations, Lynton Caldwell notes that a technological society inherently resists synthesis required in interdisciplinary planning and policy making. He notes the tendency for techniques to displace other factors in decision making. Caldwell cautions government officials to avoid accepting technical feasibility as a governing criterion, and recommends that they assert the primacy of social goals.[11]

Technique can also have negative effects in limiting the perspective of an interdisciplinary approach by the deemphasis or exclusion of disciplines. Daniel Slate considers technique to be an ideology that transcends and drives human technical activity. He identifies two characteristics of technique: *rationality*—a process, regardless of application, that tends to bring systematization (order) to bear on all that is spontaneous, judgmental, or intuitive; and *artificiality*—wherein man-devised technology becomes an imperative over nature with nature being replaced or severely modified.[12] The great majority of environmental personnel have technoscientific backgrounds, and hence may have a propensity toward technique.

There may thus be a tendency to overemphasize the technical disciplines (e.g., engineering, hydrology, forestry) over the nontechnical (e.g., social sciences, philosophy), and to require quantitative and technical orientations from the latter. But the end result may be a technique ideology that excludes important environmental and social considerations. Rationality, as a characteristic of the technique ideology, implies objectivity and freedom from values. Yet, questions might be raised on what is completely objective and what subjective in value and ethical interpretations. Views and judgments usually permeate technoscientific, statistical, and quantitative data. That is, they affect the selection of problems as well as the inferences, conclusions, and recommendations that result. Data of this nature can be manipulated to conform to a political bias. A technique ideology, moreover, has its own set of values in an interdisciplinary setting which may not be compatible with environmental values.

SOCIAL SCIENCES APPROACH*

In a value-oriented interdisciplinary environmental approach, the social sciences could make an important contribution.[13] Although technoscientific disciplines relating to environmental resources have attained a relatively "high" level by comparison, present environmental considerations call for greater emphasis on social sciences. Environmental administrators usually recognize that the majority of their problems involve people and values, and fall more in the realm of social sciences than into a given technoscientific discipline. With an ecological orientation, the social sciences could contribute scope and perspective to the interdisciplinary analysis of human problems and values relating to the environment. Technoscientific approaches to environmental problems (including computer applications) appear to be dominating environmental studies and programs. Further, many of these approaches actually involve value determinations, essentially made in a vacuum, as well as the quest for technoscientific solutions. Many environmental agencies would thus do well to establish social science divisions, staffed with professionally trained personnel whose main functions would be to analyze human values, and to coordinate with other special divisions.

Contributions to interdisciplinary environmental administration could also involve identification, articulation, and analysis of conflicting values for decision making, problem solving, and planning for the environment; in other words, the actual ends of society would be correlated with the ends of environmental administration. The social sciences are often bypassed and truly comprehensive interdisciplinary approaches are seldom utilized. Value decisions, in actuality, are usually made by technoscientific administrators, without social science input, and consequently are frequently limited to technique ideologies and platitudes. This result can be largely attributed to failure of the social sciences to respond to environmental needs. Eugene Odum, for example, notes: "Sociologists, I feel, have been too timid in suggesting goals for society. Until recently they have been content to just study situations and try to find out what went wrong after it's all over. We need also some applied human ecology that prevents malfunctions. There has to be some coercion in the management of people, but this coercion needs to be mutually agreed upon. And regulation has to be based on an objective principle to be acceptable to society in the long run."[14]

* Much of the material in this section is an extension and elaboration of material that appeared in *Bioscience* 20, no. 1 (January 1, 1970) pp. 11–16.

Given the need to involve social scientists in interdisciplinary environmental administration, there are relatively small numbers of them who are either qualified or interested.
With growing awareness of environmental problems, however, it would appear that the
numbers should increase rapidly. Many institutions of higher learning are now establishing
interdisciplinary social science–environmental programs. There is, nevertheless, some
reluctance among social scientists to recognize environmental areas as "respectable" fields
of study. The territories staked out by various disciplines, their complex jargons, traditions respecting appropriate areas of study, and specialized reward systems serve to
discourage interdisciplinary environmental approaches. Although many technoscientific
disciplines, which are better established in environmental areas, will pay lip service to the
idea of involving the social sciences, it is usually assumed that social sciences are not
scientific or objective. As a consequence, approaches that are not of a quantitative or
statistical nature are excluded. This problem also exists within the social sciences, and
may result in the exclusion of disciplines that could make definite contributions in terms
of analytical dimensions and perspectives.

The skills and insights of the nontechnical social sciences could contribute to environmental administration, and to achieving a thorough consideration of the entire environmental situation. A comprehensive interdisciplinary approach requires a common
frame of reference with an ecological orientation; the formulation and implementation of
operating principles and objectives can ensure adequate utilization of appropriate disciplines in meeting specific problems. Possible interdisciplinary arrangements include: (a) a
team of social scientists, technoscientific specialists, and experts from other disciplines
working together throughout the study process, to combine results and conclusions; and
(b) a social scientist with supporting training in secondary fields as well as in his major
discipline, or with familiarity with working concepts from other fields which could be
interwoven with technoscientific and other disciplines.

The following treatment of social science disciplines explores the possibilities of their
contributions by means of simple, working concepts of disciplines as tools for increasing
the scope and depth of value analysis in an interdisciplinary approach to the environment.
Various theoretical approaches are briefly examined for each discipline, including a
one-word conceptual framework. In addition to social science disciplines, animal behavior
and ecology are included as applicable in socioenvironmental synthesis (fig. 9.1).

Anthropology (culture). Although cultural anthropology is usually associated with
primitive societies, the central concepts can obviously be applied to complex modern
societies. Anthropological research into urban problems is on the increase. New York
State psychiatric hospitals, for example, now employ anthropologists to analyze modern
cultural problems associated with mental disease. It is quite obvious that culture, with its
institutions and attitudes, influences administration of the total environment. A thorough
administrative approach to the environment would have to encompass values, myths,
attitudes, institutional influences, and other cultural factors pertaining to man's relationship to his environment. The main contribution of a cultural approach would be toward
understanding an attitude of mind as a product of learned and institutional influences.

154

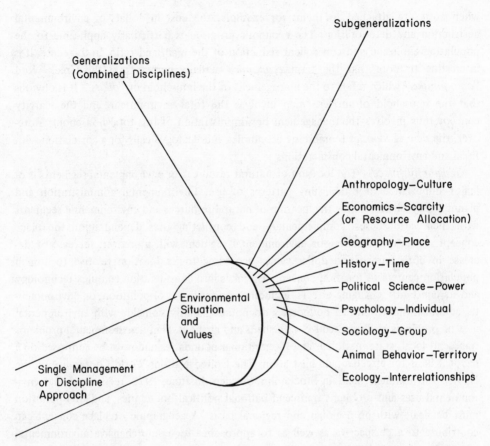

Figure 9.1. Interdisciplinary social science approach to environmental management. (From Henning, D. H. *Bioscience* 20:12, 1970.)

Thus, people and institutions could be perceived in terms of their own environmental values.

Economics (scarcity). The demand for and supply of natural resources and environmental segments by present and future generations automatically focus on their scarcity. Moreover, the limiting factor in many environmental quality measures is financing. For example, with sufficient funding the majority of polluted streams could eventually become good trout streams. Allocations of various natural resources, including those for future generations, are constantly influenced by the various economic interests and forces that compete for scarce resources. Many of the problems associated with pollution control measures undertaken by industry (as well as with identification of the social costs involved) are economic. The scarcity concept automatically affects the priority of values when costs are attached to them; for example, the cost in dollars of environmental destruction and deterioration. The economic criterion is particularly applicable to the population explosion and consequent reduction of the man/land ratio. In this sense, it is interesting to note that the term *economics* actually comes from the Greek word *"oikonomike"* which refers to the management of the household or *"oikos."* It is obvious that the household of modern man involves the total environment, and the scarcity concept thus involves the management or administration of this total household. Moreover, the *new economics* (combining economics and ecology) calls for a correlation with fiscal and environmental considerations.

Geography (place). The location of natural resources or environmental segments is of major importance in establishing patterns of use. Environmental administration and planning rely on correlating the location of natural resources and environmental segments with their various uses; complementary and conflicting uses depend upon the place concept. A natural resource or environmental segment will, moreover, increase or decrease in both human and dollar values according to its location relative to human population centers. A location concept also takes into consideration complex technology and its constantly changing effects, including various forms of pollution, on environmental administration. Political boundaries do not necessarily coincide with environmental uses or problems as illustrated by watersheds and airsheds. Many environmental problems transcend local, state, national, and international boundaries and must be addressed on a regional basis for effective administration. The United Nations World Conference on the Human Environment, held in Stockholm, Sweden, in June, 1972, recognized that environmental uses and problems transcend national political boundaries, and that pollution must be dealt with on a global and regional basis. A geographic or place concept can contribute to a perspective as well as to approaches for comprehensive environmental administration and planning.

History (time). A central concept of time is valuable in identifying past environmental patterns and values and myths associated with these patterns. With the impact of changing technology, populations, and environmental problems, outdated assumptions, values, and myths may do actual harm to environmental administration. Various agricultural agencies, for example, still operate on the myth of the family-sized farm, and the Bureau of Land Management (BLM) continues to emphasize grazing service, with little attention to recreation and environmental quality considerations in many cases. Historical analysis could place values and assumptions within a time perspective. Also, many environmental agencies' programs are managed on a public welfare basis, with emphasis on benefits for "underdeveloped" communities (e.g., a dying lumbering or mining town). In many cases, an historical analysis would actually reveal that these underdeveloped areas have had histories of over-development, and that little potential remains for specific natural resource or environmental development.

Political science (power). The concept of power provides a central focus for the

156

decision-making process in environmental administration. In the final analysis, all decisions on natural resources and environmental segments, regardless of technoscientific and other factors, are political, involving a power struggle or a conflict of competing interests and values. A human interaction process in the political arena precedes governmental decisions affecting the environment. Through the power concept, individual and group values associated with a given environmental situation could be identified and analyzed. Such analysis would include the informal dimensions of government and pressure group interaction in brokerage politics.

Psychology. Although the group is emphasized in the social sciences, there is still recognition that an individual personality committed to a given value system can have a strong influence on various environmental decisions. An analysis of key individuals in decision making, particularly through in-depth interviews, could identify values and forces behind groups in socioenvironmental situations. Norman Wengert noted that the most significant factor in the conservation movement was the leadership of individuals. Government scientists such as Gifford Pinchot, John Wesley Powell, and others were dominant forces in the formulation of public policy on conservation.[15] An intensive study of a public hunting controversy to control overpopulation in Rocky Mountain National Park revealed one individual, Harry Woodward, director of the Colorado Game and Fish Department, to be a dominant influence.[16]

Thus, the concept of the individual and his personality could provide a framework for analysis of the complex decision making and the value vs. power conflict characteristic of environmental affairs. Persistent individuals, dedicated to particular internalized values, usually form the nucleus of groups (governmental and private) and are instrumental in making decisions. An individual and his value framework may contribute to serious conflict with negative results or may offer useful input for solution of particular problems at a given time. Consequently, a systematic approach to the mental processes of a given personality, and to interaction with groups in environmental situations, could contribute to an understanding of the actual values involved. In the final analysis, all governmental decisions concerning the environment are made by individuals, based on each individual's mental picture and value system.

Sociology. The conceptual analysis of the group provides a focal point for understanding human interaction relating to environmental problems. Environmental agencies and pressure groups are basically organizations in a pluralistic society that revolve around specific value groups and interests. The group processes of organizational interaction, and of *ad hoc* problem-centered groups, can be identified under the group concept in formal and informal spheres of operation. The structural concept of groups also provides some basis for functional analysis of role frameworks. The environmental process hinges to a great extent on professionalism and specialization. Groups and individuals associated with a particular profession sometimes assume a *halo role* (a symbolic role of objectivity and esteem) and special political status, while actually making value judgments that are

157

beyond the competency or responsibility of that profession. Erving Goffman, in *The Presentation of Self in Everyday Life,* indicates that an individual in a group setting plays the role of an actor to maintain his status and interests; he presents various "masks" or images to the group. Goffman further notes that much of this occurs informally through expressions that an individual "gives" and "gives off."[17] Through this process, an environmental administrator or specialist, by virtue of his professional or specialized role, may be able to assert a personal opinion or value in a group situation and use his role status or image to avert or discourage questioning or challenging of his judgments.

Animal behavior. In Lorenz's *On Aggression,* Ardrey's *African Genesis,* and Morris's *The Naked Ape,* the concept of territory and its implications as it applies to man are considered. When man seeks to study and understand man through the social sciences, certain realistic factors seem to be overlooked. Yet it is these very factors that might contribute to a better understanding. But this requires an objective perspective of "man the animal" to be realistically incorporated into the social sciences and environmental administration. A central concept of animal behavior, as noted by the authors named above, is territory, a compulsion that has motivated *Homo sapiens* and other animals since their evolutionary beginnings. Although in modern man the territorial compulsion may include psychological, economic, and other symbolic elements in addition to spatial boundaries, he still operates under the strong influence exerted by his basic animal nature.

Applying the concept of territory to environmental administration, various clientele groups, agencies, and individuals make territorial claims on public lands and other environmental segments. However, these territorial claims may not be compatible with environmental quality considerations and may create serious conflicts for effective planning. The territorial imperative is a realistic concept affecting various segments of human populations and organizations in terms of environmental administration. It is obvious that environmental agencies are not immune from this concept, as witnessed by the rivalry, conflict, and competition among various agencies and administrators in defense of their territories. Leopold believes that man should abandon this possessiveness and ownership in favor of a *land ethic.* The crux of this ethic is that man is only one of the many living things utilizing the environment. Thus, the land ethic implies that man has a responsibility toward the land and its living forms because of his superior intelligence and his ability to manipulate the land and influence it negatively.[18]

Ecology (interrelations). The ecological approach, i.e., a central concept of interrelations with the environment, provides a theme for environmental administration. The technology of modern man, however, has placed him in a highly dynamic and manipulative role relative to the environment, with numerous negative effects ranging from air pollution to soil erosion. Yet, little real attention has been paid to man's environmental interrelationships and responsibilities in this process until a crisis has emerged.

Such interrelationships are essential to the environmental concept, particularly in operations of environmental agencies and administrators. With pressures from clientele groups and limitations on agency policy based on security and expansion, a comprehensive environmental orientation is seldom attained, except through lip service, among the federal, state, and local agencies involved in environmental affairs. Although natural resources and the environment are highly subject to administration, fragmented programs and limited policies, restricted by political pressures, may not add up to an all-encompassing approach to environmental survival and quality. An ecological approach, based on a total environment, could identify and analyze relationships essential to environmental administration.

Case study. A brief discussion of a case study on the Rocky Mountain National Park wildlife management policy will be presented to illustrate an application of the interdisciplinary concepts described above.[19] A policy vacuum was assumed because only minimal direction was available from the broad and idealistic policy statements of the National Park Service (NPS). The policy controversy hinged on the reduction of overpopulations of elk and deer. The overpopulation was primarily due to a limited winter range in and outside the park from 1930 to 1964. The major alternatives available were: (1) having the park rangers shoot the surplus elk and deer, that is, direct reduction; (2) allowing private citizens to hunt the surplus animals inside the park, that is, public hunting; and (3) having park rangers trap the surplus animals for distribution outside the park. A combination of alternatives (1) and (2) was finally selected after a great deal of controversy over public hunting.

Anthropology (culture) of the Colorado subculture indicated a strong inclination toward a frontier-exploitative outlook, with resistance to governmental control, and at the same time, a preservation-oriented attitude toward wildlife. An obvious conflict existed between the two elements. Public hunting was highly valued in the surrounding agricultural, ranching, and tourist areas. Paradoxically, some property owners objected to any reduction in animal numbers. Economics (scarcity) led to a high market value for the winter range outside the park, which absorbed a considerable number of the animals during sporadic migrations. Consequently, the animals were forced to remain in the park, leading to overpopulation and habitat destruction; those that did migrate outside the park were blamed for damage to the property of agricultural and ranching interests. Those interests, coupled with the Bureau of Reclamation's Colorado–Big Thompson Reclamation Project, made the winter range a limiting factor.

Geography (place) indicated that the central problem of the winter range was location, with conflicting uses of one area leading to various governmental and private claims based on political and real-property boundaries. History (time) indicated that values or myths from an earlier time period could affect sound wildlife management. Thus, early wildlife protection (based on large numbers) rather than later wildlife management (based on habitat) reflected a time–value lag that caused a policy conflict within the NPS as well as within public opinion. Political science (power) indicated a value conflict between wildlife protection and values associated with public hunting, with a consequent power struggle among groups seeking favorable governmental decisions. A large amount of the power struggle relating to public hunting actually occurred on the national level, as in several similar situations in national parks. However, the local park struggle involved strong efforts by the Colorado Game and Fish Department and satellite sportsmen's groups to promote public hunting in the park.

Psychology (individual) concepts suggested how the personality of the director of the Colorado Game and Fish Department was able to develop and maintain state pressure for public hunting in the park. The value frameworks of key individuals, through in-depth interviews, were important in determining the sources of conflict and solutions for the controversy. Sociology (group) revealed local and national interaction of pressure groups for and against public hunting. Socioeconomic studies of park visitors showed increasing support for modern wildlife management among the higher income and educational brackets. There was also considerable conflict on professional wildlife management roles, with individuals from various agencies claiming their individual opinions were professional ones, regardless of the alternatives or values supported.

Animal behavior (territory) indicated the territorial projections of agencies, groups, and involved individuals: (1) both the NPS and the Colorado Game and Fish Department claimed to own the wildlife in the park, with legal rights to manage it; and (2) many Colorado hunters claimed the right to hunt in the park rather than have the park rangers "slaughter" the animals. Numerous Colorado residents (many of whom insisted on wildlife protection with no reduction) felt that they had special territorial claims to the park as contrasted to people from other states. Ecology (interrelations) indicated a need for a regional environmental perspective in the analysis of a flow resource (elk and deer) in its interactions and conflicts in and outside the park. With six governmental agencies, numerous pressure groups (including governmental agencies as such), and many individuals involved in the controversy, a total framework was essential to developing an environmental approach ensuring quality of wildlife and habitat, rather than simply satisfying the specific objectives and vested interests of various agencies, pressure groups, and individuals.

Given that the disciplines described above could contribute subgeneralizations relevant in this controversial case, there remains a need for interwoven generalizations and conclusions based on an interdisciplinary approach. This would be achieved by merging the subgeneralizations or insights of the individual disciplines with an ecological overview. For example, in the case study, the major controversy hinged on a struggle for power to realize particular values through the selection of policy compatible with those values (although there was some resistance to reduction per se). Thus a value lag (time) and conflict (power) were exacerbated by limited winter range (scarcity; place), and public hunting pressures (culture). The director of the Game and Fish Department (individual) contributed to the cultural influence with pressure from sportsmen's organizations (groups) which was countered by other organizations. Value conflicts also involved agency discretion (territory) in the decision-making process, which was not correlated to an environmental or a regional approach to flow resources (interrelations).

The social sciences, particularly through interdisciplinary cooperation, can provide a conceptual framework for the identification and analysis of factors and values in environmental administration. A single discipline, or a combination of technoscientific management approaches, precludes comprehensive value and social considerations. Moreover, environmental administrators, both generalists and specialists, are actually involved in management of man's relationship to the environment. Consequently, a major concern of administrators is that of determining values for present and future generations in terms of the environmental public interest. There is a definite need for the capacity of interdisciplinary social sciences to identify and analyze underlying values in environmental decision making. This need is particularly great now, with the changing complexities of ecology, technology, economics, and the population explosion.

An interdisciplinary social science approach, with an ecological orientation, appears to be most practical when concepts from a variety of disciplines are synthesized and used to support a particular discipline. The merging of subgeneralizations from single disciplines could produce interwoven generalizations for in-depth analysis of social problems. An analogy might be made to blending or mixing several colors of paint with each color representing a different discipline. The blending should result in a multicolored mixture with each color or discipline contributing to the total result. The interdisciplinary social science approach is simply an attempt to produce a renaissance type of perspective having broad vision and scope, as well as depth, and focusing on the value spectrum. Present technoscientific specializations, disciplines, and management orientations are simply not getting at essential human values relating to the environment and especially to intangible quality considerations. In the final analysis, the human values and power competition concerned with the environment are social and political processes, and the predominant influence on the environment, which is highly subject to administration. It is obvious that the social sciences could make a contribution in this area.

ECOSYSTEM APPROACH

The *ecosystem* concept was defined by Tansley, in 1935, as the system resulting from interaction of all the living (biotic) and nonliving (abiotic) communities and factors in a given environment. Webster defines it as "a complex of ecological community and environment forming a functional whole in nature." The ecosystem concept can be applied to the examination of various levels of life; an essential criterion, however, is that everything must be included within natural or defined boundaries of an ecosystem, for example, a goldfish bowl or a prairie. The ecosystem is a basic unit of ecology. Lindeman indicated that the ecosystem is made up of various compartments called trophic, or feeding, levels. They usually include: (1) producers (green plants); (2) consumers (primary consumers which consume plants, secondary consumers which consume primary consumers, e.g., predators), and (3) decomposers (which convert dead plant and animal matter back into carbon dioxide). Energy for the system is received from the sun, and energy and matter are transferred among the various compartments.[20]

In the ecosystem concept, man is considered to belong to the consumer compartment as a herbivore (plant consumer) and carnivore (animal consumer). The place of man in the ecosystem is often referred to as that of the manipulator. Spurr notes:

> A natural resource ecosystem is an integrated ecological system, one element of which is a product of direct use to man. The product may be biological as in the case of forests, ranges, agricultural products, fish and wildlife; physical as in the case of water, air, and soil; or both. In all cases, the distinguishing facet of a natural resource ecosystem is that man has a direct involvement in the complex set of ecological interactions. Management is defined as the manipulation of the ecosystem by man. Beneficial management involves manipulation to maximize the returns to man, while exploitation is management that results in the reduction of the productivity of the ecosystem to mankind over a period of time.[21]

In this relationship, Van Dyne states:

> Man's rapidly developing technology provides him with increasing ability to manipulate the environment, e.g., traces of pesticides are now found in organisms throughout the world. But man has not had sufficient understanding of the many long-term consequences of environmental manipulation. In part, this has been because he often has not taken an ecological viewpoint: but the ecological basis of natural resource management is becoming more clearly understood, especially in multiple-use management of natural resources to increase productivity. Understanding the ecological basis of productivity in nature means understanding ecosystems. An ecosystem results from the integration of all of the living and nonliving factors of the environment for a defined segment of space and time. It is a complex of organisms and environment forming a functional whole.[27]

Van Dyne believes that the study or management of the complexities of the ecosystem requires an interdisciplinary team approach in that no single individual or discipline can encompass all the specialties required for this understanding.[23] On the other hand, the social science disciplines, which consider the values, behavior, and manipulations of man, have been notoriously absent from interdisciplinary approaches to ecosystems. While emphasis on technoscientific disciplines (forestry, hydrology, soil science, ecology, etc.) is necessary for ecosystem study and management, it is obvious that human dimensions, and consideration of man as manipulator, are not encompassed in technoscientific extrapolations. The ecosystem concept is a relatively new orientation for environmental administration, emerging as a working concept in the late 1960s. Chambers notes that the need to incorporate the social sciences is recognized and that possibilities are being discussed for various arrangements through universities, consultants, etc.[24]

The interdisciplinary approach recognizes that intricacies of ecosystem structures, components, and interrelationships need to be viewed from various angles if they are to be understood. Chambers indicates that advanced computer sciences have contributed greatly to analyzing ecosystem components, particularly at the subdivision level. He also notes that various ecological principles, basic rules, and knowledge of different ecosystems are being formulated and advanced through the International Biological Program. This program involves intensive study of selected ecosystems by large, interdisciplinary teams of scientists throughout the world. For example, worldwide studies under this program have found that the bacterial biomass in soil (which helps to break down organic matter to its mineral constituents) is 1600 to 3200 pounds per acre, yet a study in Canada revealed that the amount of these organisms was reduced by one-half with the application of chemical fertilizer on a plains ecosystem. Chambers indicates that many of the principles of and much of the knowledge from this program, through modification and adjustment, can be adapted and applied to various ecosystems in environmental administration.[25]

A relatively recent innovation in the study and management of complex ecosystems involves the Earth Resources and other Ecological Survey programs through satellites and facilities of National Aeronautics and Space Administration (NASA). Ward indicates that ecological surveys from space can provide perspective and illuminate problems; he notes that orbital investigation can provide computerized sensory data for classifying, analyzing, inventorying, and monitoring changing ecological relationships through photographic images from spacecraft. When such material is combined with other photographs and data in an interdisciplinary approach, it is obvious that new dimensions are added to the understanding of the ecosystem; for example, it is possible to identify stress conditions such as soil moisture deficiency, epidemic plant diseases, air pollution injury, and others. We are now able to observe plant growth rates, determine land surface composition and structure, assess water runoff, classify land use, document population movements and pollution, and evaluate automatic data processing techniques.[26]

While acknowledging the general applicability of various programs for the study and management of ecosystems, it is obvious that ecosystems have unique and complex characteristics. A certain amount of individual ecosystem complexity hinges upon how man manipulates energy and matter flows (including water and nutrient cycles) through the various components of the ecosystem. (The amount of living material in the different levels is known as the study crop on a food-chain basis.) Chambers notes:

> Through studying the ecosystem we see that energy cascades and matter cycles. Plants use its solar energy and minerals to manufacture living tissue which is later eaten by herbivores which in turn are eaten by carnivores. As a living tissue dies at each stage it must be broken down into mineral material which then re-enters the cycle. It is important to realize that while matter can cycle through the ecosystem repeatedly, energy passes through only once and there is energy wastage at each level of the food pyramid. The tremendous energy waste at each step is due to the fact that only a small proportion of the living tissue produced at each step is eaten by the next step. Few food pyramids have more than five levels because of this wastage. Lindeman in his work suggested the 10 percent law. Essentially, he stated that

163

if a given amount of energy is fixed by a certain trophic level, only 10 percent will be available for transfer to the next level, and so on.[27]

If productivity and stability of ecosystems and their energy and matter flows are to be maintained at optimal levels, environmental administration and management must be based on the ecosystem concept. Yet Caldwell indicates that an ecosystem approach to public land policy has seldom been attempted on a national or regional scale. Although the ambiguity and complexity of ecosystems may be a deterrant, Caldwell notes that policy of this nature has traditionally been based on juristic, economic, or demographic concepts which involve two causes.

> The first is the inability of society, because of inadequate knowledge, insufficient wealth, or incompatible institutions, to build ecologically based land policies into a general system of environmental management. The second, and more obvious, is incomparable interests among competing land users. An ecosystems approach to land policy encounters resistance to the degree that it is inconsistent with the values, assumptions, institutions, and practices that shape the prevailing social arrangements which have custody and care of the land.[28]

In considering that the ecosystem concept is not really applied effectively in land-use decisions that are developmentally or economically oriented, Caldwell indicates that ecosystem integrity has usually *followed*, rather than preceded, decisions pertaining to land-use conflicts and natural resources. He advocates including the ecosystem approach as part of public land policy on a practical, as well as theoretical, level, noting: (1) the holistic emphasis that precludes single-purpose orientations; (2) the enlistment of science into goal determination relating to public land policy, so that ecosystem criteria are based on scientific knowledge; (3) the use of administrative means based on scientific facts concerning ecosystems in preference to adjudication; (4) the finite amount of land available; and (5) the complex nature of ecosystems, with obvious negative effects from failure to recognize this imperative.[29]

Caldwell's points also apply to the necessity for extending the ecosystem concept to private lands, through policy, planning, zoning, and standards. Proposed legislation along this line involves the National Land Use Policy Act of 1971, which would authorize federal–state–local cooperation in this area. It recognizes that, "present state and local institution arrangements for planning and regulating land use of more than local impact are inadequate," with the result that important ecological and other values are being "irretrievably damaged or lost." Given that the proposed legislation provides for grants for states "to prepare and implement land use programs for the protection of areas of critical environmental concern and the control and direction of growth and development of more than local significance,"[30] there is no reference in the legislation to actual provisions for utilization of ecological principles. Moreover, many ecosystems and their effects and interrelations transcend private and political boundaries. Thus, a realistic ecosystem approach for a given public land area should, if necessary, encompass areas in private ownership, and extend beyond political boundaries.

In actuality, much of the present utilization of the ecosystem approach in environmental administration is along theoretical lines.[31] And a theory is subject to various interpretations and values. Correspondence and interview surveys by DeFrance[32] and by McQuillan[33] on the personnel of the FS, SCS, and BLM indicated a general consensus that a given agency: (1) had practiced the ecosystem approach since its beginning; (2) that multiple use was very similar to, or very compatible with, the ecosystem approach; and (3) that the interdisciplinary approach was, and had always been, used by staff specialists. Only a small portion of the personnel indicated that the ecosystem approach would require definite reorientations, or add new dimensions to their present operations.

While the actual application of the ecosystem concept to environmental administration would be time consuming and expensive, the survival of man and environment depends largely upon the regulation of the changes that man, as a natural and intricate part and manipulator of the ecosystem, induces. In this sense, the ecosystem approach encompasses and changes multiple-use and resource planning by introducing more specific criteria and ecological principles. It places natural resources and environmental manipulation in the proper perspective for more intensive and precise environmental administration and planning. In considering the implications of the ecosystem approach to management, a report of the Custer National Forest states:

> The ecosystem is the base on which all resource management activities are developed. The management objective is to create the least adverse effect possible on the ecosystem. The type and intensity of management will be determined by the individual parts of the ecosystem. These include the flora and fauna of biotic communities; climate, soils, and soil–water relationships of the abiotic environment; the inter-relationships between biotic communities and abiotic environment; and other considerations such as aesthetics and space. The concept of an ecological approach to management is a broad and flexible one. Its main function is to emphasize relationships and interdependence among organisms in the biotic community (defined as a unit or groups of various organisms which are held together by the interdependence of its members) and between these organisms and their abiotic environment. Ecosystems may be defined and studied in various sizes, or levels, depending on the objective. A pond, a lake, and a forest are examples of ecosystems that may be convenient units of study.[34]

A major, primary step in this process is to make an inventory of the biotic communities and abiotic environment of the ecosystem, the objective being to predict the potential for disturbed areas. Classification and inventory of biotic communities is usually based on plants, and involves surveying the major dominant species or species group (and trends of self perpetuation), the major life forms of dominant species, and the habitat occupied by the community. In the absence of conspicuous plants, the physical habitat may form the basis for classification, for example, a stream rapids community. A detailed narrative description covering all important components of the ecosystems, and their interrelationships, accompanies the basic inventory mappings and includes soil categories.

Inventories of individual resources (e.g., timber, range, etc.) are also made using standard methods and techniques (fig. 9.2).

Based on classification and inventory of the kind described above, numerical ratings on a scale of 0 to 4 are made for each resource within a homogeneous area. Rating criteria are kept in general terms for each resource and are based on quality (e.g., scenic values) or quantity (e.g., pounds of forage per acre). After the location and rating of the resources, an action may be proposed (e.g., timber harvesting, road construction, etc.). Ecological research is then conducted to determine what effects this action will have on the environment, and what modifications are necessary to keep the ecosystem functionally stable. If the proposed action is detrimental to the ecosystem, two alternatives exist: the proposed action can be abandoned or can be modified so that it no longer is detrimental to the ecosystem. Public involvement is sought in considering alternatives and determining needs.[36]

Although the ecosystem concept provides a framework for questioning the efficiency and advisability of existing practices and makes possible a comprehensive interdisciplinary approach, questions emerge concerning the degree to which this concept and approach are actually incorporated into environmental administration. Predetermined uses, natural resource emphasis, and resource-oriented disciplines (most natural resource personnel have only several semester or quarter hours of ecology in their specialist education), and limited and questionable public involvement, may preclude the "wholeness" necessary for a real ecosystem approach. Moreover, the public is really not permitted to enter into the formulation and planning of alternatives, but merely reviews and comments on plans and alternatives presented by natural resource specialists and administrators. Public comments are, in turn, interpreted by agency personnel who are operating under various economic constraints and value biases.

Sound environmental administration requires an interdisciplinary effort based on ecological principles, and one that recognizes that values permeate the ecosystem approach, particularly under natural resource orientations. Inventories, ratings, and proposed alternatives obviously reflect value inputs and orientations from the personnel involved. Moreover, computers, under recent systems ecology, are no more accurate or objective than the assumptions, interpretations, and values of those who do the programming and suggest the questions concerning resource allocations, uses, and alternatives. Consequently, a broad value base, with scope and depth, is needed throughout study and decision making relative to the ecosystem.

This cannot, however, come about merely by having technoscientific and natural resource specialists involved; it requires the values, skills, and knowledge of a variety of disciplines and of the public throughout the entire process. This hinges on the recognition that it is man's manipulations that are of primary concern for environmental survival and quality. In contrast to multiple-use and other approaches that emphasize economic uses of resources, the ecosystem approach does not assume that the land should be first used

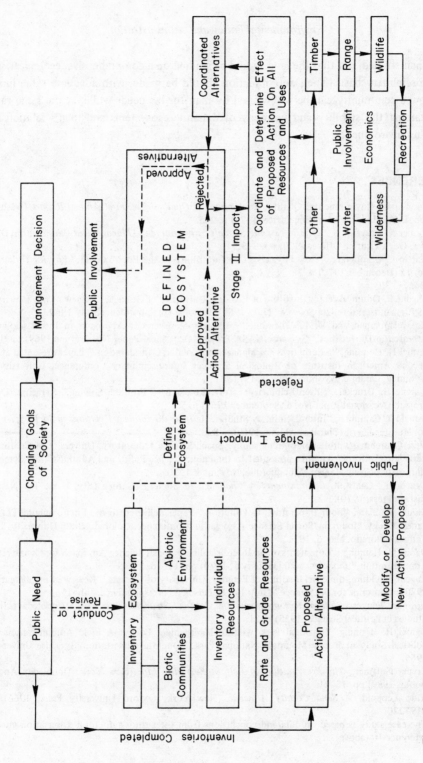

Figure 9.2. Flow chart of procedures involved in the ecological approach to land management. (From U. S. Forest Service, Custer National Forest, Billings, Montana.)

and then studied, but that the land should be studied on a comprehensive, ecological, and interdisciplinary basis. Then determination should be made, with adequate value input, on how a community can be wisely used by man for his needs while, at the same time, maintaining the stability and harmony of dynamic ecosystems and man's relationship with his environment.

REFERENCES

1. Council on Environmental Quality, *Environmental Quality: The First Annual Report* (Washington, D.C.: U.S. Gov't Printing Office, 1970) p. 245.
2. Daniel A. Dreyfus, *A Definition of the Scope of Environmental Management* (Washington, D.C.: U.S. Gov't Printing Office, 1970) pp. 3–5.
3. Martin L. Goldberger, "How Physicists Can Contribute to the Environment," *Physics Today* 23, no. 12 (December 1970) p. 26.
4. *Ibid.*, p. 30.
5. Eugene P. Odum, director, Institute of Ecology, University of Georgia, "Review of my January 1, 1970, manuscript for *BioScience*" (July 1969). Personal correspondence, July 1969.
6. R. J. Hopeman and D. L. Wilemon, "A Project Management Approach to Interdisciplinary Research in Universities," Syracuse/NASA Project, Occasional Paper No. 2 (June 1969) pp. 1–4.
7. Daniel H. Henning, "Alternatives for Management: Value Consideration." Paper presented at the Second American Institute of Biological Sciences Interdisciplinary Conference, University of Wyoming, Laramie, Wyoming, July 1, 1971.
8. Eugene E. Drucker, "Interdisciplinary Effort: Research or Problem Solving," Syracuse/NASA Project, Occasional Paper No. 6 (September 1969) p. 5.
9. Donald T. Campbell, "Interdisciplinary Studies," in *Inter-disciplinary Relations in Social Sciences*, ed. Muzafer Sherif (Chicago: Aldine, 1969) p. 328.
10. West Churchman, professor of philosophy, Space Science Laboratory, University of California, Berkeley, California. Lecture presented to the Public Science Policy and Administration Seminar, University of New Mexico, Albuquerque, November 1970.
11. Lynton K. Caldwell, *Environment: A Challenge to Society* (Garden City, N.Y.: The Natural History Press, 1970).
12. Daniel M. Slate, "Four Imperatives to Pollution." Paper delivered to the Environmental Politics Panel, Rocky Mountain Social Science Association Conference, Colorado State University, Fort Collins, Colorado, May 6, 1971.
13. Daniel H. Henning, "Comments on an Interdisciplinary Social Science Approach for Conservation Administration," *BioScience* 20 (January 1, 1970) pp. 11–16.
14. Eugene P. Odum, director, Institute of Ecology, University of Georgia, "Review of my January 1, 1970, manuscript for *BioScience*" (July 1969). Personal correspondence, July 1969.
15. Norman Wengert, *Natural Resources and the Political Struggle* (New York: Doubleday, Short Studies in Political Science, 1955) p. 21.
16. Daniel H. Henning, "National Park Wildlife Management Policy: A Field Administration and Political Study at Rocky Mountain National Park." Doctoral dissertation, Syracuse University, 1965.
17. Erving Goffman, *The Presentation of Self in Everyday Life* (New York: Doubleday Anchor Books, 1959) pp. 13–21.
18. Aldo Leopold, *A Sand County Almanac* (New York: Oxford University Press, 1966) pp. 219–220.
19. The case study is based on data and conclusions from the author's doctoral dissertation cited in reference 16 (above).

20. John W. Chambers, forest staff officer, Santa Fe National Forest, U.S. Forest Service, "Ecological Approach to Natural Resources Management." Manuscript, April 1970, and lecture presented to the Environmental Policy and Administration Seminar, University of New Mexico, Albuquerque, July 22, 1971.

21. Stephan H. Spurr, "The Natural Resource Ecosystem," in *The Ecosystem Concept in Natural Resource Management,* ed. George M. Van Dyne (New York: Academic Press, 1969) p. 3.

22. George M. Van Dyne (ed.), *The Ecosystem Concept in Natural Resource Management* (New York: Academic Press, 1969) p. vii.

23. *Ibid.,* p. vii.

24. John W. Chambers, forest staff officer, Santa Fe National Forest, U.S. Forest Service, "Ecological Approach to Natural Resources Management." Manuscript, April 1970, and lecture presented to the Environmental Policy and Administration Seminar, University of New Mexico, Albuquerque, July 22, 1971.

25. *Ibid.*

26. Robert J. Ward, "Aero Space Management Concepts and the Environmental Crisis. Master's thesis, Program for Advanced Study in Public Science Policy and Administration, University of New Mexico, 1971, pp. 36–53.

27. John W. Chambers, forest staff officer, Santa Fe National Forest, U.S. Forest Service, "Ecological Approach to Natural Resources Management." Manuscript, April 1970, and lecture presented to the Environmental Policy and Administration Seminar, University of New Mexico, Albuquerque, July 22, 1971.

28. Lynton K. Caldwell, "The Ecosystems as a Criterion for Public Land Policy," *Natural Resources Journal* 10, no. 2 (April 1970) p. 204.

29. *Ibid.,* pp. 210–211.

30. Council on Environmental Quality, *The President's 1971 Environmental Program* (Washington, D.C.: U.S. Gov't Printing Office, 1971) pp. 211–219.

31. Lynton K. Caldwell, "The Ecosystems as a Criterion for Public Land Policy," *Natural Resources Journal* 10, no. 2 (April 1970) pp. 203–221.

32. Nancy DeFrance, "Attitudes Toward the Ecological Approach." Student research paper, Public Administration of Natural Resources Seminar, Eastern Montana College, Billings, spring quarter, 1970).

33. Thomas McQuillan, "The Ecosystems Approach and Federal Personnel." Graduate student research paper, Environmental Policy and Administration Seminar, University of New Mexico, Albuquerque, May 1971.

34. Custer National Forest, U.S. Forest Service, "Ecological Approach to Land Management." Manuscript, n.d.

35. *Ibid.*

36. *Ibid.*

EPILOGUE

It is easy to attribute the serious resistance to effective environmental management to dominant interests and values of a pluralistic political system, and to identify particular economic and technoscientific pressures brought to bear on the political processes generated by environmental issues. In the same easy way, one can point to rigidity and sluggishness of bureaucracy as causes of our inadequate response to changing environmental requirements. But there seems to be a deeper cause of ineffectiveness: in practice, political instruments do not produce sound environmental policy and administration even when public concern for the environment becomes widespread and vocal. Cooley and Wandesforde-Smith[1] give a rather negative assessment of *actual* achievement under compromise and pluralism by Congress through case studies. Writers on environment from Nader[2] to Graham[3] are highly critical of governmental inaction, collusion, and resistance.

Relative to the institutional structure of the various governmental organizations involved in environmental affairs, the pattern has generally been an *ad hoc,* expedient approach, with little effort being made to formulate long-term plans for handling complex environmental problems.

Although much has been accomplished in environmental affairs during recent times (particularly in contrast to conservation activities in earlier periods), few will argue that accomplishments have been sufficiently intense or effective to deal with the magnitude of the problems. Few will dispute the fact that changes are needed. Such changes, however, depend upon degrees and priorities that reflect the individual's and society's values and perceptions. Rapid and overwhelming technoscientific change, without adequate cultural, social, and value adjustments, and allowances for time lags, have been characteristic of the past 50 years. When this historical pattern is coupled with an economic and organizational orientation, value change as a basis for effective environmental administration becomes ambiguous and difficult. Yet, sound governmental actions in this area cannot actually be accomplished without real value change and the support of society. In this sense, many environmental efforts represent a challenge to prevailing forces of society; this, in turn, results in political conflict and resistance throughout governmental processes, regardless of legal and institutional change. Society and government have difficulty in accepting environmental "limits" and imperatives as witnessed by symptomatic activity under the "energy crisis," e.g., the Alaska pipeline.

An excellent perspective on this value conflict is presented by Charles A. Reich in *The Greening of America.* Reich argues that to a great extent government and society have lost contact with reality and are dominated by technoscientific and economic forces on a dehumanized, corporate-state basis. His reality premise is based on areas of Consciousness that are present in people and society (Consciousness might be likened to value or wisdom and perception). Reich considers Consciousness I (economic individualism) and Consciousness II (organizationally and rationally oriented) to be prevalent in modern society. Yet, he considers both of these areas of Consciousness to be under the domination of the technology market and corporate-state complex. Both are given to progress and materialism, and approve of the domination of the environment by technology, a premise that naturally resists environmental concerns.

Reich, however, sees hope in the emergence of Consciousness III, which centers around the younger generation. Although evolving from today's technology, Consciousness III, according to Reich, seeks to transcend the prevailing complex, to restore the nonmaterial elements of man's existence, to place the technoscientific rationale in its proper place relative to environmental considerations, and to recognize the individual's responsibility for the actions of society. Reich considers Consciousness III to be realistic and necessary for environmental survival and quality, and Consciousness I and II to be artificial and destructive with their inherent environmental exploitation and abuses. Given the problems of categorization, it is obvious that the various states of Consciousness do greatly influence government–man–environmental relationships and that value conflicts pertaining to these states emerge and hamper constructive changes in environmental policy and administration.

Within environmental agencies, internal conflicts are present, with economically and organizationally oriented individuals opposing individuals who are oriented toward environmental quality. The latter may be younger personnel in many cases. In fact, to a great extent, the agencies and their vested interests mirror the larger value conflicts of society. Many agencies and their personnel have natural resistance to deviating from earlier organizational operations and systems and adjusting to the newer environmental policies and considerations. In the face of internalized values and pluralistic compromise approaches, some administrators may incorporate environmental requirements and concerns as an additional burden in an attempt to placate or manipulate, rather than accepting them as a new basic orientation. Despite legislation, institutional reform, and so forth, a given value orientation will not change overnight; in fact, some will never change to any effective degree. Power clusters, moreover, correlate with the value orientations of a given agency and its components. The end result may be to reduce seriously the environmental action potential, and to emphasize the technoscientific, economic spectrum. This is why due regard must be given to social systems and values that are basic sources of conflict affecting a given agency.

On the other hand, a major result of the administrative processes is to reduce, diffuse, dehumanize, and, in essence, to hide value conflicts behind technoscientific, organizational, and professional concerns, particularly under complex governmental–private relationships. The *goldfish bowl* concept of public agencies appears to relate to octopuses with ink screens. But behind this complex *adjustment–rationality–camouflage process,* value conflicts and power struggles are very much an intricate part of policy and decision making, despite the apolitical or objective claims of many agencies. Values that are compatible with agency values and interests become dominant in the behind-the-scenes power struggle for actual policy and decision making. Lip service or minor adjustments are afforded values that are not oriented toward this selective framework. Unfortunately, this selective and subtle filter process of a given agency usually precludes most environmental quality considerations; instead, emphasis is placed upon economic, technoscientific, and developmental concerns. Despite recent environmental legislation and forces, the *conflict filter* continues to operate on a somewhat impersonal and technical basis. It serves to narrow the scope of values and their alternatives that a given agency, motivated by survival and expansion imperatives, may realistically consider.

In the face of recent requirements, criticism, and demands for public participation in the environmental policy and administrative processes, more attention may be paid to the expansion of the value and power conflict, that is, there may be a shift from closed-system agencies to more open ones. Yet, many of the values surrounding public participation are somewhat incompatible with the present operations of many agencies, which are oriented toward organizational and clientele interests. Thus, realignments in power clusters would have to occur prior to effective public participation and incorporation of various environmental values. Without this power change, value inputs from public sources will continue to be relegated to minor, inconsequential roles. In this sense, the agency and its personnel have the authority and responsibility to interpret and adjust the degree and actual input of public values on a quantitative and a qualitative basis. Public participation, like any other input, is subject to the influences of power and to the political situation; it can be channeled and manipulated under given value orientations.

Thus, an environmental imperative appears to be the removal of much of the *secrecy* with which many agencies now operate. Superficial, manipulative, and public relations activities do not reduce this secrecy, which involves value judgments and decisions on environmental affairs that are of essential public concern. Many environmental decisions are irreversible in terms of ecological and other consequences; for example, construction of a dam or highway. On the assumption that the public will have to live with environmental consequences of these decisions, including the governmental and social costs involved, it would appear that the public *must* have an effective voice and value input throughout the entire processes. Yet, secrecy and hidden politics appear to underlie much of the activity in environmental policy and administration. Free communication with the public, as well as with professional colleagues outside a given agency, would remove many otherwise inevitable errors and omissions; it would also enlarge the organizational perspectives of agencies through criticism, feedback, and correction. Secrecy or selected-information releases hamper the public's knowledge and affect their values. Such mistakes or omissions on the part of the agency may eventually become public knowledge when decisions based upon them can no longer be reversed.

Many environmental agencies operate as autonomous units dedicated to their own particular organizational values and interests. It is yet to be determined how far the 80-some agencies will adjust to environmental legislation and public forces that urge supremacy of environmental considerations over economic and technical constraints. Technoscientific personnel dominate agency situations and may place economic efficiency and other biases above environmental considerations, often because of a narrow value base. A current program of the Soil Conservation Service (SCS), for example, is to remove vegetation along natural waterways of the United States, by use of herbicides and other means, with the objective of increasing water flow for economic and irrigational interests. According to numerous environmentalists, this irresponsible program is the result of the relatively recent elevation of engineers to positions of prominence throughout the agency hierarchy. Public controversy has erupted over the program, but it continues to operate, removing the natural habitat along many rivers and streams. In justifying the program to me, an engineer–administrator of the agency (SCS) stated, "We cannot afford to be a bunch of environmental idealists or theorists. We are a practical and service outfit and do what we can. People need the water, regardless of the problems and controversy involved." Yet, the very nature of environmental imperatives calls for idealism and theory that enlarges the scope, values, and ecological perspectives of agencies and restrains their autonomy.

Important factors in the autonomy and consequent unresponsiveness of agencies are the complex and impersonal organizational systems that have evolved. Personnel are increasingly limited in their capacities to bring about change, regardless of their values relative to environmental considerations. Thus, the forces, interests, power distributions, and values of the organization operate on an impersonal and dehumanized basis, emphasizing technoscientific considerations. Although the organization may be composed of people, the organizational system of interrelationships relegates little actual power to its personnel; the organization becomes a symbolic organism with a life of its own. Individuals are incorporated into the organization and expected to conform; they must think in terms of the organization's interests in order to move upward in the hierarchy, that is, they should not make waves. Position and technique are emphasized and the individual's values, creativity, professional ethics, or discipline are disregarded. The end result is to discourage personnel from contributing many important environmental alternatives in the decision-making processes of the agency. A restricted consideration of values and alternatives, reflecting and serving the organization's own interests, may not be at all creative in responding to environmental quality considerations. Many valuable ideas are lost or severely delayed through recognition by agency personnel that the individual cannot fight the autonomous system.

Autonomy is further increased owing to the multitude of agencies involved in environmental affairs. With the exception of Environmental Protection Agency (EPA), which was created in 1970 specifically to deal with environmental pollution problems, and the Council on Environmental Quality (CEQ), created in 1969, practically all federal departments and agencies are in positions of having to adapt an institutional framework to deal with environmental legislation. Most of these agencies are mission oriented and concerned with specifics, many of which involve manipulating the environment under economic and developmental policies. Many, further, have long histories and traditions of political and clientele support (e.g., the Corps of Engineers (CE)), and an extensive body of legislation to justify and defend their present policies and activities. While such policies and activities will be subject to review and change through the CEQ, it is obvious that this process will be a long and complicated one, with agencies retaining the far greater portions of their powers. This type of autonomy might be seriously questioned in light of current environmental needs, which obviously are not handled or even adequately approached under the present orientation toward pluralism, fragmentation, and interagency conflict. In essence, this autonomy produces a form of entrepreneurship, with competition and expansion of agencies, and collusion with private organizations.

Consequently, proposals to reorganize and incorporate agencies along superdepartmental lines may present more advantages than disadvantages in environmental terms. Given the complexities, problems, and power retention of established agencies and officials (as well as resistance to change in general), realignments and adjustments under superdepartments might induce a more holistic approach to the environment as well as improved interagency cooperation and coordination. Power clusters and arrangements, particularly with congressional and clientele interests, would obviously undergo some adjustments that might be beneficial. Although adequate reorganization is only one element of a complex picture, it does present possibilities for reducing agency autonomy and for bringing agencies more in line with long-range environmental responsibilities. It is also obvious that new types of coordinated arrangements among agencies are needed to approach environmental challenges. Along this line, the Intergovernmental Personnel Act might well be extended to exchange of personnel among federal agencies on an environmental problems basis, rather than on an agency basis.

In the face of present political obstacles, with associated organizational, economic, and technoscientific problems, efforts and achievements in environmental policy and administration have been mainly incremental and defensive. Intense value and political conflicts are characteristic of any new ideology or movement; yet, environment, as a growing and permanent political issue, appears to be encountering severe obstacles relative to implementation in governmental processes. Because of other governmental priorities and the resistance to change, it is obvious that fundamental changes in institutional arrangements, policies, and values, as well as political and social systems, will have to occur before these obstacles can be overcome. For example, reliance on state and local governments as major environmental pollution control institutions appears unrealistic under local political and economic domination, including that of large, local corporations. Further, control at state and local government levels is not consistent with regional and ecological realities. Obviously, new types of intergovernmental institutions and arrangements will have to be made for definite pollution control and environmental quality.

Despite political obstacles, one immediate impact of the environmental cause upon government has been to encourage and even to force consideration of values and alternatives in the administrative processes. Many of these values and alternatives hinge on quality and long-term ecological consequences, which had previously been passed over in favor of pragmatic and expedient solutions. A great many environmental abuses have occurred through inadequate consideration of values and through incomplete study of ecological effects, while technoscientific, economic, and political concerns have dominated. With new pressures to investigate alternative actions and ecological consequences, many elements of administrative procedure may actually work in the environmental public interest by making officials conscious of the ecological consequences of their actions, particularly through external inputs and criticisms.

The CEQ, however, has mainly operated on an immediate problem-solving basis. Despite accomplishments under a defensive orientation, little attention has yet been given to long-range planning and policy formulation for a comprehensive governmental approach to the environment. Technoscientific, social, and environmental assessment and evaluation, as well as preventive measures, should be encompassed in this approach. Yet, much of the time and activity of the CEQ appears to be concerned with protecting the environment from programs of federal agencies. With its review and advisory functions the CEQ also possesses considerable power to strongly influence many agencies along sound environmental lines and to do much in the way of formulating national environmental policy. This must be accomplished largely through the political process and through the support of coalitions that reflect a sufficient public value base.

Long-term considerations include an effective environmental educational program for the general public. Overall, the entire educational system of the United States has been very poor in this area, and the recent Environmental Education Act has been weakly funded. In general, the public must learn environmental attitudes and understanding outside the educational system, which reflects artificial, technoscientific, and economic values of society. A decent public information program on environmental affairs is generally not available. Ecology, the basis of environmental studies, incorporates social, intellectual, psychological, and other concerns in addition to the physical. Ecological approaches have been generally absent from the educational system, although with its holistic nature, ecology lends itself to realistic interdisciplinary approaches to environmental survival and to effective education of professionals and of private citizens. Ecology and environmental concerns are gradually being incorporated into education, ranging from units of study in elementary schools to interdisciplinary doctoral seminars in graduate schools.

Despite the urgency of environmental problems, it is a relatively slow process to make basic changes in values and systems. But environmental policy and administration require these changes. It would appear that present requirements are for qualitative changes rather than survival imperatives, with a conflict between technoscientific and economic versus ecological and esthetic values. Quality however, relates to survival in the essential recognition that all life is interdependent and interrelated. Moreover, without environmental quality, the life of man becomes artificial, shallow, and dehumanized, and the heritage to future generations becomes a curse rather than a blessing. Present conditions indicate that the processes of environmental policy and administration will continue to be permeated by value and political conflicts. On the other hand, a trend appears to indicate the emergence of a social and political consensus that reflects environmental values. It is upon institutional consequences of this trend, through the political–administrative processes, that effective environmental policy and administration depends.

REFERENCES

1. Richard A. Cooley and Geoffry Wandesforde-Smith, *Congress and the Environment* (Seattle: University of Washington Press, 1970).
2. James M. Fallows and David Zwick, *Who Runs Congress* (New York: Bantam/Grossman, 1972).
3. Frank Graham, Jr., *Since Silent Spring* (Boston: Houghton Mifflin, 1970).

A SELECTED BIBLIOGRAPHY ON PUBLIC ENVIRONMENTAL POLICY AND ADMINISTRATION

BOOKS

Allen, S. *Conserving Natural Resources, Principles and Practices in a Democracy.* New York: McGraw-Hill, 1960.

Allen, S., and Sharpe, G. W. *Introduction to American Forestry.* New York: McGraw-Hill, 1960.

Anderson, W. *Politics and Environment.* Pacific Palisades, Calif.: Goodyear, 1970.

Arvill, R. *Man and Environment: Crisis and the Strategy of Choice.* Baltimore: Penguin, 1970.

Baldwin, M., and Page, J. K., eds. *Law and the Environment.* New York: Walker, 1970.

Bates, M. *Man and Nature.* Englewood Cliffs, N.J.: Prentice-Hall, 1965.

Bauer, R. A., and Gergen, K. J., eds. *The Study of Policy Formation.* New York: Free Press, 1968.

Beckman, N., and Dworsky, L. B. "New View on Public Responsibility for Resource Development—Jurisdictions, Consequences, Remedies." *New Horizons for Resources Research,* ed. M. E. Garnsey. Denver: University of Colorado Press, 1965.

Benarde, M. A. *Our Precarious Habitat.* New York: Norton, 1970.

Bennett, G., and Hostman, J. *Bibliography of Books on the Environment—Air, Water and Solid Wastes 52.* Toledo, Ohio: Dept. of Chemical Engineering, Univ. of Toledo, 1969.

Bonifazi, C. *A Theology of Things: A Study of Man in His Physical Environment.* Philadelphia: Lippincott, 1967.

Brady, N. C., ed. *Agriculture and the Quality of Our Environment.* Washington, D.C.: American Association for the Advancement of Science, 1967.

Brennan, R. L. *Private Approaches to the Preservation of Open Land.* Waterford, Conn.: Conservation and Research Foundation, 1966.

Bresler, J. *Environments of Man.* Reading, Mass.: Addison-Wesley, 1968.

Burton, I., and Kates, R. *Readings in Resource Management and Conservation.* Chicago: Univ. of Chicago Press, 1965.

Caldwell, L. K., ed. "An Ecosystems Approach to Public Land Policy," in *Proceedings of the Western Resources Conference, 1968.* Fort Collins: Colorado State University.

Caldwell, L. K., ed. *Environmental Studies: Papers on the Politics and Public Administration of Man—Environment Relationships.* Bloomington, Ind.: Institute of Public Administration, Indiana University, 1967.

Caldwell, L. K. *Environment: Challenges to Modern Society.* New York: Natural History Press, 1970.

Caldwell, L. K. *In Defense of the Earth.* Bloomington: Indiana Univ. Press, 1972.

Chant, D. A. "The Role of Public Pressure Groups in Environmental Control." Paper delivered to the 18th Annual Ontario Industrial Waste Conference, Niagara Falls, Ontario, June 13–16, 1971.

Chretien, J. "Values and Perspectives for the World of Tomorrow." Paper delivered to the 60th Convention of the International Association of Game, Fish, and Conservation Commissioners, September 16–18, 1970.

Ciracy-Wantrup, S. V., and Parsons, J. J., eds. *Natural Resources: Quality and Quantity.* Berkeley: University of California Press, 1966.

Clawson, M. *Uncle Sam's Acres.* New York: Dodd, Mead, 1951.

Clawson, M. *Economics of Outdoor Recreation.* Washington, D.C.: Resources For the Future, Inc., 1966.

Clawson, M. *Man and Land in the United States.* Lincoln: Univ. of Nebraska Press, 1964.

Commoner, B. *Science and Survival.* New York: Viking Press, 1966.

Commoner, B. *The Closing Circle: Nature, Man, and Technology.* New York: Knopf, 1971.

Continuing Education for the Bar. *Environmental Law Handbook.* Berkeley: Univ. of Calif., 1970.

Cooley, R., and Wandesforde-Smith, G. *Congress and the Environment.* Seattle: Univ. of Washington Press, 1970.

Cooley, R. *Politics and Conservation.* New York: Harper & Row, 1963.

Cox, G. W. *Reading in Conservation Ecology.* New York: Appleton-Century-Crofts, 1969.

Darling, F. F., and Milton, J. P., eds. *Future Environments of North America.* New York: Natural History Press, 1968.

Dasmann, R. *Environmental Conservation.* New York: Wiley, 1968.

Davies, C. J. *The Politics of Pollution.* New York: Pegasus, 1970.

Day, J. A. *Dimensions of the Environmental Crisis.* New York: Wiley, 1971.

DeBell, G. *The Environmental Handbook.* New York: Ballantine, 1970.

Degler, S. E., and Bloom, S. C. *Federal Pollution Control Programs: Water, Air, and Solid Wastes.* Washington, D.C.: Bureau of National Affairs, 1969.

Dickerson, R. E. *Regional Ecology: The Study of Man's Environment.* New York: Wiley, 1970.

Disposal of Radioactive Wastes into Seas, Oceans, and Surface Waters. Vienna: International Atomic Energy Agency, 1966.

Dubos, R. *So Human and Animal.* New York: Scribners, 1968.

Ducsik, D. W., ed. *Power, Pollution, and Public Policy.* Cambridge, Mass.: MIT Press, 1972.

Ehrenfeld, D. *Biological Conservation.* New York: Holt, Rinehart & Winston, 1970.

Ehrlich, P. *The Population Bomb.* New York: Ballantine, 1968.

Ehrlich, P., and Ehrlich, A. H. *Population, Resources, Environment.* San Francisco: Freeman, 1970.

Eiseley, L. *The Immense Journey.* New York: Random House, 1957.

Ekirch, A. A. *Man and Nature in America.* New York: Columbia University Press, 1963.

Elton, C. S. *The Ecology of Invasions by Animals and Plants.* New York: Wiley, 1958.

Esposito, J. C. *Vanishing Air: The Ralph Nader Study Group Report on Air Pollution.* New York: Grossman, 1970.

Ewald, W. R., Jr., ed. *Environment for Man: The Next Fifty Years.* Bloomington, Ind.: Indiana Univ. Press, 1967.

Falk, R. A. *This Endangered Planet.* New York: Random House, 1971.

The Fitness of Man's Environment. Washington, D.C.: Smithsonian Institution Press, 1960.

Forbes, R. J. *The Conquest of Nature: Technology and Its Consequences.* New York: New American Library, 1968.

Forest Service. *Management Practices on the Bitterroot National Forests.* Washington, D.C.: U.S. Dept. of Agriculture, 1970.

Fortune Magazine Editors. *Environment: A National Mission for the Seventies.* New York: Harper & Row, 1970.

Frakes, G. E., and Solberg, C. B. *Pollution Papers.* New York: Meredith, 1971.

Garnsey, M., and Hibbs, J. R., eds. *Social Sciences and the Environment.* Boulder, Colo.: Univ. of Colorado Press, 1967.

Garvey, G. *Energy, Ecology, Economy: A Framework for Environmental Policy.* New York: Norton, 1972.

Goldman, M. I., ed. *Controlling Pollution—the Economics of a Cleaner America.* Englewood Cliffs, N.J.: Prentice-Hall, 1967.

Goldman, M. I., ed. *Ecology and Economics: Controlling Pollution in the 70s.* Englewood Cliffs, N.J.: Prentice-Hall, 1972.

Graham, F., Jr. *Disaster by Default: Politics and Water Pollution.* New York: Evans, 1966.

Greeley, W. B. *Forest Policy.* Garden City: Doubleday, 1961.

Gross, B. M., ed. *Action Under Planning: The Guidance of Economic Development.* New York: McGraw-Hill, 1967.

Gulick, L. *American Forest Policy.* New York: Institute of Public Administration, 1951.

Haar, C. *Land-Use Planning: A Casebook on the Use, Misuse, and Reuse of Urban Land.* Boston: Little, Brown, 1959.

Hamm, R. L., and Nason, L. *Ecological Approach to Conservation.* Minneapolis, Minn.: Burgess, 1964.

Headley, J. C., and Lewis, J. N. *The Pesticide Problem: An Economic Approach to Public Policy.* Baltimore: Johns Hopkins Press, 1967.

Heimann, H. *Effect of Air Pollution on Human Health.* New York: World Health Organization/ Columbia Univ. Press, 1961.

Helfrich, H. W., Jr., ed. *The Environmental Crisis: Man's Struggle to Live With Himself.* New Haven, Conn.: Yale Univ. Press, 1970.

Herfindahl, O. C., and Kneese, A. V. *Quality of the Environment: An Economic Approach to Some Problems in Using Land, Water, and Air.* Baltimore: Resources for the Future/ Johns Hopkins Press, 1965.

Herring, F. W., ed. *Open Space and the Law.* Berkeley: Univ. of California, Institute of Governmental Studies, 1965.

Holdren, J. P., and Ehrlich, P. R. *Global Ecology: Readings Toward a Rational Strategy for Man.* New York: Harcourt-Brace-Jovanovich, Inc., 1971.

Hull, W. J., and Hull, R. W. *The Origin and Development of the Waterways Policy of the United States.* Washington, D.C.: National Waterways Conference, Inc., 1967.

Ise, J. *Our National Park Policy.* Baltimore: Johns Hopkins Press, 1961.

Jackson, S. *Man and the Environment.* Dubuque, Iowa: Brown, 1973.

Jarrett, H. *Comparison in Resource Management.* Baltimore: Johns Hopkins Press, 1961.

Jarrett, H., ed. *Environmental Quality in a Growing Economy.* Baltimore: Resources for the Future/ Johns Hopkins Press, 1966.

Johnson, C. *Social and Natural Biology.* Princeton, N.J.: Van Nostrand Reinhold, 1968.

Kaufman, H. *The Forest Ranger: A Study in Administrative Behavior.* Baltimore: Johns Hopkins Press, 1960.

Kneese, A. V. *The Economics of Regional Water Quality Management.* Baltimore: Johns Hopkins Press, 1964.

Kormoney, E. *Concepts of Ecology.* Englewood Cliffs, N.J.: Prentice-Hall, 1970.

Landsberg, H. *Natural Resources for U.S. Growth: A Look Ahead to the Year 2000.* Baltimore: Johns Hopkins Press, 1964.

Leinwand, G., ed. *Air and Water Pollution.* New York: Washington Square Press, 1969.

Leopold, A. *A Sand County Almanac.* New York: Oxford Univ. Press, 1966.

Linton, R. M. *Terracide.* Boston: Little, Brown, 1970.

Lowenthal, D., ed. *Environmental Perception and Behavior,* Research Paper No. 109. Chicago: Univ. of Chicago, Dept. of Geography, 1967.

Mandelker, D. R. *Managing Our Urban Environment: Cases, Texts, and Problems.* Indianapolis: Bobbs-Merrill, 1966.

Marquis, R. W., ed. *Environmental Improvement.* Washington, D.C.: Dept. of Agriculture Graduate School, 1966.

Marx, W. *The Frail Ocean.* New York: Doubleday Anchor Books, 1967.

Meek, R. L., and Straayer, J. A., eds. *Politics of Neglect: The Environmental Crisis.* Boston: Houghton Mifflin, 1971.

Murphy, E. F. *Governing Nature.* Chicago: Quadrangle, 1967.

Murphy, E. F. *Man and His Environment: Law.* New York: Harper & Row, 1971.

Nash, R., ed. *The American Environment: Readings in the History of Conservation.* Reading, Mass.: Addison-Wesley, 1968.

179

Nash, R. *Wilderness and the American Mind.* New Haven, Conn.: Yale Univ., 1967.

National Research Council. *Resources and Man.* San Francisco: Freeman Press, 1969.

Nicholson, M. *The Environmental Revolution: A Guide for the New Masters of the World.* New York: McGraw-Hill, 1970.

Norvick, S., and Cottrell, D. *Our World in Peril: An Environment Review.* Greenwich, Conn.: Fawcett, 1971.

Odum, E. P. *The Crisis of Survival.* Glenview, Ill.: Scott, Foresman, 1970.

Odum, E. P. *The Fundamentals of Ecology,* 2d ed. Philadelphia: Saunders, 1959.

Parson, R. *Conserving American Resources.* Englewood Cliffs, N.J.: Prentice-Hall, 1965.

Perin, C. *With Man in Mind: An Interdisciplinary Prospectus for Environmental Design.* Cambridge, Mass.: MIT Press, 1970.

Perry, J. *Our Polluted World.* New York: Watts, 1967.

Popkin, R. *The Environmental Sciences Services Administration.* Washington, D.C.: Praeger, 1967.

Proceedings of the National Symposium on Quality Standards for Natural Waters. Ann Arbor: Univ. of Michigan, 1967.

Reich, C. A. *Bureaucracy and the Forests.* Santa Barbara, Calif.: Center for the Study of Democratic Institutions, 1962.

Reich, C. A. *The Greening of America.* New York: Random House, 1970.

Revelle, R., Khosla, A., and Vinovskis, M., eds. *Survival Equation: Man, Resources, and His Environment.* Boston: Houghton Mifflin, 1971.

Ridgeway, J. *The Politics of Ecology.* New York: Dutton, 1970.

Rienow, R. *Moment in the Sun, A Report on the Deteriorating Quality of the American Environment.* New York: Dial Press, 1967.

Roos, L. L. *Politics of Ecosuicide: A Reader.* New York: Holt, Rinehart & Winston, 1971.

Roslansky, J. D. *The Control of Environment.* Amsterdam: Noord-Hollandische, U.N., 1967.

Rudd, R. L. *Pesticides and the Living Landscape.* Madison: Univ. of Wisconsin Press, 1964.

Sax, J. L. *Defending the Environment: A Strategy for Citizen Action.* New York: Knopf, 1971.

Sax, J. L. *Water Law, Planning and Policy, Cases and Materials.* Indianapolis: Bobbs-Merrill, 1968.

Scenic Easements in Action, vols. 1 and 2. Madison, Wisc.: Extension Law Dept., Univ. of Wisconsin.

Schwartz, W., ed. *Voices for the Wilderness.* New York: Ballantine, 1969.

Sharkansky, I., ed. *Policy Analysis in Political Science.* Chicago: Markham, 1970.

Shepard, P. *Man in the Landscape—A Historical View of the Esthetics of Nature.* New York: Knopf, 1967.

Shepard, P., and McKinley, D. *The Subversive Science, Essays Toward an Ecology of Man.* Boston: Houghton Mifflin, 1969.

Smith, F. E. *The Politics of Conservation.* New York: Pantheon Books, 1966.

Smith, G.-H., ed. *Conservation of Natural Resources,* 4th ed. New York: Wiley, 1971.

Smithsonian Institution. *The Fitness of Man's Environment.* Washington, D.C.: The Smithsonian Institution, 1968.

Stern, A. C. *Air Pollution,* 3 vols. New York: Academic Press, 1968.

Stoddart, L. A., and Smith, A. D. *Range Management.* New York: McGraw-Hill, 1955.

Storer, J. H. *Man in the Web of Life.* New York: New American Library, 1968.

Teclaff, L. A. *The River Basin in History and Law.* The Hague: Martinies Hijhoff, 1967.

Teilhard de Chardin, P. *Man's Place in Nature: The Human Zoological Group.* Translated by Rene Hague. London: Collins, 1966.

Thomas, W. L., Jr., ed. *Man's Role in Changing the Face of the Earth.* Chicago: Univ. of Chicago Press, 1956.

Thorne, W., ed. *Land and Water Use.* Washington, D.C.: American Association for the Advancement of Science, 1963.

Tribus, M. "Integrity and the Ecological Crisis." Paper delivered to the 19th American Hydraulics Division Specialty Conference, University of Iowa, Iowa City, August 18, 1971.

Trippensee, R. E. *Wildlife Management.* New York: McGraw-Hill, 1950.

Udall, S. *The Quiet Crisis.* New York: Holt, Rinehart & Winston, 1963.

United Nations. *Papers Presented at the International Technical Conference on the Conservation of the Living Resources of the Sea.* Rome, April 13–May 10, 1955. New York: United Nations, 1956.

Von Eckhardt, W. *The Challenge of Megalopolis.* New York: Macmillan, 1964.

Wagner, R. H. *Environment and Man.* New York: Norton, 1971.

Waste Management: Generation and Disposal of Solid, Liquid, and Gaseous Wastes in the New York Region; A Report of the Second Regional Plan. Bulletin No. 107. New York: Regional Plan Association, 1968.

Water and Agriculture. Washington, D.C.: American Association for the Advancement of Science, 1960.

Watson, R. *Man and Nature.* New York: Harcourt-Brace-Jovanovich, 1969.

Wengert, N. I. *The Administration of Natural Resources.* Brooklyn, N.Y.: Asia Pub. House, 1961.

Wengert, N. I. *Natural Resources and the Political Struggle.* Garden City, N.Y.: Doubleday, 1955.

White, G., ed. *Water, Health, and Society.* Bloomington, Ind.: Indiana Univ. Press, 1969.

Whittaker, R. *Communities of Ecosystems.* New York: Macmillan, 1970.

Willhelm, S. M. *Urban Zoning and Land-Use Theory.* New York: Free Press, 1962.

Wolozin, H., ed. *The Economics of Air Pollution.* New York: Norton, 1966.

PERIODICALS

"A Model Interstate Compact for the Control of Air Pollution," Note, *Harvard Journal Legis.* 4:369, 1967.

Adams, D. A. "Environmental Law Tackles Three American Institutions," *Industrial Water Engineering* 8:4, 1971.

"Administration of Public Lands: Symposium," *Natural Resources Journal* 7:149, 1967.

"Aesthetic Zoning: A Current Evaluation of the Law," *University of Florida Law Review* 18:430, 1965.

"Aesthetic Zoning and the Police Power," *Journal of the Urban League* 46:773, 1969.

"Aesthetics in the Law," *New York Customs Brokers' Assoc.* 22:607, 1967.

"Aesthetics v. Free Enterprise—A Symposium," *Practical Lawyer* 15, 1969.

"Agricultural Pesticides: The Need for Improved Control Legislation," *Minnesota Law Review* 52:1242, 1968.

"Air Pollution as a Private Nuisance," *Casenote, Washington and Lee Law Review* 24:314, 1967.

"Air Pollution—Automobile Smog: A Proposed Remedy," Note, *DePaul Law Review* 14:436, 1965.

"Air Pollution, Bibliography of Congressional Materials," Note, *Law Library Journal* 62:84, 1969.

"Air Pollution Control: A Symposium," *Law and Contemporary Problems* 33, 1968.

"Air Pollution Symposium," *Arizona Law Review* 10, 1968.

"Aircraft Noise: Unrelenting, Unremitting, Intolerable," *Environmental Science and Technology* 1:976, 1967.

"Airplane Noise, Property Rights, and the Constitution," Note, *Columbia Law Review* 65:1426, 1965.

Aitken, L. L., Jr. "Public Land Law Review Commission: Public Participation," *Rocky Mountain Mining Law Institute* 13:41, 1967.

American Society for Public Administration, "Symposium on Environmental Policy," *Public Administration Review* 28:301, 1968.

"America's Changing Environment," *Daedalus* 96:1003, 1967.

Arkin, M. B., Burdick, G. M., and Joyner, S. A. "Sonic Boom—A Legal Nightmare," *Oklahoma Law Review* 19:292, 1966.

Beazley, R. "Conservation Decision Making: A Rationalization," *Natural Resources Journal* 7:345, 1967.

Beham, R. W. "Succotash Syndrome, or Multiple Use: A Heartfelt Approach to Forest Land Management." *Natural Resources Journal* 7:473, 1967.

Bennett, E. F. "Public Land Policy: Reconciliation of Public Use and Private Development," *Rocky Mountain Mining Law Institute* 11:169, 1966.

Bermingham, P. E. "The Federal Government and Air and Water Pollution," *Business Law* 23:457, 1968.

Beverly, R. G. "Development and Legislation of Environmental Regulations for Mining," *Rocky Mountain Mining Law Institute* 15:311, 1966.

Blaustein, A. D. "Arguendo: the Legal Challenge of Population Control," *Law and Society Review* 3:107, 1968.

Bolle, A. W. "Public Participation and Environmental Quality," *Natural Resources Journal* 11:3, 1971.

Bosselman, F. J. "Control of Surface Mining: An Exercise in Creative Federalism," *Natural Resources Journal* 9:138, 1969.

Boston, W., Jr. "A Cause for Injunction," *JAG Journal* 20:47, 1965.

Bower, B. T. "Some Physical, Technological, and Economic Characteristics of Water and Water Resource Systems: Implications for Administration," *Natural Resources Journal* 3:215, 1963.

Broesche, T. C. "Land-Use Regulation for the Protection of Public Parks and Recreational Areas," *Texas Law Review* 45:966, 1966.

Brooks, D. L. "Environmental Quality Control: A Statement of the Problem," *BioScience* 17:December, 1967.

Brown, P. "Pollution and Attendant Problems," *Oklahoma* 40:47, 1969.

Bultena, G. L., and Taves, M. J. "Changing Wilderness Images and Forest Policy," *Journal of Forestry* March 1961.

Burhenne, W. E., and Irwin, W. A. "The Coordination of Legislative Policy and the Regulation of Private Interests: Some Suggested Pragmatic Principles for Environmental Policy," *Natural Resources Journal* 11:3, 1971.

Burton, I. "The Quality of the Environment: A Review," *Geographical Review* 58:473, 1968.

Burton, I., and Kates, R. W. "The Perception of Natural Hazards in Resource Management," *Natural Resources Journal* 3:412, 1964.

Cain, S. A. "Environmental Management and the Department of the Interior," *Public Administration Review* 28:301, 1968.

Caldwell, L. K. "Authority and Responsibility for Environmental Administration," *Annals of the American Academy of Political and Social Science* 389:107, 1970.

Caldwell, L. K. "Environment: A New Focus for Public Policy?" *Public Administration Review* 23:132, 1963.

Caldwell, L. K. "Environmental Policy in a Hypertrophic Society," *Natural Resources Journal* 11:3, 1971.

Caldwell, L. K. "Environmental Quality as an Administrative Problem," *Annals of the American Academy of Political and Social Science* 400:103, 1972.

Caldwell, L. K. "Problems of Applied Ecology: Perceptions, Institutions, Methods, and Operational Tools," *BioScience* 16:524, 1966.

Caldwell, L. K. "Restructuring for Coordinative Policy and Action," *Public Administration Review* 28:301, 1968.

"Can Law Reclaim Man's Environment?" *Trial* 5:10: 1969.

Carmichael, D. M. "Forty Years of Water Pollution Control in Wisconsin: A Case Study," *Wisconsin Law Review* 350, 1967.

Carter, L. J. "Technology and the Environment: A New Concern on Capitol Hill," *Science* 157:784, 1967.

Carver, J. A., Jr. "Administrative Law and Public Land Management," *Administrative Law Review* 18:7, 1965.

Carver, J. A., Jr. "Role of the Federal Government in Land Management," *Rocky Mountain Mining Law Institute* 11:345, 1966.

Carver, J. A., Jr. "Pollution Control and the Federal Power Commission," *Natural Resources Law* 1:32, 1968.

Caulfield, H. P., Jr. "Environmental Management: Water and Related Land," *Public Administration Review* 28:306, 1968.

Ciriacy-Wantrup, S. V. "The Economics of Environmental Policy," *Land Economics* 1:47, 1971

"Citizen Participation in Public Land Decisions," *St. Louis University Law Journal* 9:372, 1965.

Clark, H. H., Jr. "Law as an Instrument of Population Control," *University of Colorado Law Review* 40:179, 1968.

Clary, J. T. "Air and Water Interstate Compacts," *Natural Resources Law* 1:60, 1968.

Cliff, E. P. "The Role of Forest Recreation in Forest Land Management," *Journal of Forestry* 59:491, 1961.

Clogger, T. J. "Noises that Assail Us," *Contemporary Review* 711:113, 1967.

Clyde, E. W. "Legal Problems Imposed by Requirements of Restoration and Beautification of Mining Properties," *Rocky Mountain Mining Law Institute* 13:187, 1967.

Coleman, W. "Science and Symbol in the Turner Frontier Hypothesis," *American Historical Review* 72:22, 1966.

"Commercial Feedlots–Nuisance, Zoning, and Regulation," Note, *Washburn Law Journal* 6:493, 1967.

"Constitutional Law–Governmental Regulations of Surface Mining Activities," *North Carolina Law Review* 46:103, 1967.

Corbridge, J. "Weather Modification: Law and Administration," *Natural Resources Journal* 8:207, 1968; *County Officer* 30:16, 1965.

Craik, K. H. "Environmental Dispositions of Environmental Decision Makers," *Annals of the American Academy of Political and Social Science* 389:87, 1970.

Craine, L. E. "Natural Resources and Government," *Public Administration Review* 16:212, 1968.

Craine, L. E. "The Inner-Directed Field Man," *Public Administration Review* 22:4, 1960.

Craine, L. E. "The Muskingum Watershed Conservancy District: A Study of Local Control," *Law and Contemporary Problems* 22:323, 1957.

Craine, L. E. "Water Management and Urban Planning," *American Journal of Public Health* 50:427, 1961.

Craine, L. E., and Fox, I. "Organizational Arrangement for Water Development," *Natural Resources Journal* 2:1, 1962.

Croker, T. D. "Some Economics of Air Pollution Control," *Natural Resources Journal* 8:236, 1968.

Dana, S. T. "Multiple Use, Biology, and Economics," *Journal of Forestry* September 1943.

Delogu, O. E. "The Taxing Power as a Land Use Control Device," *Denver Law Journal* 45:279, 1968.

Dovies, J. C., III. "Some Political Characteristics of Pollution Control," *American Journal of Public Health* 61:7, 1971.

Dunkelberger, H. E. "Federal–State Relationships in the Adoption of Water Quality Standards Under the Federal Pollution Control Act," *Natural Resources Law* 2:47, 1969.

Edelman, S. "Federal Air and Water Control: The Application of the Commerce Powers to Abate Interstate and Intrastate Pollution," *George Washington Law Review* 33:1067, 1965.

Edwards, M. N. "The Legislative Approach to Air and Water Quality," *Natural Resources Law* 1:58, 1969.

Egler, F. E. "Pesticides in Our Ecosystem," *American Scientist* 52:110, 1964.

Eliassen, R. "Future Planning of Water Resources at the Regional Water District Level," *Journal of the American Waterworks Association* 59:433, 1967.

"Environment and Behavior," *American Behavioral Scientist* 10:3, 1966.

"Environment Control: A Symposium," *Denver Law Journal* 45:145, 1968.

"Environmental Legislation: 1971 Not A Year for Conclusive Action," *Science* 174:4013, 1971.

"Environmental Policy: New Directions in Federal Action," *Public Administration Review* 28:301, 1968.

"Federal Regulation of Air Transportation and the Environmental Impact Problem," *University of Chicago Law Review* 35:317, 1968.

First, M. W. "Environmental Hazards," *New England Journal of Medicine* 275:1478, 1966.

Fishbein, G. "The Future of Environmental Health at the Federal Level," *American Journal of Public Health and the Nation's Health* 58, 1968.

Fisher, J. L. "Resource Policies and Administration for the Future," *Public Administration Review* 21:74, 1961.

Fisher, J. L. "The Natural Environment," *The Annals of the American Academy of Political and Social Science* 371:127, 1967.

Forer, L. G. "Preservation of America's Park Lands: The Inadequacy of Present Law," *New York University Law Review* 41:1093, 1965.

Fraser, Darling F. "Conservation and Ecological Theory," *Journal of Ecology* 52:March, 1963.

Frauenglass, H. "Environmental Policy: Public Participation and the Open Information System," *National Resources Journal* 11:3, 1971.

Freeman, A. M. "Advocacy and Resources Allocation Decisions in the Public Sector," *Natural Resources Journal* 9:166, 1969.

Frye, J. C. "Geological Information for Managing the Environment," *Texas Quarterly* 11:55, 1968.

Galbraith, J. K. "Economics and Environment," *American Institute of Architects* 66:September, 1966.

Galbraith, J. K. "The Polipollutionists," *Atlantic Monthly* 219:52, 1967.

Gilliam, H. "The Fallacy of Single-Purpose Planning," *Daedalus* 96:1142, 1967.

Goodman, D. "Ideology and Ecological Irrationality," *BioScience* 20:23, 1970.

Goodman, M. "National Radiation Health Standards—A Study in Scientific Decision Making," *Atomic Energy Law Journal* 6:217, 1964.

Green, H. P. "Technology Assessment and the Law: Introduction and Perspective," *George Washington Law Review* 36:1033, 1968.

Green, L. C. "State Control of the Interstate Air Pollution," *Law and Contemporary Problems* 33:315, 1968.

Hagevik, G. "Legislation for Air Quality Management: Reducing Theory to Practice," *Law and Contemporary Problems* 33:369, 1968.

Hall, G. R. "Conservation as a Public Policy Goal," *Yale Review* 51:400, 1962.

Halprin, L. "The Engineer and the Landscape," *International Science and Technology* November 1967.

Halprin, L. "Public Policy and Environmental Administration," *BioScience* 27:December, 1967.

Hamill, L. "The Process of Making Good Decisions About the Use of the Environment of Man," *National Resources Journal* 8:279, 1968.

Hammer, S. "Defense of Explosion or Vibration Damage Cases," *Defense Law Journal* 14:1, 1965.

Hammond, J. H., Jr. "The Wilderness Act and Mining: Some Proposals for Conservation," *Oregon Law Review* 47:447, 1968.

Hampton, C. R. "Environmental Control Problems and the Oil Industry in the Rocky Mountain Region," *Rocky Mountain Mining Law Institute* 15:621, 1969.

Headley, J. "Environmental Quality and Chemical Pesticides," *Journal of Soil and Water Conservation* 21:130, 1966.

Henning, D. H. "Comments on an Interdisciplinary Social Science Approach for Conservation Administration," *BioScience* 20:1, 1970.

Henning, D. H. "Natural Resources Administration and the Public Interest," *Public Administration Review* 30 March–April 1970.

Henning, D. H. "The Administration of Wilderness in a Democracy," *Congressional Record* September 23, 1968.

Selected Bibliography

Henning, D. H. "The Politics of Natural Resources Administration," *The Annals of Regional Science* 2, 1968.

Henning, D. H. "The Public Land Law Review Commission: A Political and Western Analysis," *Idaho Law Review* 7:77, 1970.

Henning, D. H. "Wilderness: Its Meaning to Man," *Naturalist* 18:120, 1967.

Hill, J. D. "Liability for Aircraft Noise—the Aftermath of *Causby* and *Griggs,*" *University of Miami Law Review* 19:1, 1964.

Horton, J. E. "The Tactics of Ecotokenism," *Outdoor America* 36:8, 1971.

Huffman, R. E. "Public Policy for Resource Development in the West," *Journal of Farm Economics* 35:719, 1953.

Jackson, H. M. "Environmental Policy and Congress," *Natural Resources Journal* 11:3, 1971.

Jaffe, L. L. "Citizen as Litigant in Public Actions: The Non-Hohfeldian or Ideological Plaintiff," *University of Pennsylvania Law Review* 16:1033, 1968.

Jordan, Frederich J. E. "Recent Developments in Environmental Pollution Control," *McGill Law Journal* 15:279, 1969.

Juergensmeyer, J. C. "Control of Air Pollution Through the Assertion of Private Rights," *Duke Law Journal* 1126, 1967.

Klausner, S. Z., ed. "Society and its Physical Environment," *Annals of the American Academy of Political and Social Science* 389:entire issue, 1970.

Kleiman, H. S. "Planning Growth for a Changing Society," *Battelle Research Outlook* 3:1, 1971.

Knelman, F. H. "A Policy for Survival," *Alternatives: Perspectives on Society and Environment* 1:2, 1971.

Knelman, F. H. "Pollution and the Technological Order," *Canadian Dimension* 7:7, 1971.

Knetsch, J. L. "Economic Aspects of Environmental Pollution," *Journal of Farm Economics* 48: December, 1966.

Knodell, J. D., Jr. "Liability for Pollution of Surface and Underground Waters," *Rocky Mountain Mineral Law Institute* 12:33, 1967.

Kramer, H. P. "Environment: Past, Present, Future," *Environmental Science and Technology* 2: August, 1968.

Krutilla, J. V. "Some Environmental Effects of Economic Development," *Daedalus* 96:1058, 1967.

"Land-Planning and the Law: Emerging Policies and Techniques—A Symposium," *U.C.L.A. Law Review* 12:707, 1965.

"Land-Use Symposium," *Iowa Law Review* 50, 1965.

Lee, L. K. "Federal Legislation in the 1960s," *Parks and Recreation* 6:8, 1971.

"Legal Control of Water Pollution," *U.C.D.L. Review* 1:1, 1969.

Leopold, A. "Land-Use and Democracy," *Audubon Magazine* 64:259, 1942.

Lessing, L. "Systems Engineering Invades the City," *Fortune* 77:154, 1968.

Lester, A. P. "River Pollution in International Law," *American Journal of International Law* 57:828, 1963.

Lewis, W. R., Sr. "The Phantom of Federal Liability for Pollution Abatement in Condemnation Actions," *Mercer Law Review* 17:364, 1966.

Libby, W. F. "Man's Place in the Physical Universe," *Bulletin of the Atomic Scientists* 21:12, 1965.

Lieberman, J. A., and Belter, W. G. "Waste Management and Environmental Aspects of Nuclear Power," *Environmental Science and Technology* 1:June, 1967.

Llewelyn-Davies, R. "Ekistics, the Future Pattern of Human Settlements," *Architectural Review* 138:399, 1965.

"Local Zoning of Strip Mining," *Kentucky Law Journal* 57:738, 1968.

Long, P. P. "Power and Administration," *Public Administration Review* 9:Autumn, 1969.

Loucks, D. P. "Residuals—Environmental Quality Management: A Framework for Policy Analysis," *Natural Resources Journal*, 11:3, 1971.

Lynch, K. "City as Environment," *Scientific American* 213:209, 1965.

185

Maloney, F., and Plager, S. "Diffused Surface Water, Scourge or Bounty?" *Natural Resources Journal* 8:72, 1968.

Mann, D. "Political Implications of Migration to the Arid Lands of the United States," *Natural Resources Journal* 9:212, 1969.

Martin, P. P. "Conflict Resolution Through the Multi-Use Concept in Forest Decision Making," *Natural Resources Journal* 9:228, 1969.

McArdle, R. E. "Multiple Use–Multiple Benefits," *Journal of Forestry* May, 1953.

McCarthy, R. D. "Recent Legal Developments in Environmental Defense," *Buffalo Law Review* 19:195, 1970.

McCaull, J. "The Politics of Technology," *Environment* 14:2, 1972.

McCloskey, J. M. "A Landscape Policy for Public Lands," *Denver Law Journal* 45:149, 1968.

McCloskey, J. M. "Can Recreational Conservationists Provide for a Mining Industry?" *Rocky Mountain Mining Law Institute* 13:65, 1967.

McCloskey, J. M. "Wilderness Act of 1964: Its Background and Meaning," *Oregon Law Review* 45:288, 1966.

McConnell, G. "The Multiple-Use Concept in Forest Service Policy," *Sierra Club Bulletin* October, 1959.

McElrath, D. "Public Response to Environmental Problems," Indiana Univ., Institute of Public Administration. Environmental Studies, I:January 1967.

Middleton, J. T. "Man and His Habitat: Problems of Pollution," *Bulletin of the Atomic Scientists* 21:March, 1965.

Mitchell, B. "Behavioral Aspects of Water Management," *Environment and Behavior* 3:2, 1971.

Mock, H. B. "Human Obstacles to Utilization of the Public Domain," *Rocky Mountain Mining Law Institute* 12:187, 1967.

Morgan, R. J. "Pressure Politics and Resource Administration," *Journal of Politics* 18:1, 1956.

Moses, R. J. "What Happened to Multiple-Purpose Resource Development?–A Plea for Reasonableness," *Land and Water Law Review* 3:435, 1968.

Murray, W. J. "Recent Conservation Developments: Technical, Economic, and Legal," *Tulane Tidelands Institute* 7:3, 1963.

Nace, R. L. "Water Resources: A Global Problem with Local Roots," *Environmental Science and Technology* 1:550, 1967.

"Natural Resources Symposium," *Oregon Law Review* 45, 1960.

Nebolsine, R. "Today's Problems of Industrial Waste Water Pollution Abatement," *Natural Resources Law* 1:39, 1968.

"Neglected Ninth Amendment: The 'Other Rights' Retained by the People," *Marquette Law Review* 51:121, 1967.

Netherton, R. D. "Implementation of Land Use Policy: Police Power vs. Eminent Domain," *Land and Water Law Review* 3:33, 1968.

Norton, T. M. "Police Power, Planning, and Aesthetics," *Santa Clara Lawyer* 7:71, 1967.

Olpin, O. "Recent Developments Affecting Public Lands of the States–1968," *Natural Resources Law* 2:229, 1969.

"Open Space Legislation: Suggestions for a Model Act," *Georgia Law Review* 2:83, 1967.

O'Riordan, T. "Public Opinion and Environmental Quality," *Environment and Behavior* 3:2, 1971.

"Park Planning and the Acquisition of Open Spaces: A Case Study," *University of Chicago Law Review* 36:642, 1969.

Pearl, M. A. "Historical View of Public Land Disposal and the American Land Use," *California Western Law Review* 4:65, 1968.

Plager, S. J., and Handler, J. F. "The Politics of Planning for Urban Redevelopment: Strategies in the Manipulation of Public Law," *Wisconsin Law Review* 724, 1966.

"Population, Pressure, Housing and Habitat," *Law and Contemporary Problems* 32:191, 1967.

Reagan, M. D. "Toward Improved National Policy Planning," *Public Administration Review* 23:10, 1963.

Selected Bibliography

"Recreational Planning: A Symposium," *Kentucky Law Journal* 55, 1967.

Reich, C. A. "Law of the Planned Society," *Yale Law Journal* 75:1227, 1966.

Reis, R. I. "Policy and Planning for Recreational Use of Inland Water," *Temple Law Quarterly* 40:155, 1967.

Reitze, A. W. "Pollution Control: Why Has it Failed?" *American Bar Association Journal* 55:923, 1969.

"Reorganizing to Fight Urban Pollution," *Environmental Science and Technology* 2:504, 1968.

Rhodes, H. N. "Engineering and Economics in Conservation," *Rocky Mountain Mining Law Institute* 12:425, 1967.

Rhodes, H. N. "Need for Meaningful Control in the Management of Federally Owned Timberlands," *Land and Water Law Review* 4:121, 1969.

Rogers, "Administrative Law–Expansion of 'Public Interest' Standing," *North Carolina Law Review* 45:998, 1967.

Rohrman, D. F. "Law of Pesticides: Present and Future," *Journal of Public Law* 7:351, 1968.

Rohrman, D. F. "Pesticide Laws and Legal Implications of Pesticide Use," *Food and Drug Commission Law Journal* 23:142, 1968.

Sax, J. L. "Environment and the Courts of Law," *Ecology Today* 1:7, 1971.

Schiller, H. I. "Social Control and Individual Freedom," *Bulletin of the Atomic Scientists* 24:16, 1968.

Schmitz, T. M. "Pollution, Law, Science, and Damage Awards," *Cleveland State Law Review* 18:456, 1969.

Schoonover, B., and Stienriff, D. J. "Public Relations, Law, Environmental Pollution," *Cleveland State Law Review* 18:467, 1969.

Searles, S. Z. "Aesthetics in the Law," *New York State Bar Journal* 22:607, 1967.

"Sierra Club Political Activity, and Tax Exempt Charitable Status," *Georgetown Law Journal* 55:1128, 1967.

Sigler, J. A. "Controlling the Use of Pesticides," *Journal of Public Law* 15:311, 1966.

Sillin, L. F. J. "Environmental Considerations Facing the Public Utility Industry," *Natural Resources Law* 2:20, 1969.

Spater, G. A. "Noise and the Law," *Michigan Law Review* 63:1373, 1965.

Spengler, J. J. "Megalopolis: Resource Conserver or Resource Waster?" *Natural Resources Journal* 7:376, 1967.

Spilhaus, A. "Control of the World Environment," *Geographical Review* 66 October, 1956.

"Standing to Appeal Zoning Determinations: the 'Aggrieved Persons' Requirement," *Michigan Law Review* 64:1070, 1966.

"Standing to Sue and Conservation Values," *University of Colorado Law Review* 38:291, 1966.

Steck, H. "Power and the Liberation of Nature: The Politics of Ecology," *Alternatives* 1:1, 1971.

Stein, "Regulatory Aspects of Federal Water Pollution Control," *Denver Law Journal* 45:267, 1968.

"Stream Pollution–Recovery of Damages," Note, *Iowa Law Review* 50:141, 1964.

"Symposium: The Impact of Science and Technology on International Law," *California Law Review* 55:419, 1967.

Symposium: "Long-range Concerns Resulting from the Deteriorating American Environment," *Daedalus* 96, 1967.

Symposium: "Oil Shale Resources," *National Resources Journal* 8:569, 1968.

Symposium: "Technology Assessment," *George Washington Law Review* 36:1033, 1968.

Symposium, "Water Law," *Willamette Law Journal* 3:295, 1966.

Symposium: "Water Resources Research," *Natural Resources Journal* 5:218, 1968.

Thomas, Pearl, Williams, and Van Dersal. "Conservation of Natural Resources: A Panel," *Law Library Journal* 60:362, 1967.

Tichenor, P. J. "Environment and Public Opinion," *Journal of Environmental Education* 2:4, 1971.

Tippy, R. "Preservation Values in River Basin Planning," *Natural Resources Journal* 8:259, 1968.

Trelease, F. "Policies for Water Law: Property Rights, Economic Forces, and Public Regulation," *Natural Resources Journal* 5:1, 1965.

Tribus, M. "Power is Not in the Hands of Technically Qualified People," *Professional Engineer* 4:41, 1971.

Twiss, R. H., and Litton, R. B. "Resource Use in the Regional Landscape," *Natural Resources Journal* 6:76, 1966.

Tyler, R. "Methods for State Level Enforcement of Air and Water Pollution Laws," *Texas Bar Journal* 31:905, 1968.

"Urban Problems and Prospects," *Law and Contemporary Problems* 80:1, 1965.

Utton, A. E. "Environmental Policy and International Institutional Arrangements: A Proposal for Regional and Global Environmental Protection Agencies," *Natural Resources Journal* 11:3, 1971.

Waggoner, P. E. "The Environmental Dilemma," *Horticulture* 49:5, 1971.

Walsh, J. "Environmental Pollution: West Germany, U.S. Cooperate," *Science* 157:529, 1967.

Walsh, J. "Pollution: PSAC Panel Takes a Panoramic View," *Science* 150:1006, 1965.

Wandesforde-Smith, G. "The Bureaucratic Response to Environmental Politics," *Natural Resources Journal* 11:3, 1971.

Warne, W. "Water Crisis is Present," *Natural Resources Journal* 9:53, 1969.

"Water for Recreation: A Plea for Recognition," *Denver Law Journal* 44:228, 1967.

"Water Use—A Symposium," *Boston College Industrial and Commercial Law Review* 9:531, 1968.

Wengert, N. "The Ideological Basis of Conservation and Natural Resources Policies and Programs," *Annals of Science* 364: November, 1962.

Wengert, N. "Political and Social Accommodation: The Political Process and Environmental Preservation," *Natural Resources Journal* 11:3, 1971.

Wilson, H. A. "Sonic Boom," *Scientific American* 206:36, 1962.

Wolf, E. L. "Legal Aspects of Air Pollution," *Trial Law Quarterly* 5:22, 1968.

Wolman, A. "Impact of Population Changes on the Environment," *Public Administration Review* 28 July—August 1968.

Wolman, A. "Pollution as an International Issue," *Foreign Affairs* 47:164, 1968.

Wolozin, H. "The Economics of Air Pollution: Central Problems," *Law and Contemporary Problems* 33:227, 1968.

Wood, R. C. "Federal Role in the Urban Environment," *Public Administration Review* 28 July—August 1968.

Woodcock, L. "Labor and the Politics of Environment," *Sierra Club Bulletin* 56:10, 1971.

Wright, D. S. "Intergovernmental Action on Environmental Policy: The Role of The States," Indiana Univ., Institute of Public Administration, Environmental Studies, II, March 1967.

Zielinski, " 'Public Interest' Standing for the Federal Taxpayer: A Proposal," *Buffalo Law Review* 17:887, 1968.

Zimmerman, "Political Boundaries and Air Pollution Control," *Journal of the Urban League.* 46:173, 1968.

Zivnuska, J. A. "The Multiple Problems of Multiple Use," *Journal of Forestry* 59:555, 1961.

GOVERNMENT PUBLICATIONS

Bureau of Land Management Library. *Public Lands Bibliography* 106 (suppl. 1965), 1968.

Burgin, V. *Decisions and Opinions of the U.S. Department of the Interior.* Washington: Dept. of the Interior, 1969.

Caldwell, L. *A National Policy for the Environment.* U.S. 90th Cong., 2d sess., S. Doc. 35. Washington: U.S. Gov't Printing Office, 1968.

Citizens' Advisory Committee on Environmental Quality. *Report to the President and to the President's Council on Environmental Quality.* Washington: U.S. Gov't Printing Office, 1969.

Selected Bibliography

Citizens' Advisory Committee on Recreation and Natural Beauty. *Annual Report to the President and to the President's Council on Recreation and Natural Beauty.* Washington: U.S. Gov't Printing Office, 1968.

Commission on Organization of Executive Branch. Washington: (First Hoover Commission). *Task Force Report on Natural Resources.* Washington: U.S. Gov't Printing Office, 1949.

Committee on Environmental Quality of the Federal Council for Science and Technology. *Noise— Sound Without Value.* Washington: U.S. Gov't Printing Office, 1968.

Committee on Pollution of the National Academy of Sciences, National Research Council. *Waste Management and Control.* Washington: National Academy of Sciences, 1966.

Committee on Resources and Man, National Academy of Sciences—National Research Council. *Resources and Man, Summary of Findings and Recommendations.* Washington: National Academy of Sciences, 1969.

"Congress and Federal Pollution Controls." *Congressional Digest* 49:193, 1970.

Council on Environmental Quality. *Environmental Quality: First Annual Report.* Washington: U.S. Gov't Printing Office, 1970.

Council on Environmental Quality. *Monitor* 102(October 1971)p. 9.

Degler, S. E., and Bloom, S. C. *Federal Pollution Control Programs: Water, Air, and Solid Wastes.* Washington: Bureau of National Affairs, 1969.

Democratic Study Group. *Federal Water Pollution Control Act, Fact Sheet 92–93: Analysis of Human Resources 11896.* Washington: U.S. Gov't Printing Office, 1972.

Donnelly, W. H. *Effect of Calvert Cliffs and Other Court Decisions upon Nuclear Power in the United States.* Washington: U.S. Gov't Printing Office, 1972.

Eliason, R.: *Solid Waste Management: A Comprehensive Assessment of Solid Waste Problems, Practices, and Needs.* Washington: U.S. Gov't Printing Office, 1969.

Legislative Reference Service. *Congressional White Paper on a National Policy for the Environment Submitted to the U.S. Congress, 90th Cong., 2d sess.* (Comm. Print, 1968).

Massachusetts Institute of Technology. *Papers on National Land Use Policy Issues.* Washington: U.S. Gov't Printing Office, 1971.

National Academy of Sciences. *Waste Management and Control: A Report to the Federal Council on Science and Technology* Pub. 1400. Washington: National Academy of Sciences, 1966.

National Academy of Sciences, National Research Council. *Disposal of Radioactive Waste on Land* Pub. 519. Washington: National Academy of Sciences, 1957.

National Academy of Sciences, National Research Council. *Weather and Climate Modification— Problems and Prospects* Pub. 1350, 2 vols. Washington: National Academy of Sciences, 1966.

National Referral Center for Science and Technology. *Directory of Information Resources in the United States: Water.* Washington: U.S. Gov't Printing Office, 1970.

Office of Science and Technology. *Considerations Affecting Steam Power Plant Site Selection.* Washington: U.S. Gov't Printing Office, 1968.

Office of Science and Technology. *Control of Agriculture-Related Pollution.* Washington: U.S. Gov't Printing Office, 1969.

Pell, C., and Case, C. P. *United Nations Conference on the Human Environment.* Washington: U.S. Gov't Printing Office, 1972.

Perry, H., Beard, D., and Brown, H. *A Review of Energy Policy.* The Activities of the 92d Congress, 1st Session. Washington, D.C.: U.S. Gov't Printing Office, 1972.

"Pollution Control—Evolution of the Present Federal Law." *Congressional Digest* 49:194, 1970.

President's Committee on Population and Family Planning. *The Transition From Concern to Action.* Washington: U.S. Gov't Printing Office, 1968.

President's Council on Recreation and Natural Beauty. *From Sea to Shining Sea: A Report on the American Environment—Our Natural Heritage.* Washington: U.S. Gov't Printing Office, 304, 1968.

President's Materials Policy Commission. *Resources for Freedom,* vol. I. Washington: U.S. Gov't Printing Office, 1952.

President's Science Advisory Committee. *The Use of Pesticides, Report of the Life Sciences Panel.* Washington: U.S. Gov't Printing Office, 1963.

President's Science Advisory Committee. *Use of Pesticides.* Washington: U.S. Gov't Printing Office, 1966.

President's Science Advisory Committee, Environmental Pollution Panel. *Restoring the Quality of Our Environment.* Washington: U.S. Gov't Printing Office, 1965.

President's Water Resources Policy Commission. *A Water Policy for the American People,* vol. I. Washington: U.S. Gov't Printing Office, 1950.

Presidential Advisory Committee on Water Resources Policy. *Water Resources Policy.* Washington: U.S. Gov't Printing Office, 1955.

Presidential Message to Congress on Population. Delivered by President Richard M. Nixon on July 18, 1969, at the White House. Washington: U.S. Gov't Printing Office, 1969.

"Program on Environmental Quality Control," *U.S. Congressional Record* 114, no. 17, Tuesday, February 6, 1968.

Public Land Law Review Commission. *Administrative Procedures and Public Lands.* Study Report. Charlottesville: Univ. of Virginia, Institute of Government, 1969.

Public Land Law Review Commission. *Digest of Public Land Laws.* Colorado Springs, Colo.: Shepard's Citations, Inc., 1968.

Public Land Law Review Commission. *Federal Public Land Laws and Policies Relating to Use and Occupancy,* by Daniel, Mann, Johnson, and Mendenhall. Study Report, ch. 3, pts. IID, IIE. Washington: U.S. Gov't Printing Office, 1970.

Public Land Law Review Commission. *History of Public Land Law and Development,* by P. W. Gates and R. W. Swenson. Study Report. Washington: U.S. Gov't Printing Office, 1968.

Public Land Law Review Commission. *Legal and Administrative Framework for Environmental Management of the Public Lands,* by I. M. Herman and R. H. Twiss. Study Report. Washington: U.S. Gov't Printing Office, 1970.

Public Land Law Review Commission. *Regional and Local Land Use Planning,* by D. R. Herman and Associates. Study Report, ch. IV. Washington: U.S. Gov't Printing Office, 1970.

Revelle, R. *The Quality of Human Environment.* Washington: U.S. Gov't Printing Office, 1968.

Secretary of Health, Education and Welfare, *Automotive Air Pollution.* Washington: U.S. Gov't Printing Office, 1967.

Shaw, E. W. *A Review of Energy Resources of the Public Lands, Based on Studies Sponsored by the PLLRC.* Washington: U.S. Gov't Printing Office, 1971.

Sherman, H. R., and Abbasi, S. R. *The Need for a World Environmental Institute.* Washington: U.S. Gov't Printing Office, 1972.

Udell, G. G., ed. *Laws Relating to Forestry, Game Conservation, Flood Control, and Related Subjects.* Washington: U.S. Gov't Printing Office, 1971.

United Nations, Economic and Social Council. *Intergovernmental Conference of Experts on the Scientific Basis for Rational Use and Conservation of the Resources of the Biosphere* (SC/MD/9), January 6, 1969.

U.S. Army Corps of Engineers, Coastal Engineering Resource Center. *Shore Protection, Planning, and Design.* Washington: U.S. Gov't Printing Office, 1966.

U.S. Bureau of International Scientific and Technological Affairs. *U.S. National Report on the Human Environment.* U.S. State Department Report No. 8588. Washington: U.S. Gov't Printing Office, 1971.

U.S., Congress. Joint Committee on Atomic Energy, Subcommittee on Legislation. *AEC Licensing Procedure and Related Legislation.* Hearings, 92d Cong., 1st sess., 1971. Washington: U.S. Gov't Printing Office, 1971.

U.S., Congress. Joint Economics Committee. *The Economics of National Priorities.* Hearings, 92d Cong., 1st sess. Washington: U.S. Gov't Printing Office, 1971.

U.S., Congress, Joint Economics Committee. *The Economics of Recycling Waste Materials.* Hearings, 92d Cong., 1st sess. Washington: U.S. Gov't Printing Office, 1972.

Selected Bibliography

U.S., Congress. Joint Economics Committee. *Natural Gas Regulation and the Trans-Alaska Pipeline.* 92d Cong., 2d sess. Washington: U.S. Gov't Printing Office, 1972.

U.S., Congress, House. *Ad Hoc* Subcommittee on Urban Growth of the House Committee on Banking and Currency. *Population Trends.* Hearings, 91st Cong., 1st sess., on H. 803. Washington: U.S. Gov't Printing Office, 1969.

U.S., Congress, House. Committee on Agriculture. *Cooperative Forest Programs.* 92d Cong., 1st sess., H. Rept. 8817 to accompany H.R. 8817. Washington: U.S. Gov't Printing Office, 1971.

U.S., Congress, House. Committee on Government Operations. *Protecting America's Estuaries.* Hearings, 92d Cong., 1st sess., on H. 1761. Washington: U.S. Gov't Printing Office, 1971.

U.S., Congress, House. Committee on Interior and Insular Affairs. *Intergovernmental Cooperation.* Hearings, 90th Cong., 1st sess. Washington: U.S. Gov't Printing Office, 1967.

U.S., Congress, House. Committee on Interior and Insular Affairs. *National Land Policy, Planning and Management Act of 1972.* 92d Cong., 2d sess. Washington: U.S. Gov't Printing Office, 1972.

U.S., Congress, House. Committee on Interior and Insular Affairs. *Policies, Programs, and Activities of the Department of Interior.* Hearings, 90th Cong., 1st sess. Washington: U.S. Gov't Printing Office, 1967.

U.S., Congress, House. Committee on Merchant Marine and Fisheries. *Acquisition of Lands for Recreational and Natural Resources Protection Purposes at Fish and Wildlife Conservation Areas.* 92d Cong., 1st sess. Washington: U.S. Gov't Printing Office, 1971.

U.S., Congress, House. Committee on Public Works. *Water Pollution Control Legislation.* 92d Cong., 1st sess., H.R.9. Washington: U.S. Gov't Printing Office, 1971.

U.S., Congress, House. Committee on Science and Astronautics. *The Adequacy of Technology for Pollution Abatement.* 89th Cong., 2d sess. Washington: U.S. Gov't Printing Office, 1966.

U.S., Congress, House. *Environmental Pollution: A Challenge to Science and Technology.* 89th Cong., 2d sess., H. Washington: U.S. Gov't Printing Office, 1966.

U.S., Congress, House Document Room. *Laws Relating to Forestry, Game Conservation, Flood Control, and Related Subjects.* [Aug. 24, 1912–Nov. 8, 1966] Washington: U.S. Gov't Printing Office, 1966.

U.S., Congress, House. Subcommittee on Science Research and Development of the Science and Astronautics Committee. *Environmental Quality.* Hearings, 90th Cong., 2d sess., on H.R. 7796, H.R. 13211, H.R. 14605, and H.R. 14627. Washington: U.S. Gov't Printing Office, 1968.

U.S., Congress, House. Subcommittee of House Committee on Government Operations. *Effects of Population Growth on Natural Resources and the Environment.* Hearings, 91st Cong., 1st sess., on H. 256. Washington: U.S. Gov't Printing Office, 1969.

U.S., Congress, House. Subcommittee of Science, Research, and Development of the Committee on Science and Astronautics. *Environmental Quality.* Hearings, 90th Cong., 2d sess., on H.R. 7796, H.R. 13211, H.R. 14605, and H.R. 14627. Washington: U.S. Gov't Printing Office, 1968.

U.S., Congress, House. Subcommittee on Conservation and Natural Resources of the Committee on Government Operations. *Increasing Protection for Our Waters, Wetlands, and Shorelines: The Corps of Engineers.* 92d Cong., 2d sess., H. Rept. 17. Washington: U.S. Gov't Printing Office, 1972.

U.S., Congress, House. Subcommittee on Environment of the Committee on Interior and Insular Affairs. *Proposed Amendments to the Land and Water Conservation Fund Act.* 92d Cong., 1st sess., H. Res. 6730 and related bills. Washington: U.S. Gov't Printing Office, 1971.

U.S., Congress, House. Subcommittee on Environment of the Committee on Interior and Insular Affairs. *Public Land Policy Act of 1971.* 92d Cong., 1st sess., H.R. 7211. Washington: U.S. Gov't Printing Office, 1971.

U.S., Congress, House. Subcommittee on Fisheries and Wildlife Conservation of the Committee on Merchant Marine and Fisheries. Hearings, 91st Cong., 1st sess. Washington: U.S. Gov't Printing Office, 1971.

U.S., Congress, House. Subcommittee on Forests of the Committee on Agriculture. *Forest Law*

Enforcement. Hearing, 92d Cong., 1st sess., on H.R. 1399, H.R. 3146, H.R. 6400, H.R. 7259, and H.R. 730. Washington: U.S. Gov't Printing Office, 1971.

U.S., Congress, House. Subcommittee on National Parks and Recreation of the Committee on Interior and Insular Affairs. *Policies, Programs and Activities of the National Park Service and the Bureau of Recreation.* Hearings, 92d Cong., 1st sess. Washington: U.S. Gov't Printing Office, 1971.

U.S., Congress, House. Subcommittee on Public Health and Environment of the Committee on Interstate and Foreign Commerce. *Safe Drinking Water.* Hearings, 82d Cong., 2d sess., on H.R. 14899. Washington: U.S. Gov't Printing Office, 1972.

U.S., Congress, House. Subcommittee on Public Lands of the Committee on Interior and Insular Affairs. *Designation of Wilderness Areas.* 92d Cong., 1st sess., H.R. 3838 and other bills. Washington: U.S. Gov't Printing Office, 1972.

U.S., Congress, House. Subcommittee on Science, Research, and Development of the Committee on Science and Astronautics. *Managing the Environment.* 90th Cong., 2d sess. Washington: U.S. Gov't Printing Office, 1968.

U.S., Congress, Senate. Committee on Agriculture and Forestry. *National Forest Wilderness Areas Act of 1972.* 92d Cong., 2d sess., S Rept. 1214 to accompany S. 3973. Washington: U.S. Gov't Printing Office, 1972.

U.S., Congress, Senate. Committee of Commerce. *Conservation and Protection of U.S. Fish Resources.* 92d Cong., 1st sess., S. Rept. 582 to accompany S. 2192. Washington: U.S. Gov't Printing Office, 1971.

U.S., Congress, Senate. Committee on Commerce. *Creation of a National Program for Coastal and Estuarine Zone Management.* 92d Cong., 1st sess., S. Rept. 526 to accompany S. 582. Washington: U.S. Gov't Printing Office, 1971.

U.S., Congress, Senate. Committee on Commerce. *Endangered Species Conservation Act of 1972.* 92d Cong., 2d sess., S. Rept. 1136 on S. 3818. Washington: U.S. Gov't Printing Office, 1972.

U.S., Congress, Senate. Committee on Commerce. *National Coastal Zone Management Act of 1972.* 92d Cong., 2d sess. Washington: U.S. Gov't Printing Office, 1972.

U.S., Congress, Senate. Committee on Government Operations. *Establish a Department of Natural Resources.* Hearings, 92d Cong., 1st sess., on S. 1431. Washington: U.S. Gov't Printing Office, 1971.

U.S., Congress, Senate. Committee on Interior and Insular Affairs. *Amending the Mining and Minerals Policy Act of 1970.* 92d Cong., 1st sess., S. 635. Washington: U.S. Gov't Printing Office, 1971.

U.S., Congress, Senate. Committee on Interior and Insular Affairs. *A Brief Presentation of the Committee's History and Jurisdiction, and a Summary of Its Accomplishments During the 90th Congress.* 90th Cong., 2d sess., S. Doc. 61. Washington: U.S. Gov't Printing Office, 1968.

U.S., Congress, Senate. Committee on Interior and Insular Affairs. *A Definition of the Scope of Environmental Management.* Washington: U.S. Gov't Printing Office, 1970.

U.S., Congress, Senate. Committee on Interior and Insular Affairs. *Energy Research Policy Alternatives.* Hearing, 92d Cong., 2d sess., on S. Res. 45. Washington: U.S. Gov't Printing Office, 1972.

U.S., Congress, Senate. Committee on Interior and Insular Affairs. *Joint House-Senate Colloquium to Discuss a National Policy for the Environment.* Hearings, 90th Cong., 2d sess., on S. 233. Washington: U.S. Gov't Printing Office, 1968.

U.S., Congress, Senate. Committee on Interior and Insular Affairs. *Land Use Policy and Planning Assistance Act of 1972.* 92d Cong., 2d sess., S. 632. Washington: U.S. Gov't Printing Office, 1972.

U.S., Congress, Senate. Committee on Interior and Insular Affairs. *Legislation to Revise the Public Land Laws.* Hearings, 92d Cong., 1st sess., on S. 921, S. 2401, S. 2450, and S. 2542. Washington: U.S. Gov't Printing Office, 1972.

U.S., Congress, Senate. Committee on Interior and Insular Affairs. *National Environment Policy.* Hearings, 91st Cong., 1st sess., on S. 234. Washington: U.S. Gov't Printing Office, 1969.

U.S., Congress, Senate. Committee on Interior and Insular Affairs. *National Fuels and Energy Policy.* 92d Cong., 1st sess., S. Res. 45. Washington: U.S. Gov't Printing Office, 1971.

U.S., Congress, Senate. Committee on Interior and Insular Affairs. *National Land Use Policy.* Hearings, 92d Cong., 1st sess., on S. 632 and S. 992. Washington: U.S. Gov't Printing Office, 1971.

U.S., Congress, Senate. Committee on Interior and Insular Affairs. *A National Policy for the Environment: A Special Report.* 90th Cong., 2d sess., S. Rept. 35. Washington: U.S. Gov't Printing Office, 1968.

U.S., Congress, Senate. Committee on Interior and Insular Affairs. *Natural Gas Policy Issues.* Hearings, 92d Cong., 2d sess., on S. Res. 45. Washington: U.S. Gov't Printing Office, 1972.

U.S., Congress, Senate. Committee on Interior and Insular Affairs. *Reclamation Feasibility Studies, 1972.* 92d Cong., 2d sess., Senate report to accompany S. 3959. Washington: U.S. Gov't Printing Office, 1972.

U.S., Congress, Senate. *Report of Select Committee on National Water Resources.* 87th Cong., 1st sess., S. Rept. 29. Washington: U.S. Gov't Printing Office, 1961.

U.S., Congress, Senate. Subcommittee on Parks and Recreation of Committee on Interior and Insular Affairs. *Land and Water Conservation Fund Act of 1965.* Hearing, 92d Cong., 2d sess., on S. 990 and S. 2473. Washington: U.S. Gov't Printing Office, 1972.

U.S., Congress, Senate. Subcommittee on Public Lands of the Committee on Interior and Insular Affairs. *"Clear-cutting" Practices on National Timberlands.* Hearings, 92d Cong., 1st sess., on management practices on public lands. Washington: U.S. Gov't Printing Office, 1971.

U.S., Congress, Senate. Subcommittee on Public Lands of the Committee on Interior and Insular Affairs. *Management Practices on Public Lands.* 92d Cong., 1st sess., on S. 350 and S. 1734. Washington: U.S. Gov't Printing Office, 1971.

U.S., Congress, Senate. Committee on Interior and Insular Affairs. *Outer Continental Shelf Policy Issues.* Hearings, 92d Cong., 2d sess., on S. Res. 45. Washington: U.S. Gov't Printing Office, 1972.

U.S., Congress, Senate. Subcommittee on Public Lands of the Committee on Interior and Insular Affairs. *Preservation of Wilderness Areas.* Hearings, 92d Cong., 2d sess., on S. 2453. Washington: U.S. Gov't Printing Office, 1972.

U.S., Congress, Senate. Subcommittee on Reorganization and International Organizations of the Committee on Government Operations. *Interagency Environmental Hazards Coordination: Pesticides and Public Policy.* Washington: U.S. Gov't Printing Office, 1966.

U.S., Congress, Senate. Subcommittee on Flood Control, Rivers, and Harbors of the Committee on Public Works. *The Effect of Channelization on the Environment.* Hearing, 92d Cong., 1st sess., on S. 24. Washington: U.S. Gov't Printing Office, 1971.

U.S., Congress, Senate. Subcommittee on Investigations and Oversight of the Committee of Public Works. *Red Tape—Inquiring into Delays and Excessive Paperwork in Administration of Public Works Programs.* Hearings, 92d Cong., 1st sess., S. 15. Washington: U.S. Gov't Printing Office, 1971.

U.S., Congress, Senate. Subcommittee on Oceans and Atmosphere of the Committee on Commerce. *Effects of Mercury on Man and the Environment.* Hearings, 91st Cong., 2d sess., on S. 73. Washington: U.S. Gov't Printing Office, 1970.

U.S., Congress, Senate. Subcommittee on Oceans and Atmosphere of the Commerce Committee. *Ocean Mammal Protection.* Hearings, 92d Cong., 2d sess., on S. 685 and other related legislation. Washington: U.S. Gov't Printing Office, 1972.

U.S., Congress, Senate. Subcommittee on Parks and Recreation of the Committee on Interior and Insular Affairs. *Preservation of Historical Archeological Data and Preservation of National Monuments.* Hearing, 92d Cong., 1st sess., on S. 1245 and S. 1152. Washington: U.S. Gov't Printing Office, 1971.

U.S., Congress, Senate. Subcommittee on Rural Development of the Committee on Agriculture and Forestry. *Rural Development.* Hearings, 92d Cong., 1st sess. Washington: U.S. Gov't Printing Office, 1971.

U.S., Congress, Senate. *Surface Mining Reclamation Act of 1972.* 92d Cong., 2d sess. Washington: U.S. Gov't Printing Office, 1972.

193

U.S., Congress, Senate. Subcommittee on Intergovernmental Relations of the Senate Committee on Government Operations. *Intergovernmental Cooperation Act of 1967 and Related Legislation.* Hearings, 90th Cong., 2d sess., on S. 536. Washington: U.S. Gov't Printing Office, 1968.

U.S. Department of Agriculture. *A Place to Live—The Yearbook of Agriculture 1963.* Washington: U.S. Gov't Printing Office, 1963.

U.S. Department of Agriculture, Graduate School. *Environmental Improvement: Air, Water and Soil.* Washington: U.S. Gov't Printing Office.

U.S. Department of Agriculture. *Public Access to Public Domain Lands: Two Case Studies of Landowner-Sportsman Conflict.* Washington: U.S. Gov't Printing Office, 1968.

U.S. Department of Commerce, Environmental Services Administration. *Man's Geophysical Environment: Its Study from Space.* Washington: U.S. Gov't Printing Office, 1968.

U.S. Department of Commerce, Environmental Services Administration Economic Research Service. *Science and Engineering,* July 13, 1965—June 30, 1967.

U.S. Department of Health, Education and Welfare, Public Health Services. *Air Pollution Control, Field Operations Manual.* Washington: U.S. Gov't Printing Office, 1962.

U.S. Department of Health, Education and Welfare, Public Health Service. *Handbook on Air Pollution. Education, and Outdoor Recreation.* Washington: U.S. Gov't Printing Office, 1968.

U.S. Department of Health, Education and Welfare, Public Health Service. *Proceedings of the National Conferences on Air Pollution.* Washington: U.S. Gov't Printing Office, 1968.

U.S. Department of Health, Education and Welfare. *Public Health Service Symposium, Environmental Measurements: Valid Data and Logical Interpretation.* Washington: U.S. Gov't Printing Office, 1964.

U.S. Department of Health, Education and Welfare. *Proceedings: The National Conference on Water Pollution.* Washington: U.S. Gov't Printing Office, 1960.

U.S. Department of Health, Education and Welfare. *Report of the Subcommittee on Water Supply and Pollution Control.* Washington: U.S. Public Health Service, 1962, pub. no. 980.

U.S. Department of Housing and Urban Development. *Urban Land Policy—Selected Aspects of European Experience.* Washington: U.S. Gov't Printing Office, 1970.

U.S. Department of the Interior. *Federal Water Pollution Control Administration.* Washington: U.S. Gov't Printing Office, 1964.

U.S. Department of the Interior. *The Quest for Quality, Conservation Yearbook No. 1.* Washington: U.S. Gov't Printing Office, 1965, no. 96.

U.S. Department of the Interior. *The Population Challenge, Conservation Yearbook No. 2.* Washington: U.S. Gov't Printing Office, 1966, no. 80.

U.S. Department of the Interior. *The Third Wave, Conservation Yearbook No. 3.* Washington: U.S. Gov't Printing Office, 1967, no. 128.

U.S. Department of the Interior. *Man—An Endangered Species, Conservation Yearbook No. 4.* Washington: U.S. Gov't Printing Office, 1968, no. 100.

U.S. Department of the Interior. *The Public Land Record.* Washington: U.S. Dept. of the Interior, 1959.

U.S. Department of the Interior. *Surface Mining and Our Environment.* Washington: Sup't. of Documents, 1967.

U.S. Department of the Interior. *Noise and the Sonic Boom in Relation to Man.* Washington: U.S. Gov't Printing Office, 1960.

U.S. Department of the Interior. National Park Service. *Our Vanishing Shoreline.* Washington: U.S. Gov't Printing Office, 1956.

U.S. Department of the Interior. *Recreation Land Price Escalation.* Washington: Dept. of Interior, 1967.

U.S. Department of the Interior, Federal Water Pollution Control Administration. *Water and Water Pollution Control: A Selected List of Publications.* Washington: U.S. Gov't Printing Office, 1968.

U.S. Environmental Protection Agency. *The Economics of Clean Air.* 92d Cong., 1st sess. Washington: U.S. Gov't Printing Office, 1971.

Selected Bibliography

U.S. Environmental Protection Agency. *The Economics of Clean Water—Summary and Analysis.* 92d Cong., 2d sess. Washington: U.S. Gov't Printing Office, 1972.

U.S., Library of Congress, Congressional Research Service of the Environmental Policy Division. *An Analysis of Forestry Issues in the First Session of the 92d Congress.* Washington: U.S. Gov't Printing Office, 1972.

U.S., Library of Congress, Congressional Research Service of the Environmental Policy Division. *A Bibliography of Non-technical Literature on Energy,* by F. Dean. Washington: U.S. Gov't Printing Office, 1971.

U.S., Library of Congress, Congressional Research Service of the Environmental Policy Division. *Congress and the Nation's Environment—Environmental Affairs of the 91st Congress.* Washington: U.S. Gov't Printing Office, 1971.

U.S., Library of Congress, Congressional Research Service of the Environmental Policy Division. *Considerations in the Formulation of National Energy Policy,* by D. P. Beard. Washington: U.S. Gov't Printing Office, 1971.

U.S., Library of Congress, Congressional Research Service of the Environmental Policy Division. *National Land Use Policy.* 92d Cong., 2d sess. Washington: U.S. Gov't Printing Office, 1972.

U.S., Library of Congress, Congressional Research Service of the Environmental Policy Division. *The Evolution and Dynamics of National Goals in the United States,* by F. P. Huddle. Washington: U.S. Gov't Printing Office, 1971.

U.S., Library of Congress, Congressional Research Service of the Environmental Policy Division. *Science, Technology, and American Diplomacy; the Mekong Project; Opportunities and the Problems of Regionalism,* by F. P. Huddle. Washington: U.S. Gov't Printing Office, 1972.

U.S. Office of Economic Opportunity, *Catalog of Federal Programs for Individual and Community Improvement,* no. 414. Washington: U.S. Gov't Printing Office, 1965.

U.S. Water Resources Council, Special Task Force. *Procedures for Evaluation of Water and Related Land Resource Projects.* Washington: U.S. Gov't Printing Office, 1971.

U.S. White House Conference on Natural Beauty. *Beauty for America.* Washington: U.S. Gov't Printing Office, 1965.

Vawter, W. R. *Second Hoover Commission: Task Force Report on Water Resources and Power,* vol. 3, *Interstate Compacts—The Federal Interest.* Washington: U.S. Gov't Printing Office, 1955.

Water Resources Council. *The Nation's Water Resources, First National Assessment.* Washington: U.S. Gov't Printing Office, 1968.

Whyte, W. H., *Open Space Action,* Study Report no. 14 of the Outdoor Recreation Resources Review Commission. Washington: Supt. of Documents, 1962.

INDEX

Daniel H. Henning

Dr. Daniel H. Henning is Associate Professor of Political Science at Eastern Montana College, Billings, Montana. He has authored or edited several books on environmental policy and related subjects and has written numerous articles and papers for leading legal and scientific journals. A recipient of many fellowships and awards, Dr. Henning has also held high-ranking positions in a number of national and international organizations. Some of the organizations include the Northwest Scientific Association for which he served as Trustee and Chairman, the International Union for the Conservation of Nature and Natural resources at which he was a delegate, and the American Society for Public Administration of which he was a Chairman. Dr. Henning received his B.S. degree in Social Science and Biology from Bowling Green University, his M.S. in Public Administration and Conservation from the University of Michigan, and his Ph.D. in Public Administration, Political Science and Natural Resources from Syracuse University.